Kieren McCarthy is a freelance
following and reporting on the evolution of the Internet
since the late 1990s. He is a specialist in the legally
undecided issue of domain names, as well as the complex
issues surrounding governance of the Internet. Kieren has
written for, among others, *The Guardian*, *The Times*, *The
Independent*, *New Scientist*, *The Register*, *PC Week*,
Practical Internet, *Computeractive* and *Techworld*.

Over the course of the past ten years, he has interviewed
many of the early pioneers of the Internet as well as more
recent figures who have shaped the direction of the Internet.

A highly regarded blogger on the Internet's political
processes, Kieren is often asked to give his expert opinion
to other media, and recently acted as official blog-watcher
at the inaugural meeting of the Internet Governance Forum.

He currently lives in Oxford, England.

SEX.COM

One Domain, Two Men, Twelve
Years and the Brutal Battle for the
Jewel in the Internet's Crown

Kieren McCarthy

Quercus

Quercus
21 Bloomsbury Square
London
WC1A 2NS

A CIP catalogue record for this book is available
from the British Library.

ISBN 1 905204 66 3
ISBN-13 978 1 905204 66 3

10 9 8 7 6 5 4 3 2 1

Printed and bound in
Great Britain by Clays Ltd, St Ives plc.

PREFACE

It's difficult now to imagine a time before the Internet. But it was just over a decade ago that people outside the military and academic worlds first heard about this rapidly expanding international network of computers.

Academics loved its ability to share vast amounts of information; governments discovered a remarkable communications device; and the rest of us, well, we used it to go shopping, talk about our lives, and look for sex.

The Internet has given sex or, more accurately, pornography, an enormous new outlet. Web browsers brought top-shelf magazines direct to every computer screen. It wasn't long before they did the same with videos. And then the Net really hit its stride: real-time webcams and instant messaging meant direct interaction with complete strangers. The gap between reality and pornography had been narrowed still further.

Sex on the Net is one of the great dirty secrets of our time. A quarter of all search-engine requests are for pornography, at least a fifth of adults online have accessed a porn site, and there are an estimated 400 million Web pages out there catering for the demand. The adult industry is worth $57 billion worldwide, and the United States – which remains the world centre for pornography – claims $12 billion of it.

The bulk of that industry is based in California, in particular Los Angeles, so it is particularly apt that Stephen Michael Cohen was born in the City of Angels and has spent most of his life living in and around it.

It was also in California, in San Francisco, that the website that for many years was the focal point for the new online sex industry – sex.com – was registered. Gary Kremen was the most unlikely porn baron ever born, a geek businessman with a computer degree. But Kremen recognised way back in 1994 that the domain – given to him entirely free of charge – might become valuable one day. Just how valuable he was to find out when Stephen Cohen stole it from him just prior to the dotcom boom and made it the centre of an enormous international empire.

The millions of dollars made by sex.com every month at its peak were reason enough for a fight, but its ownership meant more than just a worldly fortune to both men.

Sex.com had provided Stephen Cohen with the life he'd always dreamed of and helped put to rest his bitter hatred of society. For Gary Kremen, the theft of the domain undermined everything he held dear. But at the same time it presented him with a challenge, and a worthy opponent. Neither man was used to losing, and neither was prepared to back down, even for a second. So the case began to take over their lives, and then started to suck in those of friends, families and employees, and, for a short while, even the US legal system and the Internet itself.

But the Internet domain name sex.com represents far more than just the biggest name in an explosion of worldwide pornography – it became the epicentre of a fight over the main building block of the Internet and how these electronic addresses fit into our society and our legal systems.

The battle for ownership of sex.com is set against the back-drop of an extraordinary period of modern history – the dotcom boom, a digital gold rush where fortunes were made and lost faster than ever before in human history. A seemingly worthless property situated on an invisible computer network, and handed over free of charge, suddenly became worth millions of dollars. Within months, every investor, every pioneer, every chancer, crook, bookmaker, moneylender, brothel owner, legal advisor and snake-oil salesman had descended on the Internet boomtown.

Most forays turned up nothing but fools' gold, but there was never any doubt sex.com was the real thing. And when the fight broke out for its ownership, the result was a dramatic retelling of the ancient tales of what men will do, and are capable of doing, when confronted head on with their most basic desires: sex and power.

Despite its name, it was violence that first drew attention to the fact that the battle for sex.com was much more than a petty argument over an Internet address.

In June 2001 reports started to appear that the former owner of sex.com, Stephen Michael Cohen, was in fear of his life after two bounty hunters had come looking for him at his Tijuana home. A gunfight with the Mexican police had ensued.

The bounty hunters were in pursuit of a $50,000 reward from the new – and, it turns out, original – owner of sex.com, Gary Kremen. Why the reward? Who got shot? What were the Mexican police doing there? Had the adult industry resorted to Mafia-style violence?

Every question produced more questions, and each of those provoked more. Every step along the line, the story became more incredible. Kremen claimed the event never happened. Cohen says he had the evidence that showed it had, and had supplied to the court, but the judge refused to accept it.

Investigating the truth meant stepping into the tornado of truth and fiction circling the two men – a chaotic area where dozens of lawyers, partners, friends and family swirled about.

Bitter disputes are the hardest to unravel. Each actor has a different recollection of the same event and, over time, retelling carves inaccurate details in stone. People behave childishly, viciously, under pressure and later seek to hide it. Accepting errors can become impossible as a matter of personal pride.

But what made this story especially difficult to pin down was the extraordinary gift for obfuscation possessed by Stephen Michael Cohen, a gift that has been behind a great deal of his lifelong success as a con man. His lies are compulsive and brilliant. Even when pinned down, he has an immediate explanation to hand. And then an explanation for why that one also turns out to be false.

Unlike other members of his profession, Cohen has not come clean or sought to relieve his conscience. Finding the truth therefore consists of discarding every other possibility. In many cases, it is only possible to reconstruct a vague sense of what actually happened.

One example of this peculiar reality was to haunt Kremen's case for years. An army of lawyers had carefully dissected every detail, and yet only when the method by which Cohen had stolen the domain became the entire focus of a second court case did one of the smartest lawyers in the United States uncover the truth. Even now, after years of fighting, and four different lawsuits and four different appeals all focused on the theft of sex.com, no one apart from Stephen Cohen really knows exactly how he managed to steal the most valuable domain in the world.

What appears in these pages is what I have managed to piece together from years of extensive research, tens of thousands of pages of court documents, dozens of interviews, and an extended spell in the tornado that surrounds the brutal battle for sex.com.

1

A BIG GUY

"I'm just a small guy," the 38-year-old Gary Kremen told reporters waiting outside the San Jose courthouse. "I'm just a small guy and this is a huge guy who has built an empire based on fraud and deceit."

He was half right. Stephen Michael Cohen *is* a huge guy. A guy who counts some of America's smartest criminals among his closest friends; a guy who sits on top of a vast and sprawling web of companies, businesses and offshore bank accounts; a guy who in just two years pushed, kicked and threatened his way to the top of the multi-billion-dollar adult sex industry and has since moved into hotels, casinos and international stock scams; a guy who has talked his way out of almost as many jails as he has into people's bank accounts. This is a *huge* guy.

But then so is the unassuming geek-turned-businessman – and now pornographer – talking to the media on the corner of East San Carlos Street and South 1st Street.

Gary Kremen had chased down one of the greatest conmen of all time and won. Not only that but he had done it through the prohibitively expensive and complex US legal system, in an entirely new area of law, and against a man who had very deep pockets, an army of lawyers, and a lifetime of screwing people behind him. Kremen's only weapons had been raw determination, coupled with and fed by moral outrage.

Moments earlier, Judge James Ware of the Northern District Court of California ended years of furious fighting when he ordered the defendants Stephen Michael Cohen, Ocean Fund

International, Ynata and Sand Man Internacional – who were, in fact, all the same person – to jointly pay Kremen a total of $65 million.

Forty million dollars was "by way of restitution and disgorgement for the profits generated through use of the sex.com domain name", and the remaining $25 million was punitive damages for having stolen Kremen's property. A huge fine for a huge guy.

On one Tuesday afternoon in 2001, the entire legal landscape of the Internet had changed. But the impact on Gary Kremen was far greater. Having spent five years living in the shadow of bankruptcy and having battled through a crippling addiction to crystal meth (methamphetamine), he was now the owner of the Internet's most valuable real estate – the almost mythical sex.com.

Even better, Kremen was due a mind-blowing $65 million from the very man that had done everything in his power to ruin him. A reporter asked Gary Kremen how he felt. "I feel pretty good about it," he replied.

But the reality was that this was not the end of the case, and Kremen knew it. It wasn't even the beginning of the end. It was, as Winston Churchill put it, just the end of the beginning.

Contained in the same judgment that had awarded Kremen his historic win, came the following announcement: "The warrant of arrest issued on March 2, 2001 shall remain outstanding until defendant Stephen M. Cohen surrenders the property of each defendant to this Court."

Having tackled and beaten every obstacle put in his way, chased and menaced powerful men and companies into a corner, sold everything he had to keep the legal fight going, and finally having triumphed, Kremen wasn't to get the ultimate satisfaction of seeing his nemesis beaten.

Honourable defeat is not in Cohen's dictionary – the very idea of it is distasteful, something for weak and foolish people. Stephen Michael Cohen, you see, is a con man – a very, very good con man. Having separated people from their cars, their cash, their computers, even their homes, he knew that the solution to every problem was to keep fighting, never stop, never admit defeat, and never, ever, play by their rules. If you fight harder, for longer, you will eventually win.

So while Kremen stood on the courtroom steps in San Jose answering questions about his remarkable legal victory, Cohen was hard at work 400 miles away and just across the Mexican border emptying every last cent from his US bank accounts and liquidating his assets so Kremen couldn't get his hands on them.

The next stage in the brutal battle for sex.com had begun.

2

CAGED

"I never stole it. He stole it!" Cohen cries, pointing at Gary Kremen. "Let's get this real clear, I have had sex.com since 1979. It was you guys that went into court and explained that there was some cockamamie list and therefore he was the owner. The name sex.com has always been mine."

It was just plain bad luck, no doubt, that the United States District Court for Northern California, the United States Court of Appeals for the Ninth Circuit, and the United States Supreme Court had all decided things were the other way around – that it was Cohen who had stolen sex.com from Kremen.

There was another clue: it was Cohen and not Kremen who was sitting in an orange jumpsuit that had stencilled on the front, in black:

SANTA CLARA CO.
DEPARTMENT OF CORRECTION
MAIN JAIL

It was December 2005, 56 months since Cohen had been ordered to pay Kremen $65 million in damages, and he was stuck in the one place that he had been carefully avoiding ever since: a US jail. Sitting facing Gary Kremen.

Sixty-five million dollars was a lot of money, Cohen had decided five years earlier, and there was no way he was going to pay it to the man that had not only beaten him in court but

4

who had also taken away his beloved sex.com. Kremen had the domain, but he would keep the cash. He had still won.

So Cohen fled the United States and moved outside both the court's and Gary Kremen's reach. It was the start of a chase then went on for five long years, across the United States, Mexico, Europe and Asia until, finally, fate intervened and Stephen Cohen found himself being handed over to the US marshalls at the Mexican border.

A fortnight later he was shipped to San Jose jail, and a month after that, there he was, facing the man that he had met only once before in person but with whom he had been battling for ten years: Gary Kremen. Kremen and his lawyers wanted to know where the money was. Cohen thought he would tackle the issue rather differently. "I take great offence that you're under the belief that sex.com was ever stolen," he told them. "I'm the true owner of sex.com. I lost this case by default."

They might as well have asked Cohen to cut off his arms and legs, because to a man like Stephen Cohen, it is the money – every single cent of it – that justifies the lifetime of lies, the cold deception of friends and family, and the painful process of living outside society. "In all the years you've been chasing me," Cohen told Kremen, "you have never got a single asset in my name. And you never will."

3

THEFT

"So one day, the name disappeared," explains Gary Kremen. "One day it said one thing, one day it said another. I saw some guy's name next to it, but if you looked through it my information was still there. I just thought, you know, it's some bureaucratic screw-up and that eventually they'd figure it out."

It was September 1995 and the new name that had appeared on the electronic ownership records for sex.com was Stephen Cohen and, unknown to Kremen, he had just stolen the domain name after several days of concerted effort. Kremen's email address had also changed from gkremen@netcom.com to steve@liberty.com.

What gave Kremen peace of mind was that his home address was still there. He decided it was probably an accidental over-write of information on the database – this was, after all, the early days of the Internet and its systems were still very far from 100 per cent reliable. Kremen reasoned that when the mistake was noticed, the company in charge would simply revert back to an earlier saved version and his name would be restored.

But it was not to be. Kremen kept checking sex.com's details, and for a fortnight it stayed the same: a mix of Kremen and Cohen's information. And then, one day, his address also disappeared, replaced with one he didn't recognise. Shortly after, Stephen Cohen's name also changed, this time to a company name, Sporting Houses Management. And that was it. Gary Kremen had just become one of the first men in the world to be conned over the Internet. He had lost the Net's most valuable property, silently, on a computer screen, right before his very eyes.

So he did what anyone would do and called the number listed as the contact for sex.com to find out what the hell was going on. And he spoke for the first time to the man he would spend the next ten years chasing. According to Kremen, Cohen told him straight off that he had trademark rights in the name sex.com, but Kremen didn't believe him and immediately called the company that ran and sold all dotcoms at the time, Network Solutions, asking to be given the domain back. Cohen recollects an altogether different version of events. "It only lasted maybe ten seconds, the whole call," Cohen says. "He made some off-the-wall comment: 'I'm sex.com, you're not sex.com.' I told him to go fuck himself and hung up."

Whatever happened, Kremen did call NSI, "and they said they'd investigate and I said fine, get back to me. And then they never got back." But Kremen was persistent and kept calling and arguing, refusing to be put off until he finally reached the head of investigations, Sherry Proehl. Proehl told him that if what he said was true, he shouldn't worry, and the domain name would be returned.

So far, so good. Except Kremen had no idea who he was dealing with. He had blithely entered the foggy world of Stephen Michael Cohen, where nothing is certain except for the fact that Stephen Michael Cohen will come out of it better off. Just two days after discussing the situation with Sherry Proehl, Kremen received a call out of the blue from a Bob Johnson, who identified himself as Proehl's supervisor. Johnson advised Kremen that NSI would not be returning the domain because Stephen Cohen did indeed have a trademark in the name and so possessed greater rights to it.

"This was just when the issue of people registering other people's trademarks hit," Kremen explains years later. It was November 1995, and domain names were just beginning to enter people's consciousness because Network Solutions had started charging $50 a year for them. Thousands of people suddenly all had the same thought: if people were willing to pay money for a space on this computer network, there must be a market for other goods. And so company lawyers started making a lot of noise about how currently anyone could register company names and trademarks as domain names without authorisation. Network Solutions was desperate to avoid a fight with corporate America, and the issue had inevitably found its way into the press. The trademark issue was therefore timely and struck a chord with Kremen. "It was a believable story. I believed it. I didn't realise how dumb that was until later on."

It wasn't really so dumb of Kremen to believe the story, but even so it *was* baloney. There was no Bob Johnson at NSI – it had been none other than Stephen Cohen on the telephone. Cohen had already spent a decade posing as everyone from government officials to FBI agents to lawyers. He was so good at it that, according to one story, he had even impersonated a judge in Colorado, heard real cases in court, and let people off before he was finally discovered by an embarrassed judiciary. Kremen simply had no idea he was dealing with a master criminal who was prepared to say or do anything, legal or not, in order to keep the property he'd stolen.

And the phone call from "Bob Johnson" was all it took for Cohen to secure ownership of sex.com. It stopped Kremen from chasing NSI for several valuable months, during which time Cohen managed to jump the last hurdle – Proehl's *real* boss. David Graves was looking at the change in sex.com's ownership and had told Cohen he wanted proof that it was legitimate. Cohen told him he had a signed document that handed over ownership to him, so Graves asked him to send a copy. Nearly three months after he had stolen the domain, and under increasing pressure to prove his claim, Cohen finally faxed NSI what was to become the most controversial and bitterly fought-over document in the battle for sex.com.

How was the most valuable domain name on the Internet stolen? With a one-page forged letter.

ONLINE CLASSIFIEDS, INC.
(FOR YOUR ONLINE AD'S)
242 COLE STREET
SAN FRANCISCO, CA 94117

October 15, 1995

Stephen Cohen
1261 North Lakeview Drive
Suite J-825
Anaheim, CA 92807

Re: SEX.COM

Dear Mr. Cohen:

Per our numerous conversations, we understand that you have been using sex.com on your French Connections BBS since 1979 and now you want to use sex.com as a domain name on the internet. Our corporation is the owner of sex.com as it relates to the internet.

At one time, we employed Gary Kremen who was hired for the express purpose of setting up our system. We allowed Mr. Kremen to be our administrative and technical contact with the internet, because of his vast experience with computers and their connections to the internet.

Subsequently, we were forced to dismiss Mr. Kremen. At no time, was Mr. Kremen ever a stockholder, officer, nor a director of our corporation and as such, Mr. Kremen has no rights, titles or interest in our domain name. Further, the internet shows that sex.com is listed in our corporation and not in Mr. Kremen's personal name. In fact, Mr. Kremen is the president of a different and unrelated corporation called Electric Classifieds, which is located at 340 Brandon Street in San Francisco, California. Further, Mr. Kremen's corporation owns match.com which is listed with the internet registration.

We never got around to changing our administrative contact with the internet registration and now our Board of directors has decided to abandon the domain name sex.com.

Because we do not have a direct connection to the internet, we request that you notify the internet registration on our behalf, to delete our domain name sex.com. Further, we have no objections to your use of the domain name sex.com and this letter shall serve as our authorization to the internet registration to transfer sex.com to your corporation.

Sincerely,

Sharon Dimmick
Sharon Dimmick, President

It was from the president of Online Classifieds Inc., the company name under which Gary Kremen had registered sex.com, and it was addressed to Stephen Cohen. The president, a Sharon Dimmick, wrote that she was handing over ownership of the

9

sex.com domain to Cohen in recognition of his existing trademark for no consideration i.e. for free. She pointed out that Gary Kremen had been fired, and the company had decided not to do anything with sex.com, and so was turning it over to Cohen. The most crucial part of the letter, however, stated that it – the letter itself – should be used as proof of Online Classifieds' intent and should be presented to Network Solutions as evidence of the agreed transfer.

The whole thing was a fake produced on Cohen's home computer, and printed out and faxed to NSI from his workplace. It was sent on 5 December 1995, but dated 15 October of that year – two days before Cohen actually stole sex.com.

It was a cunning ploy, appearing to give Network Solutions all the justification it needed to change ownership, while also explaining why Gary Kremen had complained – because he was an aggrieved ex-employee. However, while the letter was a clever piece of high-wire balancing, it suffered from one major defect that would ultimately lead to Cohen's downfall: it was appallingly written.

Cohen possesses an unnatural gift of persuasion, but he left school early with a poor education, no qualifications and dreadful literacy. He can't spell, and he has never learned the art of writing. As a result, he simply types verbatim what he would say to someone, never fully recognizing the difference between what people say and how they express the same thing in print.

The letter heading itself possessed a glaring mistake. It read: "Online Classifieds, Inc. (For your online ad's)". The extra apostrophe in "ads" is a basic grammatical error, and one that would be understandable in the body of a letter, but almost inconceivable in a company's official letter heading, reproduced thousands of times on company stationery. It also contained no phone number or email address or website. And, as Kremen's lawyers were to discover, the letter heading was printed in an unusual font that Cohen had been using in his letters, both forged and real, for years.

The rest of the letter is just as sloppy, and the syntax frequently childish. It began: "Per our numerous conversations, we understand that you have been using sex.com on your French Connections BBS since 1979 and now you want to use sex.com as a domain name on the internet. Our corporation is the owner of sex.com as it relates to the internet."

Would the president of a company really write an important letter so poorly? Cohen also hadn't done his homework – the ".com" extension only came into existence in 1984. Considering that this phoney letter was being faxed as proof to the very company that ran all dotcoms, such a glaring error was bound to raise eyebrows.

It continued just as badly: "At one time, we employed Gary Kremen who was hired for the express purpose of setting up our system. We allowed Mr Kremen to be our administrative and technical contact with the internet, because of his vast experience with computers and their connections to the internet.

"Subsequently, we were forced to dismiss Mr Kremen. At no time was Mr Kremen ever a stockholder, officer nor a director of our corporation and as such, Mr Kremen has no rights, titles or interests in our domain name. Further, the internet shows that sex.com is listed in our corporation and not in Mr Kremen's personal name. In fact, Mr Kremen is the president of a different and unrelated corporation called Electric Classifieds, which is located at 340 Brandon Street in San Francisco, California. Further, Mr Kremen's corporation owns match.com which is listed with the internet registration.

"We never got around to changing our administrative contact with the internet registration and now our Board of Directors has decided to abandon the domain name sex.com."

While the concept behind the letter was brilliant, its execution was poorly handled. What company would claim that it "never got around" to doing something? Why would the president of Online Classifieds talk about match.com? In a phone conversation, the slang would be fine and the tangents about Gary Kremen, complete with precise facts, would give the listener greater confidence in the speaker. But when put down on paper, such persuasive techniques jar. Cohen had completely over-egged it by going on about Kremen when the letter was only supposed to be handing over ownership of rights in sex.com.

The final paragraph in which Cohen sought to have the letter itself act as a passport to the domain change was too blunt and blew the whole scam:

"Because we do not have a direct connection to the internet, we request that you notify the internet registration on our behalf, to delete our domain name sex.com. Further, we have no objections to your use of the domain name sex.com and this letter shall serve as our authorization to the internet registration to transfer sex.com to your organization."

The likelihood that a company called Online Classifieds, which was handing over ownership of an Internet domain, did not have an Internet connection was so remote it would be bound to set off alarm bells. Cohen's motive was also immediately obvious: this was sex.com, the most transparently desirable Internet domain in existence. NSI only had Cohen's word that the transfer was legitimate, and the proof of this was a highly unusual and unorthodox letter sent to Cohen, and faxed by Cohen.

And that should have been the end of the matter. The remarkable tale of sex.com reduced to a few weeks of irritation before Kremen was handed back the domain and things continued as they were previously. The domain transfer had already been flagged up as suspicious. The original owner had complained, and the apparent proof of its legitimate transfer was a transparent forgery. Handing the domain back really was no more than typing a few details into their system and hitting Save.

But it never happened. There was no investigation – not one that NSI has ever admitted to, anyway. Kremen was ignored, and Cohen was allowed to continue running sex.com, which even back in 1995 was making him hundreds of thousands of dollars every month. Why?

That was the question that would haunt Gary Kremen for the next eight years.

4

GARY KREMEN

Gary Alan Kremen is a remarkable man. Born 20 September 1963 in Skokie, Illinois – just outside Chicago – to two teachers, it was obvious early on that he had a prodigious intellect. A sharp, driven and inquisitive child, he used to sit for hours in his back garden looking through a homemade telescope at the stars.

At eight, he was reading physics books intended for children twice his age. At twelve, he built his first PC. While at high school, he was nearly expelled for hacking into the school's computer system. He once decided on a whim to go to the highest point in each of California's 59 counties – and he knows that there are really only 58 counties because Klamath County was dissolved in 1874. He is, put simply, the quintessential geek – highly intelligent, obsessed with the intricacies and forever looking to push back the frontiers of what is allowed.

Inevitably he was also a socially awkward boy, with just a handful of friends. Cross-country running – where the stamina and drive of the individual is paramount – was his sport of choice. But like the most famous geek in the world, Bill Gates, Gary possesses an unusual drive and determination that overrides his natural shyness. Gary Kremen decided early on in his life he was going to make it big in business, and he was going to do it at the sharp edge. And, like Gates, that meant the new and exciting world of computers.

He took degrees in both computer science and electrical engineering at Chicago's Northwestern University, graduating in 1985, and went straight into his first job, aged 23, as a member of the technical staff at the headquarters of Aerospace Corporation in El Segundo, California. The corporation did a lot of government-funded research, so it was in the unique position of being one of only 200 or so bodies that were connected together by one of the predecessors of the Internet, the ARPAnet. The World Wide Web wouldn't exist for another seven years, but Kremen got to learn about the new computer networks that were breaking out while he passed his time in an extremely dull job.

Not long after, he decided to broaden his options, and started taking night classes in accounting. And then he quit to go to business school, taking a full-price place at the spiritual home of technological entrepreneurship, Stanford. He was cocky and arrogant, turning down a full scholarship from the University of Chicago because he had already decided, in his own words, "to make my millions in Silicon Valley".

It was a life-changing decision. His peers at Stanford between 1987 and 1989 became the driving forces behind a series of new computer companies that are now household names – Microsoft and Sun Microsystems being but two. Far from leaping straight into a glittering job however, Kremen left Stanford in the middle of a recession from which Silicon Valley didn't recover for another four years. He took a job as a financial controller at one of the few businesses to survive during this tough patch – bio-technology. It was well paid, although nothing special by Silicon Valley standards, but Kremen remembers it fondly because the CEO allowed him to sit in on board meetings, and it was there that Kremen suddenly realised he wanted to be an entrepreneur, spotting new business opportunities, forming a company around them, selling up and then moving on to the next thing. The Internet at the time was still no more than a few hundred computer companies, universities and government off-shoots communicating with one another, but thanks to a flatmate who worked at Sun as an engineer, Kremen had full access. And it was while looking about the network one day that he suddenly came up with a business plan – one of the very first hatched over the Internet.

We now take it pretty much for granted that a computer is connected or can be connected to the Internet. But back in the late 1980s and early 1990s, the opposite was true: there were hundreds of thousands of computers, but only a small percentage of them were connected to anything beyond a printer. One of the advantages of being on the early Internet was that information and files were shared freely among users, and since most of the people on the network were computer scientists, it was awash with software programs they had written in their spare time to do various jobs made freely available to everyone. Kremen reckoned that if he put together a suite of these software programs, people not on the network might be willing to pay for it. So he downloaded and tested a wide range of programs, put together about ten different packages catering for different needs, and advertised them for $99. Full Source Software thus became possibly the first open source software company in the world.

Kremen's hunch proved right, and soon he was selling $1,000 to $2,000 worth of software a day. He then expanded his small-scale enterprise by buying the rights to a series of security programs that he again sold as a complete package. His timing was immaculate: in November 1988 a previously unsuspected threat – a computer virus – appeared from nowhere and promptly infected ten per cent of all computers attached to the Internet. Internet protocols had been designed to survive a nuclear blast, but it was never considered that the threat might come from within the network itself. The antivirus market was born and Kremen, through a hunch, was one of the first onboard. Neither venture made Kremen a lot of money but they had an enormous impact on the young entrepreneur and gave him the confidence to trust his instincts about where these new computer networks were going.

And there was one thing Gary Kremen was sure about: it wouldn't be long before everyone was connected to these networks. It would mean the end of his software business model, but just imagine the possibilities if hundreds of thousands of people were all able to interact with one another using their computers. You could buy and sell stuff over it, just like you did in the real world. In fact you could buy something from a complete stranger on the other side of the country as if they were sitting at a terminal right next to you. It seemed amazing, even ridiculous, but it was clearly possible because that's what they were already doing – communicating directly, and with virtually no delay, to people thousands of miles away.

And so Kremen started thinking about how to create a business that would make money over the networks themselves, and the solution he came up with says much about the fledgling Internet itself: classified ads. The simple fact was that no one knew what use was going to be made of the Internet – whether it would be purely academic and just for serious work, or if it would become more personal and everyday. Kremen was sure that the Internet was going to reach far beyond work tasks and become a part of people's lives, and that hunch was backed up by the increasingly frivolous way computer scientists were using electronic mail on the network at the time.

Email was for serious information exchange, the employees were told. The computer networks were not a toy, they were expensive, hi-tech links. This staid approach was quickly blown away, though, thanks to familiarity – perhaps the best example being the introduction of the "smiley" in September 1982 to denote a joke or something funny. Of course being computer scientists, there was some serious discussion about how precisely you could signify a joke. "Maybe we should adopt a convention of putting a star (*) in the subject field of any notice which is to be taken as a joke," argued one, who had clearly failed to get a joke emailed to him earlier. Another disagreed: "I believe that the joke character should be % rather than *."

The conversation went on:

"How about using * for good jokes and % for bad jokes?"

"No, no, no! Surely everyone will agree that '&' is the funniest character on the keyboard. It looks funny (like a jolly fat man in convulsions of laughter)."

"I think that the joke character should be the sequence {#} because it looks like two lips with teeth showing between them."

Finally it was a man named Scott E. Fahlman who hit on the right idea: "I propose the following character sequence for joke markers: :-) Read it sideways." The smiley was born.

It was clear people were taking to the Internet in an informal way, but even so no one knew what they should expect to find there, or even what it would provide that other media such as newspapers, radio or television didn't. Classified ads in this context was a masterstroke. If people didn't know what was there, Kremen would simply provide them with a notice board and let them decide on their own – while taking a small fee for everything that appeared.

And so with the proceeds from his software business, he hired a lawyer, formed Electric Classifieds Inc., and embarked on a tour of Silicon Valley venture capitalists, attempting to sell them his vision of adverts carried over the Internet. He eventually raised $1.3 million, but a condition of the money was that he lost his position as CEO to a more experienced businessman, becoming chairman instead. It wasn't long, though, before Kremen and the CEO, retired newspaper editor Alan D. Mutter, clashed. Mutter didn't think Kremen was qualified enough to act as the company's marketing director as well as chairman, and Kremen disagreed. Loudly.

The personality clash was all the more difficult thanks to the enormous speed with which the Internet was changing. Tim Berners-Lee had just invented the World Wide Web. A company called Netscape then released something that many of us now think of as *being* the Internet – the Web browser (although Berners-Lee, among others, was very annoyed to discover that this piece of software allowed pictures to be viewed alongside text). In barely a few months, millions of dollars were being thrown into projects on the new computer networks. No one knew where it was going – or those that were foolish enough to claim they did were soon proved hopelessly wrong.

This frenzy of action made it impossible to draw up robust business plans, so people simply went with their gut feeling. Kremen's boss Alan Mutter did the same and, since he was an ex-newspaperman, felt that newspapers should be the focus of Electric Classifieds' business. That approach was backed up by the press themselves, with several newspapers marking out Electric Classifieds as the future of business on the Internet. And Kremen got his first taste of publicity – entered at number 36 in a poll of the top 100 people working on the World Wide Web. In July 1995, he was the focus of a two-page feature in the businessman's bible, *Forbes*. *Fortune* magazine devoted a page to Electric Classifieds; the hip new *Wired* magazine did the same.

But while Kremen's head was swelling, things grew more and more difficult within the company. Mutter was pushing the company in a direction that Kremen was certain was wrong, and tension grew. It finally came to a head when the company decided to ditch Kremen's pet project: a dating service he had set up at another of his domain names, match.com.

Kremen had built the dating side of the business from scratch, first over email, then through the very earliest browser, called Mosaic, and finally over the World Wide Web. He had acquired the domain name match.com at the same time he registered sex.com, and decided it was perfect for the service. But Mutter didn't like it. "He was very religious and he was embarrassed by Match.com," Kremen explains with irritation. "He wanted to go after the other classifieds. And I said 'dude, we've got to be like eBay and the newspapers have to be our enemies'. And we had big fights over that, and the board voted to sell Match.com."

Not that Kremen took the rejection graciously. "I screamed and screamed and screamed. I hit someone I think, I was so angry. I said: 'I think this is the one, let's forget the other classifieds, we've got traction here, we've got real income, it's growing like this every day. Let's back the successful horse.' But the old-timers were embarrassed by dating." Kremen was difficult, sometimes impossible to deal with, but his hunch had been right yet again. The board of Electric Classifieds sold Match.com for $8 million to a company called Cedant, but just a year-and-a-half later Cedant sold it on for $50 million. It is now the market leader in an enormous international online dating industry and makes hundreds of millions of dollars every year. Kremen retains a lifetime account, logging in as "The Founder".

The sale of Match.com marked the end of Kremen's association with the company he had started. He resigned and sold a small portion of his stock in a private sale, making just $50,000 from what was supposed to be a leading new-wave company, and immediately started another company, NetAngels, which produced what is now known as spyware – software that tracks what websites Internet users visit. He also acted as a broker for two of the biggest domain name sales of all time: computer.com for $500,000 and altavista.com for $3.35 million.

It was in domain names that Kremen's future lay. He was one of the very first people to recognise their commercial value, and had registered more names than most, including jobs.com, autos.com, housing.com, notices.com. The problem was that all these domains were now the property of Electric Classifieds Inc., the company he had just walked away from. Except, that is, for one.

"I kept sex.com in my name, because I remember saying to Peng [Ong, the co-founder of Electric Classifieds], 'we'll keep that in your and my name,' and he goes, 'Oh, no, in Singapore, they'll execute me!' And I went, fine, I'll take it."

Kremen registered sex.com under the name Online Classifieds Inc. because he thought at the time you had to register as a company or organisation, rather than an individual. It was an off-the-cuff decision that unwittingly opened the way for Stephen Cohen to steal the domain name.

Aside from sending a few test emails to make sure the domain worked, Kremen had never even put up a website on sex.com. But it was to sex.com that he turned once Electric Classifieds fell apart and he had moved on from NetAngels. The rumble of the approaching dotcom boom was already being felt, and in 1996, Kremen did a quick stock-take of the past two years. It was then that he suddenly realised his most valuable possession all along had been sex.com and that he still wasn't exactly sure why he didn't still own it.

5

SEX TRADE

By the time Kremen had come to this conclusion, Stephen Cohen was having the time of his life. Control of sex.com didn't just mean money – tons and tons of it – it was the golden key that unlocked his dreams.

Cohen is obsessed with sex, his other driving force being power. So having its number-one property on the biggest and newest marketplace in the world was mind-blowing. He instantly became a player in the adult industry, a seductive and extravagant business whose rewards are ready money, good times and easy sex. The gloss soon fades for most, but Cohen was in his element.

Perhaps surprisingly, considering his imagination and foresight, Cohen did nothing innovative with sex.com – he simply plastered it with ads for other porn websites. But then he didn't have to do anything more – this was sex.com, it was the days before search engines like Google, and millions of people arrived at the site every day by simply typing "sex.com" into their Web browsers and hitting return. He could afford to let everyone else do the running.

Besides which, Stephen Cohen possesses an odd sort of laziness. When there is a scam to be pulled off, or a deal to be made, he will go to extraordinary lengths to cover every possible angle. But once the buzz is over and the scam pulled, in everyday life Cohen is hopelessly sloppy.

So he covered sex.com with paying ads when he could have established the biggest pornography website on the Internet and stolen the market. The very earliest version of sex.com that went up on the Internet, back in 1996, featured a garish mixture of fonts in different sizes, styles and colours on a dark blue patterned background. It was basic and poorly designed even by the standards of the time.

The entry page threatened (in an intriguing fashion of course) that if you weren't 18 years old and tried to enter the site you would be in trouble. There was plenty of pseudo-legal language ("... you NOW understand that YOU hereby certify, state and acknowledge to all, that you are familiar with the laws pertaining to the viewing of sexually explicit material in your community ..."). There were also lots of spelling mistakes, and – this being Stephen Cohen's site – a number of complete falsehoods.

A nice touch was that the "Exit" button (for minors and prudes) went to a sex chat room that paid Cohen for any visitors from his website. If you clicked on "Enter", you hit another page – this time with a pink background of cartoonish breasts – and were asked a second time if you were sure you wanted to "view explicit, sexually oriented materials". The Exit button this time went to a different website, which also paid Cohen per visitor. This second page was entirely superfluous, but had the effect of doubling the number of "hits" on the website before people had even got inside – something Cohen would use to claim more visitors than he really had, and so charge advertisers more.

Once inside sex.com, you were hit by a barrage of slim rectangular ads for other porn sites featuring explicit photos and crude language. They ran, one after the other, all the way down the page and cost $45,000 each a month. A column on the left let you sign up for "free memberships" by typing in your email address and then, as you went down, there was a series of text links for things like "Teen hardcore fucking!", "Gay Sex Boys", "Gang Bang Cam" and so on, which took you to more paying websites. These ads cost $10,000 a month.

There was a "Sex in the news" link that led to a short summary of news stories with the general theme of sex, bought-in for a few thousands dollars a month. There were also two pictures of the day, a cartoon of the day, and a story of the day, all of which were updated less than once a month and after the first few months ditched altogether. Even this small amount of work was too much trouble for Cohen.

Lastly, right at the very bottom, were small text links to the "Sex.Com Members Area", "Join Sex.Com", "Advertising Info", "HOW TO!", and "Copyright Info". The members' area was a pretty poor deal by all accounts: Cohen had very little material on sex.com, but you were still charged the going rate of $25 per month on your credit card. And, if later court documents are to be believed, often more than once.

The "How To" area was the only area where Cohen left his mark, in the form of a series of five short guides by the master himself. One, "Anal Intercourse and Analingus. By Stephen Cohen", was no more than a plain orange webpage with black text. Hemingway it was not: "For many people, anal sex is the ultimate taboo. Buttfucking makes it sound crude and dirty, sodomy sounds technical. But some people love anal sex. Others hate it. Others haven't tried it yet and are curious ..." Cohen then goes into some detail. The guides for oral sex (male and female) and hand jobs were written by "Tammy, Linda and Nicole", but had an oddly Stephen Cohen ring to them. And a guide to US law and sex was little more than a copy of state sodomy laws copied from another website.

The entire site was designed to get maximum money for minimum effort. And it barely changed over the five years that Cohen ran sex.com, going through two redesigns but retaining exactly the same approach – dozens of paid-for ads to other sites. What was extraordinary about this complacency was that the adult industry itself was rocketing ahead with the very latest Internet technologies – webcams, live link-ups, instant messaging, streaming video – in order to attract customers.

Cohen simply used sex.com's billboard status to promote other peoples' efforts for a healthy profit.

Cohen now likes to paint himself as a great businessman when he was in charge of sex.com, but the fact was that he made his mark on the adult business not by producing better goods or services but by scaring the bejesus out of his competitors. And he did it through trademark law, using the same line that he had used against Kremen.

When you apply for a trademark, it goes through an initial approval process, and then the claim is published in specialist journals to see if anyone has an objection. If there is no opposition, the trademark application then goes through a second, more thorough, checking system. And if it emerges from that unchallenged, it is then approved.

Since this process can take years, however, and since trademarks exist to protect companies from others stealing their ideas, the system has evolved so that the mere application for a trademark holds legal weight.

Filled with this knowledge, Cohen applied his criminal mind. He claimed to have trademark rights to "sex.com", and to have had it since 1979 – a claim that he still repeats to this day despite not having a shred of evidence. On the trademark application, he stated that an earlier bulletin board computer system he had run included a section called "sex.com" which stood for "Sex Communications". Cohen then provided testimony and printouts to prove his point. Unfortunately the documents were forgeries and the testimony worthless.

But that was beside the point. If he had a trademark application to point to, he could work his magic. In May 1996 – eight months after he had stolen sex.com – Cohen applied to the United States Patent and Trademark Office (USPTO) for the trademark "sex.com" and received application number 75106638. The application was immediately spat back at him by a patent investigator for containing none of the information required. So Cohen hired a specialist law firm to rewrite the application and resubmitted his claim. It was rejected a second time for being too similar to an existing trademark for "Sex Net". So Cohen simply forged an agreement between him and the owner of that trademark and faxed it to the USPTO.

Cohen knew it didn't matter whether the application was legitimate or not – all that mattered was that it was going through the process. What he did then took his unique audacity and confidence to pull off. Despite having no basis in fact or reality, he devised a plan that worked against some of the toughest businessmen in the adult world – people that no one can accuse of being naive or easily intimidated. He simply contacted anyone that owned a dotcom domain that contained the word "sex" and informed them, in no uncertain terms, that they were infringing his trademark, and, as a result, unless they wanted to face his lawyers for infringement proceedings, they would have to pay him "licensing fees". Sometimes, he simply demanded ownership of the domain.

In the late 1990s, no one was sure of the value of domain names, apart from the fact they only cost $100 to buy. Faced with a businessman earning millions of dollars threatening to bring hell down on you unless you complied, the majority of people that Cohen cornered capitulated and handed the domains over. After all, it would cost five times the cost of the thing just to get a lawyer to reply.

An early target was FT Inc., which owned sexsex.com and sexysex.com. Cohen asked the company for licensing fees. When he heard nothing back, he sued. On 10 February 1997, FT Inc. received a complaint for trademark infringement and unfair competition, alongside a request for a jury trial.

"Since at least 1979, plaintiff has continuously used the SEX.COM mark in interstate commerce in connection with providing access to adult entertainment material on computer bulletin board systems (BBS), the Internet and the World Wide Web," the complaint read.

It was more BS than BBS, but it caught people's attention.

The complaint then accused FT Inc. of "wilful, wanton, malicious, intentional" conduct while asking for damages, threatening directors, staff and customers, and demanding all profits made by the company while it had been "infringing" the sex.com mark – which, according to Cohen, was 1979. It was a particularly heavy-handed approach, and was designed to be, scaring the hell out of small companies that thought there might be something in this Internet business but who didn't have the experience, courage or pockets to deal with a heavy legal action.

Once successful, Cohen repeated this approach over and over again, amassing a huge portfolio of domains effectively for free. Inevitably he came up against other big guns in the adult industry who weren't as easily intimidated and who had the funds to wage a legal battle. Cohen was, as ever, one step ahead, and had already prepared for the confrontation.

6

THE OREGON WAY

Everyone knows or has met someone who is able to get seemingly impossible things done, from finding some luxury item in the middle of nowhere, to persuading someone to do something out of the ordinary, often against their better judgment. A shortcut, a tip, the man with the inside track. Stephen Cohen is that person.

An easy manner, a splash of charm, the ability to read people instantly and a very, very quick mind is what you need if you are to make a living conning people out of their possessions. But they are all as nothing without the right knowledge and careful planning. Stephen Cohen possesses an extraordinary ability to acquire snippets of information and then weave them together to create an entirely different, and entirely convincing, picture about what is happening or has just happened.

It makes him an extraordinary storyteller, and he will literally tell you tale after tale for hours. He will tell you about meeting Bill Gates. "I know him. I went to Comdex one year – I arrived on the Tuesday and I couldn't get a badge because it was late, around 5.30 p.m. There were some old farts on security, about 65, so I just walked in. And I saw a group of people watching big screen TV but with the sound turned off. So I walked up to this guy, introduced myself and started talking ..."

He will tell you about his Rolls Royce: "It was a 1979 Silver Cloud. But I remember the insurance company asked me for the horse power of the car because it wasn't listed anywhere, so I wrote to Rolls Royce's headquarters in England saying 'What is the horsepower of my car, I need to know for my insurance company' and they wrote me a letter back. It contained one word: 'sufficient'."

He will tell you about charming the most beautiful woman in the world in a lift in Nicaragua. He will leave pregnant pauses in an intriguing story about how a Caribbean plane due to take off returned to a terminal to let on several mysterious American-speaking men dressed exactly alike. Whatever the subject, whatever the country, whatever the moment, Stephen Cohen has a story to tell about it. And every story has in it a kernel of truth, a fascinating snippet that he has picked up from somewhere that he then weaves a tale around.

But while this most human of gifts makes Stephen Cohen a great man to chat to, it is also the basis of his criminal enterprise. He has learnt that if you talk to someone long enough they will relax and be more likely to break confidences. The sheer amount of time he spends talking on the phone is extraordinary. He has new phone lines installed in every place he lives; he has become an expert on the latest technology that runs calls over the Internet; when in jail he made literally dozens of phone calls every day. Stephen Cohen was born with a phone attached to his ear.

This mastery of the phone and ability to draw out secrets achieves remarkable results. Cohen would often taunt Kremen by calling him up and providing small details of Kremen's legal tactics, often just hours after they had been discreetly prepared. Talk with him about a wide range of subjects, and he will have a comment to make on something that happened only hours earlier. Cohen picks up interesting titbits before they become public knowledge and uses them to give the impression of knowledge and authority. The catch is that there is almost no depth to that knowledge – something that becomes increasingly obvious the more you speak with him.

An old friend and lawyer of Cohen's, Frank Butler, knows this better than most. "Steve is the sort of person that has read the first page of every book ever written. He would pick your brain for all of the salient points of an issue and then regurgitate them back to you. And he could use them to his advantage. He is a very bright person." One of Kremen's lawyers, James (Jim) Wagstaffe, is less complimentary: "If you lit a match in front of his mouth, the whole room would explode it is so full of gas."

Nonetheless, through a potent combination of careful planning, bald untruths, aggressive legal pressure and endless phone calls, Cohen manages to achieve seemingly impossible results, getting people to hand over money, cars, even houses in return for nothing. And he has done it over and over again for nearly 40 years.

It is an old maxim that you can't con an honest man. As a result, conmen are often viewed as loveable rogues, even though they feed off people's weaknesses, because the person who loses out knew they were up to no good in the first place. Cohen doesn't fit this model of con man. He is certainly devastatingly charming when he needs to be, he can spin a yarn and have you believe it's true, but Stephen Michael Cohen prefers – loves – to fox, bewilder and cajole honest people into making mistakes. People aren't complicit in a Stephen Cohen scam – he takes you for what you're worth and then turns around and grins, defying you to try to get your possessions back. The result is that Cohen's skills at avoiding people – creditors, bailiffs, lawyers, angry husbands, sheriffs – are even more honed than those he uses to con people in the first place.

California has no fewer than four district courts and is home to one of twelve Appeals Courts of the United States. Cohen knows every one. But even though he, most of his businesses, and most of the adult industry are based in and around Los Angeles, he decided to sue the owners of domains containing the word "sex" in the state of Oregon, over 1,000 miles north. The state of Oregon has just one district court, no Appeals Court, and a culture of law practice that is a million miles away from the tough-talking, ruthless existence of LA lawyers so frequently portrayed in films and on television. In Oregon things also go much, much faster.

"In Oregon, I tried a murder case in three days," exclaims Charles Carreon – another of Kremen's lawyers. "I won a $300,000 verdict after a four-day trial: the jury was out for two hours! It takes them all day in LA just to pick the foreman! Here, they *move* your ass."

Cohen had learnt about the speed of the courts of Oregon and decided to use it to his advantage. While he was hoping that his application for a "sex.com" trademark would be approved, he also knew he had faked the supporting documents so there was a big risk it would be turned down. So he decided to go in fast and go in hard with anyone that stood up to him. If someone refused to hand over their "sex" domain or pay the licensing fees, Cohen came good on his threat and took them to court – no fewer than eleven times in two years.

He hired a tough and aggressive law firm to make sure people took him seriously: DuBoff Dorband Cushing & King. Leonard DuBoff is a highly experienced Oregon notable, and an acknowledged expert in trademark law, albeit one without sight or a right hand, thanks to an explosion in his youth. He led the initial charge.

One of the first people to benefit from this personal attention was porn giant Serge Birbrair and his company Signs Signs Signs. Cohen wanted Birbrair's "sexia.com" domain but Birbrair had refused.

The next thing Birbrair knew, on 10 February 1998, Signs Signs Signs received no fewer than five legal documents: a trademark infringement complaint; a discovery order requesting that he hand over all relevant information concerning sexia.com; a motion for a temporary restraining order preventing him from using the domain; a memorandum in support of the motion for a temporary restraining order; and an affidavit from Cohen's company again backing up the call for a temporary restraining order.

Just two days later, the issue appeared before an Oregon judge, who set a calendar for the case to be heard. Just seven days after that, the hearing took place, and the very next day Cohen was granted a preliminary injunction. Cohen immediately provided this injunction to the dotcom registry, Network Solutions, and sexia.com was dead.

And that was it – in just ten days, Birbrair went from having a leading adult website to having nothing. And he hadn't even begun to fight Cohen. The combination of his distant Oregon lawyers and an overwhelming first action was a knockout punch and the combination was so successful that Cohen used it again and again and again, building a huge number of premium domain names through pure, raw aggression. No one had seen anything like it, particularly not over the fledgling Internet.

Before Birbrair's case had even ended, Cohen had taken another company to court: Netsphere and its freesex.com domain. He used the exact same approach: five legal documents outlining the claimed infringement, three of them requesting an injunction. The only difference was the name of the domain in the documents. Just two days after lodging the complaint in court, the case was in front of a judge. It was a Wednesday and the first case conference was arranged for that Friday. The case conference was carried out by telephone and gave Netsphere just eleven days to respond.

Netsphere was completely overwhelmed and decided the best thing to do was hide. Cohen's lawyers tried to serve the company with the legal papers but couldn't find them. After three weeks of looking, they informed the court they had only located one of the three defendants. But Cohen didn't stop at that. A week later, Netsphere was tracked down and presented with the court documents. The very next day, the hearing took place without the defendants present.

The judge gave Netsphere another eleven days to respond, but the case was already won. It handed over the domain before the second deadline was up.

There was no stopping Cohen. Just eight days after filing suit against Netsphere, the same process was repeated all over again with another company, Netside, for the domain "sexcom.net". Again the five documents arrived. Again, just two days later, the judge laid down a calendar for the case.

The process was so fast each time that companies barely had time to formulate a response before their domain was put on hold. Netside at least tried to slow the process down: being a Florida company and so on the other side of the United States, it argued Oregon was an improper venue. But just a week later it decided it couldn't handle the legal pressure and simply handed over the domain to Cohen.

This approach hadn't gone unnoticed in the adult industry. People were running scared, but a few were getting increasingly angry. It didn't help that Cohen did almost nothing with the domains he acquired, often simply putting up a single page that redirected to sex.com. Everything was maximum profit for minimum effort.

The domain-name crusade was suddenly halted in its tracks, however, when one company – the owner of "hotsex.com" – decided to take the fight to Cohen before Cohen had the chance to sue him. Three days after Cohen had launched his third court case, against Netside, he was named as the main defendant in a civil case brought against him by Michael Davon of Web-Depot, who faced him with his own tactics: Web-Depot was based in Cambridge, Massachusetts – the opposite end of America.

Davon also hired a trademark specialist to argue his case. Unfortunately for him, the speed of law was more Californian than Oregonian in Massachusetts, so it took another two months for the case to come before a judge.

This wasn't the only challenge Cohen faced. The undisputed king of online porn, Ron Levi, saw his chance and got involved. Levi had been watching Cohen's progress in the adult industry, and when Cohen stopped his rampage against other "sex" domains thanks to Web-Depot lawsuit, Levi jumped in. Levi owned "wwwsex.com". So those that typed in the "www" web address but didn't hit the full stop, would be taken to http://www.wwwsex.com. It sounds stupid, but it was incredibly effective. More importantly than that though, the name tackled a fundamental element of trademark law.

An intriguing aspect of trademark – often abused by companies to explain unethical behaviour – is that a company has to defend any misuse of its mark if it is to keep it. So if Cohen didn't react to someone using a domain that included the term "sex.com", he couldn't then go and attack someone else later for having a dotcom with the word "sex" in it. Levi knew this and so launched a site at wwwsex.com while Cohen was waiting for the Web-Depot case to come to court.

But Cohen – who had been carefully avoiding the notoriously tough Levi – had noticed the sudden appearance of the site, realised what it meant, and so sued. Ron Levi received the same five legal papers, but this time with the domain "wwwsex.com" filling in the blanks. Levi had his Californian attorney immediately apply for permission to represent him in an Oregon court, and the two found themselves in a stand-off. Both decided that the fight was for another day, however, and a month later Cohen withdrew his complaint and Levi took down his site. It was a wary truce, and one that finally broke down when Cohen found out that Levi had started funding Gary Kremen's legal battle against him.

Cohen then fought for another three months with Web-Depot and Michael Davon in Massachusetts, gradually losing ground. Eight months in and just days before the trial date, Cohen settled and hoped that no one on the West Coast would notice.

Cohen then continued as if nothing had happened, sending out another long list of demands to "sex" domain owners threatening them with legal action unless they capitulated. This time, however, Cohen found a more defiant adult industry that refuse to simply cave in when they received a letter from

DuBoff Dorband Cushing & King. On 29 July 1999 his legal team filed no fewer than five trademark infringement lawsuits and kicked the whole process off again.

By 2001, Cohen owned, among many, many other domains: lovemysex.com, wwwsex.net, wesex.com, 4sexy.com, ezhotsex.com, sexq.com, sexonline.com, hardsexonline.com, sexxlist.com, sexxxlist.com, trysex.com and truesex.com.

It is difficult to underestimate how happy Cohen was during this period – possibly for the first time since his childhood. He had spent his whole adult life pulling scams and then rapidly avoiding the fallout. No matter how much Cohen had congratulated himself on his prowess at not being caught, there had always been people after him. And despite all his feelings of superiority, it was quite clear society had thought little of him.

Now, however, sitting on top of sex.com, he found both the buzz he craved and, for the first time, a measure of respectability in the eyes of at least some of the rest of the world. It may have been the sleazy adult industry, and he may have been basing his entire legal crusade on a domain name he had stolen, using a trademark application he knew to be fraudulent, but he was successfully screwing people and didn't have to watch his back while he did it. The money, power and sense of legitimacy was intoxicating.

Unfortunately for Cohen, the more Gary Kremen saw him using sex.com to build a fortune and found a business, the more determined he became to take it off him. A strange intensity started building between the two, as each put more and more store in having control of the domain.

7

PHONE CALLS

If it hadn't been for the allure of sex.com, Gary Kremen and Stephen Cohen would most likely never have met one another nor ever even been in the same room. They lived only a short distance apart but inhabited entirely different worlds. Kremen was a respectable Stanford-educated business brain, used to cutting high-level business deals in the fast-moving technology field; Cohen was a street hustler, on the make and always looking for the easy score.

They were both enormously driven, highly intelligent and determined to make millions by whatever means they could and yet they could not be more opposite. Even as the two men fought their battles through proxies, neither could resist finding out more about who was directing the troops. Cohen and Kremen had spoken twice very briefly: the first time when Kremen called to find out what the hell was going on with sex.com, and a second time when Cohen pretended to be from NSI.

But driven by a fascination of the other, the phonecalls were soon to become a regular feature, starting with one call Kremen received early on in the case. "I remember he called and left a message. He said, 'This is Steve Cohen, give us a call.' And I thought, oh he's calling to settle. And then he'd just call and start going into, you know, he's owned this since 1979 and how he could prove it with some trademark documents and he had witnesses and he also had sexonline.com. But you know – you want to hear it – because it's intelligence. Even if your enemy or the other side is trying to confuse you – you want to hear it."

That experience is something that everyone who has known Stephen Cohen recognises. He loves the sound of his own voice and will call at any time, day or night, and talk for hours. Cohen gave Kremen his phone number, and a few days later, just out of interest, Kremen called Cohen and they talked again. "He can be interesting," Kremen explains. "And in the beginning, he mostly called me."

Soon, however, Kremen started growing tired of hearing the same old story. Even though he would always have an entertaining tale to tell, Cohen always got back to the fact that he had the rights to sex.com. "He talks, and talks, and talks, and talks," Kremen continues. "He'll go on with his own fantasies, and it's kinda convincing. It's like a Gestapo effect – if you hear it enough, you will believe it. There is a Goebbels part to him."

It was Goebbels who said: If you tell a lie, big enough, often enough, people will believe it. It could be Stephen Cohen's motto. But while the phone calls were Stephen Cohen's way to try to shake Kremen's belief in his ownership of sex.com by repeating the same mantra over and over again, they soon became something else entirely.

Sometimes before and sometimes after hearings in the case, Cohen called Kremen to tell him how he was going to have his ass kicked. Sometimes he would call before, and then if Charles Carreon, one of Kremen's lawyers, had had a bad day, he would call Kremen again after, rubbing it in. Cohen also swamped everyone else with calls: he'd call Carreon and tell him tales of derring-do; he'd call up legal secretaries and court clerks and post-room boys posing as various people and sweet-talk them into providing any information about the case they had. He called another of Kremen's lawyers, Sheri Falco, pretending to be from NSI. He occasionally called Jim Wagstaffe (yet another of Kremen's lawyers), although Wagstaffe played it very formally: "First I would check with his lawyer that it was okay to talk with him. Then I'd always have someone else listening in on the conversation. I would always tell him someone was listening. But then he always said he was recording the conversation. This wasn't confidential."

It was how Cohen had always operated, and then whenever he picked up an interesting snippet of information, he would wend a tale around it and call Kremen to inform him why he was going to lose the case. And it worked. Kremen – who became increasingly worried about where his case was going and how much money he was spending on it – would get mad or he would get depressed. If Cohen outlined why his new legal tactic was going to be a disaster, Kremen would call his attorneys and demand they explain why it wasn't. If Cohen called when Kremen was on a comedown from crystal meth, it hurt, and only increased the sense of depression, which in turn led to Kremen taking more methamphetamine to pull out of it. But, like Kremen said, he wanted to hear it. Cohen had got hold of his mobile number and Kremen would answer it.

It reached the point where Cohen even called Kremen to tell him what he was going to do in order to toy with him, although this mind-game occasionally backfired, such as when he told Kremen about his plans to put a company of Kremen's through bankruptcy. Cohen wanted to hear Kremen's reaction as he gave him the news. Although in that case, forewarned was forearmed and Kremen's lawyers managed to beat Cohen at his own game, albeit with some help from an alert magistrate.

The calls slipped into a strange bond between the two men that remained even when the case started turning back the other way and it was Kremen who started calling Cohen to goad and mock. It became even stranger when Kremen managed to take control of Cohen's mansion. Cohen couldn't stand the idea of Kremen calling him from his own home, crowing about it, so he smashed the place to pieces. At least he would know that Kremen would be calling from a wreck.

One night, a few months after he had moved in, Kremen found in a drawer some of Cohen's personal possessions that had been missed, including a number of menus from his favourite restaurants. Some of Kremen's friends were over so he called Cohen on speakerphone and after some chit-chat, started reading out items from the menus asking Cohen what he wanted and if he'd like to come over for dinner. Cohen exploded with rage; Kremen and his friends fell about laughing.

Kremen did the same about a year later when he learnt from Cohen's credit-card records that his favourite restaurant had been the Samurai sushi restaurant on Lomas Santa Fe Drive, about ten minutes' drive from the house. Cohen had eaten there every night for years. So Kremen paid it a visit and then called Cohen in the middle of the meal to tell him what he was having for dinner and where he was having it. "He didn't call back for six months," Kremen says with some amusement but also a little sadness. The next time Kremen was in the restaurant, something occurred to him and he gave the owner his card and asked him to call him if he ever saw his old customer Steve Cohen in there. The next thing he knew he had a call from Cohen. "I'm way ahead of you," he told Kremen. The owner had called Cohen to tell him about the visitor.

For ten years, the twists and turns, the ups and downs were all played out between the two in long, sometimes tortuous phone conversations. Even when Kremen won sex.com back, Cohen would call telling him in a hundred different ways how he had screwed up the business and how he would never make it. "Look at his peers in the sex industry – he's a joke," Cohen said at the time. "He makes lots of press but he's a joke. A lot of them are taking advantage of him. It's not a pretty picture: allowing a site to go from the top site on the Internet to the toilet. The best thing would be to bury it." Ten minutes later, he was back on the same subject: "It's barely running on life support. The decent thing to do would be to let it run until it dies."

When Kremen was after his money and Cohen shifted it just in time to another bank, within hours his number would flash up on Kremen's phone and Kremen knew then that the plan his investigators had been working on for two months had failed.

Equally, when Cohen saw Kremen's number he knew something had gone wrong for him. The desire for both of them was to leave it, but at the same time they were both desperate to know what had happened.

Kremen recognises in retrospect that he shouldn't have answered Cohen's calls or let him into his head. "His genius is in wearing people down. And he's very good at that." And did he wear Kremen down? "He did. But he didn't win."

8

ANATOMY OF A THEFT

It's become widely accepted Net folklore that sex.com was stolen by a forged letter. But the truth is that the letter was produced several months after the domain had already been stolen.

How do we know? Because Network Solutions has never produced the original letter. Why? Because it was never sent to the company. The letter was written in December 2005 by Cohen, backdated to October, and only ever faxed to NSI. It was no more than Cohen's ingenuous after-the-fact attempt to get past company checks.

If it wasn't the letter that provided authorisation, how exactly did Stephen Cohen steal sex.com?

There is only one man who knows for sure, but he prefers to argue, even now, that the letter is legitimate. However, thanks to the legal right of discovery, NSI was obliged to hand Gary Kremen all documents – including emails and records of telephone calls – relating to the transfer of the domain name, and from these it has become possible to piece together what happened more than a decade ago, on 18 October 1995.

How did Stephen Cohen steal sex.com? By hacking Network Solutions' systems. Except being Stephen Cohen he did it the opposite way to normal. Hackers use what they call "social engineering" to break into computer systems. This is no more than calling someone up at the company and persuading them to hand over useful details, such as a username and password by, say, pretending to be an IT administrator and so a figure of authority, or by telling a tale and appealing to someone's sympathies. Once the hacker has an entry point into a system, he can then use his computer skills to work his way into other parts of the system.

Unfortunately, Stephen Cohen's coding skills – while significantly better than most of the population's – were not enough for him to crack the first version of NSI's domain automation software. And so he settled for causing the system to throw up a query over the sex.com domain, and then used his extraordinary skills of manipulation to persuade a human at the other end that the change should go through.

Because of the huge interest in domain names, it rapidly became impossible for Network Solutions to go through all the applications for domain names manually, and so the company designed and built a system for automating the registration of new names. This system was in a constant state of change, going rapidly through different versions as software engineers made it better and faster.

At the time Stephen Cohen stole sex.com, the system comprised a single one-size-fits-all Web form. If you wanted to make a change to your details (i.e. change your physical address, or telephone number) you used one part of the form. If you wanted to delete your domain registration, you used a different part of the form.

There was also a whole manner of shorthand, incomprehensible to anyone unfamiliar with the system, but which Cohen had learned by talking to, and charming, Network Solutions employees on the phone. He also learnt NSI's unpublished methods and procedures, lending him a sense of easy authority and believability when talking to employees on the phone.

Cohen actually made several attempts to change the ownership of sex.com in the days before 17 October 1995, trying out a number of different combinations until he struck lucky. In the end, he put in two contradictory requests on the same form: a "D" for delete order, meaning the whole domain-name ownership information should be deleted; and an "N" order, for new information, which contained a new email address and telephone number for sex.com. As a result, he received an email from NSI asking for confirmation of the changes.

Network Solutions' automated system in fact responded to both email addresses – Kremen's and the new email address (Cohen's) asking for a confirmation of the changes and asking for any response to be titled "urgent resubmission". Cohen immediately sent back a response – but Kremen did not. He says he never received the email. What's more, since Kremen had registered the domain by mail, he expected any future changes would be relayed to him the same way (the ability to buy a domain name with a credit card through a website was still some way off in 1995).

Nonetheless the reason Kremen never received the email covering Cohen's changes was because, by some bizarre coincidence, Kremen's Netcom account had been taken over months earlier by infamous hacker Kevin Mitnick, who used it to hide his identity while online. Just hours before Mitnick was finally arrested by the FBI in North Carolina in February 1995, he had been logged on as Kremen and was hacking into a number of companies' computer servers. Kremen never received email at his Netcom address from that point on.

But this is all beside the point because Network Solutions should never have accepted only Cohen's response as sufficient to change the details. So why did it? Because Cohen called NSI up and persuaded whoever was on the other end that the change was legitimate because the Netcom email address was not in use and because Kremen had been "fired".

We can't be sure who gave the green light because all the depositions with NSI employees have been sealed by court order, but it is clear Cohen had built up an affinity with someone authorised to put the changes through. He was a regular customer of the company and so, during the course of buying several domain names, had developed a certain level of trust with a number of individuals. Cohen went on to exploit these relationships when he sued other "sex" domains and contacted NSI to get them suspended once he had a court order. To NSI's eyes, Stephen Cohen was a respectable and regular customer. So when he asked for one small procedural element to be overlooked, it went through.

Once Gary Kremen's name and email address had been changed, Cohen was in a position to authorise other changes to sex.com. And so, gradually, carefully, he did make changes, until there were no remnants of Kremen's ownership left.

Even now, Network Solutions prefers to pretend the whole thing never happened. The company and its lawyers steadfastly refuse to make any comment on the matter, and requests are met either with contemptuous silence or a period of lengthy consideration followed by a refusal to discuss even the slightest detail. And so it was when Gary Kremen called the company in 1995 to ask what had happened to his sex.com domain.

"They said they'd investigate, I said fine. But they never got back to me, so I called again. They kept on saying, we're gonna investigate, we're gonna investigate, we're gonna investigate."

And investigate they did. The director of business affairs, David Graves, contacted Stephen Cohen. Cohen assured him everything was above board and he would send proof, and then called Kremen pretending to be from NSI. He left it a fortnight to see if anything happened, and when nothing did, Cohen faxed the forged letter to Network Solutions.

NSI must have known at that point that the transfer was fishy. A subsequent review by the Appeals Court refused to believe that the company could have thought it was legitimate. But with Kremen not chasing it up, they let the matter drop. The last thing the company needed was news getting out that someone had found a way to bypass its checking system because, quite simply, it could ruin the company's entire plan to make billions of dollars from selling domains.

By the time Kremen realised his mistake and called NSI again, his problem had been buried under a million other issues. The domain-name market had taken off, and in just a year had gone from registering 1,400 domains a month to a blistering 30,000. Not only that, but a whole range of novel legal questions involving domain names had started appearing. NSI was expanding at an enormous rate, it was never out of the newspapers, and even governments were starting to investigate it. It had far bigger problems than one guy trying to dig up an old problem the company thought had been settled.

And so NSI fobbed Kremen off. "It got to the point where I wasn't getting any answers, so I hired a lawyer," Kremen recalls. Kremen had met Greg Raifman through his legal work for an early Internet service provider. So he hired him, and Raifman started chasing Cohen and NSI, sending letters asking for copies of any transfer requests regarding the domain. Both Cohen and NSI refused. So Raifman sent more letters and made more phone calls. Cohen's attorney, Michael Mayock, still refused, but NSI's David Graves promised he would look into it. Raifman kept the pressure on, and finally, eventually, eight months after Cohen had stolen the domain and more than six months since NSI had received the forged letter purporting to be from Sharon Dimmick of Online Classifieds handing over ownership of the sex.com domain to Cohen – the apparent evidence that the transfer was legitimate – the company sent Kremen a copy.

And it was then, for the first time, and despite everything Kremen thought he knew about Stephen Cohen, that it suddenly sunk in. He wasn't facing a man who had got lucky and now refused to hand over sex.com because it was valuable; he had strayed into the path of a calculating, determined, ruthless and brilliant con man. With a mixture of fury and trepidation, he picked up the phone to his attorney.

Raifman immediately called NSI and explained the letter was a forgery. This Sharon Dimmick had nothing to do with Online Classifieds, and nothing to do with sex.com – she was no more than an old flatmate of Gary Kremen's, he insisted. She didn't even spell her name that way, it was Sharyn with a "y". What's more, Stephen Cohen was a convicted felon and a crook and they had the court records to prove it. Raifman demanded that NSI hold an immediate investigation and return the domain to Kremen. But NSI remained silent. He called a week later, furious. And then again the next day, a Friday. And again on the Monday. And again on the Tuesday.

NSI had had the forged letter for six months. It delayed sending it to Kremen but had already made its decision before it finally handed it over. Taking into account NSI's unquestioned authority, the dangerous chain of events that an investigation might set in motion, and the fact that Kremen was just one, small domain owner, it was the smart choice.

But Jim Wagstaffe, the lawyer brought in years later to review exactly what happened with NSI, has a less conspiratorial explanation. "Why didn't NSI hand it over? People like having things a certain way. My father was a lawyer, he's dead now, and he couldn't understand why people didn't still use carbon paper when Xerox came in. When faxes came, he didn't understand why people were sending faxes. He'd say: 'Give them a call!' I gave him a computer, a laptop, three years before he died, but he never even took it out of the box. And he was a very good lawyer, a very intelligent man. People don't take change well. It's difficult." Either way, NSI refused an investigation.

Raifman wrote to Cohen's lawyer and demanded the return of the domain, but it was a waste of time. Nonetheless, the fact that Kremen had the forged letter in his hand worried Cohen enough to set up another new company and to move ownership of sex.com for a fourth time in just eight months – from Nevada-based Sporting Houses to Ocean Fund International, a company based in the notorious offshore tax haven of the British Virgin Islands.

NSI had refused an investigation and the domain name had changed ownership to an offshore holding company. "And that was when I knew we had big problems, big problems," Kremen confesses.

9

DIMMICK'S DILEMMA

In fact, Graves' decision very nearly killed the whole matter stone dead. Kremen just didn't have the money to take the Internet's biggest and most powerful company to court. Letters were one thing – official complaints, witnesses, law courts, judges, juries and top-notch lawyers quite another.

It wasn't until nearly a year later that Kremen restarted the whole process. His burning sense of injustice lent him the fire for a fight. "I'd had enough. And I knew about the statute of limitations – I wanted my name back. I was ready. I was thinking about doing a sluttier version of Match.com."

Raifman had since moved onto other cases and clients, so Kremen hired another lawyer. This was Sheri Falco, just out of law school and with lots to prove. She worked from an office in the building where Kremen's businesses were based. "I said Sheri, I've got this problem, they're not responding, can you send some letters?" He paid her $5,000.

"I had just graduated law school and started my own intellectual law practice," Falco recalls. "I was doing Internet law and multimedia law, and graphic designers and things like that." She also recalls when she got involved in the case. "At some point Gary came up to me and he said, 'I've got this case that I want you to look at,' so he kept saying that for a month or two, and then at some point he brought in this piece of paper, which was – you know – the infamous fraudulent letter.

"So I looked at that document, and it was clearly fraudulent, so I started to do a little bit of investigation about the sex.com trademark. And at that very moment – I mean it was fortuitous, really – Stephen Cohen had applied to the United States Patent and Trademark Office for a federally registered trademark for the name 'sex.com'. And so I filed an opposition to that trademark."

If it had been a few months earlier or later, the whole case would have been stillborn, but with Falco's name on a document opposing Cohen's "sex.com" trademark application, and with Kremen emailing anyone with "sex" in their domain to tell them about his situation, she suddenly started receiving calls from people who had been threatened by Cohen and wanted to get their own back.

"It all kind of escalated rather quickly," Falco remembers. Among the most interesting phone calls was one from Serge Birbrair, who had lost his sexia.com domain to Cohen but done his own research on the man and uncovered a long criminal history going back to the 1970s. Other phone calls wished Kremen luck, some asked what they could do to help end Cohen's campaign of plunder. The news about Kremen's claim started appearing on adult industry websites, giving him some notoriety but there remained a very big problem: he couldn't afford a proper legal action. Whenever he had a few thousand dollars spare, he put it into the case, but rather naively hoped that the threat of legal action would be enough to get sex.com back.

Greg Raifman had managed to get the forged letter out of NSI, and Falco had blocked Cohen's trademark application, but with Cohen making it quite clear he wouldn't hand over sex.com without a fight, and NSI refusing to hand over the domain, Kremen had run out of options.

It looked hopeless. Until, that is, he received a discreet offer of financial help from two of the adult industry's most colourful characters, both of whom wanted Cohen brought down: Ron Levi and Seth Warshavsky.

Levi is a driving force in the adult industry. A calm, controlled and intelligent man, Levi keeps his private life private and is not a man to cross lightly. Levi had already clashed with Cohen over "wwwsex.com" and exchanged lawsuits before both warily backed down. He didn't like the look of Cohen and realised it was only a matter of time before Cohen would try to screw him, so he decided to get his shot in first. In terms of personality, Seth Warshavsky could not be more different to Levi. In many respects an odious man (one school friend describes how Seth tried to persuade him to drink a milkshake that he had urinated in), Warshavsky was a big mouth and a show-off with a gift for self-promotion.

Painted as the "Larry Flint of the Internet", Warshavsky courted the limelight with a series of publicity-seeking ideas on the new medium, including posting nude photos of prudish US radio commentator Dr Laura Schlessinger, broadcasting sex-change and brain surgery online, and webcasting a couple supposedly losing their virginity. But he became most famous for posting on the Internet a homemade sex video of actress Pamela Anderson and her rock star husband Tommy Lee Jones on their honeymoon.

It's uncertain why Warshavsky wanted to get involved in funding Kremen's lawsuit, most likely he just wanted to be a part of the action. But with Kremen desperate for cash, Warshavsky and Levi stamped out an agreement with Falco by which they would fund Kremen's legal action to the tune of $100,000 each and in return would receive a controlling 51 per cent of sex.com.

Neither Levi nor Warshavsky wanted Cohen to be aware of what they were doing. For one thing, they were still buying lucrative advertising space on sex.com for their own websites. And they didn't want Cohen as an enemy. So they set up a limited company together called KVI to fund a set of more experienced lawyers to take the case to trial.

Thus a new set of lawyers – Kathryn Diemer, Joel Dichter and Sean Moynihan – became involved in the case. Dichter was Warshavsky's lawyer, and Moynihan was already making a name for himself advising adult websites about the state of Internet law at any given time. "I still represented Gary," Falco explains. "I was Gary's voice, but they were really Seth's attorneys."

Although Kremen was finally in a position to sue Cohen, it came at a high price. "He never really felt that they were hearing him," Falco recalls. "He had a lot of ideas about how to do strategy, but they didn't particularly find his input valuable or interesting, and they didn't solicit it. He felt kind of shut out by the process. And so my job was to continually try to figure out ways to get him heard and seen, because it was really his case."

Kremen reflects: "You have to understand I didn't understand anything about the law at that point. I know now, but at the time it was a mystery. To most people I know in business, it's a big mystery."

Nonetheless, Falco and Kremen had already researched and written the bulk of what would become the lawsuit against Stephen Michael Cohen. Before taking that final step, however, they made one last effort to get hold of sex.com: Sheri Falco tracked down Sharyn Dimmick – the woman who had purportedly signed the transfer letter as president of Online Classifieds, but who, in reality, had been no more than an ex-housemate of Kremen's.

Dimmick and Kremen had not parted on the best of terms. Even though Kremen is not, by any estimation, the easiest person to get along with in a confined space, Sharyn Dimmick was obsessive about seemingly random things, and had a very short fuse. As proof of her writing and signature, Kremen admitted into evidence a series of increasingly deranged and threatening notes left by Dimmick while he was living with her, which for some reason he had kept. Kremen eventually moved out when Dimmick threatened to cut off his testicles while waving a knife about. (She ended up hospitalizing her next flatmate.)

Dimmick had had nothing to do with sex.com, or Online Classifieds, and Cohen came across her name by calling the phone company and asking who was on the telephone bill for the address registered as Online Classifieds' office. Unfortunately, he only heard the name and so wrote it with the more common spelling – "Sharon".

Eventually Sheri Falco tracked Dimmick down. "She was in a trailer outside of San Francisco, about an hour, two or three hours north of the city, with her husband. So Sean [Moynihan] and I took a little road trip to interview her in her trailer." Sharyn Dimmick denied having anything to do with the letter and signed an affidavit stating she had no connection with the letter, or Online Classifieds, or anything else remotely connected to the case.

On Friday 21 November 1997, Falco put a copy of the affidavit in an envelope with a note asking that NSI return sex.com immediately to her client Gary Kremen. It was sent certified mail to David Graves, Business Affairs Office, Network Solutions, 505 Huntmar Park Drive, Herndon, Virginia 22070.

It was the last possible exit route prior to litigation, but yet again NSI refused to budge. But Graves was concerned enough to contact Cohen for the third time. We know this because shortly after Falco received a phone call from NSI's infamous "Bob Johnson" asking if she could confirm what information they had sent her. It was Stephen Cohen trying to find out what the opposition knew but Falco spotted the deception and cut the conversation short.

From that point on Cohen started actively stalling and disrupting Kremen's efforts. Cohen had been in control of sex.com for over two years, during which time he had made at least $1 million in profit. And the Internet was just beginning to skyrocket as hundreds of thousands of people worldwide joined the network for the first time. It was late 1997, and every day that Cohen stalled the process he made an extra $10,000 from sex.com.

Nonetheless, Falco kept pushing. She did the legwork while Warshavsky's lawyers discussed how to approach the legal fight. Eventually, four months after he had received Sharyn Dimmick's affidavit, NSI's David Graves was forced to take a very small step backwards. In a letter dated 17 March 1998, he refused to hand over the domain, or suspend its use, or provide any more information surrounding the transfer, but he did agree that, on receipt of a formal legal complaint lodged against Stephen Cohen, NSI would hand control of sex.com to the court and comply with any discovery requests for further information on the transfer.

Graves' concession fell far short of what Kremen had been demanding. His team had incontrovertible proof that the domain had been wrongly handed over, and yet Cohen would continue to be able to run the domain exactly as he wished until the court made its final decision. Cohen would also be free to use the money he made from the domain to fight the case – and that meant he could hire the very best lawyers to drag it out.

Graves' letter didn't end there though. Aware now that the issue was not going away, he issued a stark warning to Kremen: "Please understand however that if Network Solutions is named as a party to this civil action, we will not be limited to the above actions. In such an event, we reserve the right to raise any and all defences we deem appropriate, and take any other action necessary to defend ourselves."

There could be no mistake about it. Network Solutions had thrown its lot in with Stephen Cohen, and if Gary Kremen wanted to get sex.com back, he would have to do it on his own. The chances of success were tiny: Cohen was aggressive, canny, and had millions to spend on the legal case. Besides, the only company capable of handing the domain back had made it clear it was actively hostile towards sex.com's original owner.

The Dimmick affidavit was a last-ditch effort to end the dispute without litigation and it failed. And so on 9 July 1998, an incredible 995 days after Cohen had stolen sex.com, Gary Kremen, an individual, and Online Classifieds Inc., a Delaware company, sued Stephen Cohen and five of his companies – Ocean Fund International, Sand Man Internacional, Sporting Houses Management, Sporting Houses of America and Sporting Houses General – for stealing his property.

The District Court of the Northern District of California based in San Jose – chosen specifically because of its reputation for hearing cutting-edge technology cases – gave it case number 20718, and Judge James Ware was assigned. The legal battle had begun.

10

STEPHEN MICHAEL COHEN

Stephen Michael Cohen is a psychiatrist's nightmare. With the IQ of a genius, an obsessive attention to detail, tremendous drive and insurmountable optimism, he could have been anything in life. But his broken family background pushed him away from society's arms and into emotional seclusion and a career of heartless, predatory crime.

Born on 23 February 1948 to a wealthy Jewish family in Los Angeles, Cohen's family was torn apart when his father, an accountant, left with his secretary to start a new life just over the Santa Monica hills in posh Beverly Hills. It had an enormous impact on the young boy forced to live with a bitter mother and two older sisters, and Cohen began to idolise his absent father, who was driving around in a Rolls Royce while his son was doing the dishes.

The experience never left him. Years later he would proudly claim his father did his accounts, but the fact was that Cohen had just hired someone with the same name, David Cohen. One of Cohen's earliest lawyers, Frank Butler, also recalls a strange connection with his father: "Winning was everything to Steve. Just because you prevailed in a case against him that did not mean that you would ever collect anything. He always counted himself a winner if he was ahead of you. Something deep inside of Steve simply makes him that way. I can't imagine what, but it has something to do with his father."

While Cohen built a fantasy around his successful, happy-go-lucky father, he also took a determined dislike to his mother, describing Renee Cohen as a hopeless gambler and a drunk, although Cohen's ex-wife Susan Boydston always thought she was charming. Cohen sometimes claims his mother is dead, when in fact she still lives in the house in Las Vegas that he gave her. At other times, he claims she is half-crazy. As for Cohen's sisters, they refuse to talk about their younger brother. His ex-wives are equally unwilling to drag up old memories.

Stephen Michael Cohen has married five times – each time to a woman of lesser intelligence whom he initially charmed but then manipulated and conned with callous disregard, leaving behind unpaid loans and sometimes children whom he then failed to support. Nevertheless, having been raised by three women, Cohen has an instinctive feminine under-standing. He has an unusually comfortable chatting style, but remains incapable of forming lasting emotional relation-ships or even friendships with women. Instead, throughout his life, he has treated women as no more than fronts for his phoney businesses, as a source of ready cash, and for his unending, pubescent desire for uncomplicated, disconnected sex.

The roots of his emotional weaknesses lie in the angry, out-of-control teenage Cohen. In desperate need of a father figure, he hated school, and, although clearly highly intelligent, he paid little attention and did badly. There is a certain irony in the fact that as he arrived at Van Nuys High School in San Fernando Valley, the young men who would go on to invent the Internet were just leaving. Vint Cerf, Jon Postel and Steve Crocker had left Van Nuys for the country's top universities and careers as software engineers, later designing the founda-tions of the Internet for the benefit of all. Stephen Cohen left Van Nuys for a career as a criminal, and later designed ways to use the Internet for the benefit of one man. "So many wonderful people have done wonderful things for society," he said once. "I'm not one of them."

Cohen's lack of education was to hamper and frustrate him for the rest of his life, but at the time he couldn't care less. He became obsessed with sex, talking endlessly about it and bragging to classmates about how much he was "getting". But the reality was that he was a loner who sat at the back of the class feeling superior because he knew he was so much smarter than everyone else. His arrogance made him unpopular, and this in turn made him increasingly bitter and introverted when no one recognised his brilliance. But suddenly something in the teenage Cohen switched on and he emerged from his snide, mocking outward persona with a startling gift for persuasion.

Cohen found he was able to talk with absolute conviction about something he had made up just seconds earlier, and he was smart enough to see where people's minds were going, and get there before them. At first he just told lies to amuse himself by highlighting others' gullibility, but it soon extended to manipulation, particularly with girls. It was a magical fit – the one thing that he truly excelled at helped him get the one thing he wanted. Sex and lies. But before Cohen had much of a chance to enjoy his new-found skill, high school came to an end and he was forced to enter the real world.

With only a high-school diploma and poor grades, Cohen's options were severely limited. There was no way he was going back into education, and the thought of having to work for someone less intelligent than himself – someone who would tell him what to do – was too much. The only thing he did have, apart from a very large chip on his shoulder, was an uncanny confidence and an unconfined willingness to lie to get whatever he wanted. Add it all up and it was inevitable that crime beckoned.

We don't know what Cohen's first scam was, or who was its victim, or even where it was perpetrated, as Cohen refuses to discuss or sometimes even acknowledge his extensive criminal past. But what we do know is that he was 19, freewheeling and living in California during the Summer of Love, 1967. Cohen had hit the jackpot. Not only did the free-love philosophy mean uncomplicated and bountiful sex, but the multitude of stoned hippies – usually naive middle-class kids – presented Cohen with a golden opportunity to get back at the people he hated. He worked his magic and soothed his soul by ripping them off. The result was that he didn't have to work, adding to his general feeling of euphoria. The experience forever forged his personality.

But there was one more crucial experience that Cohen was to go through before the hippies left town for the history books: his first brush with the law. Someone of Cohen's age, with his name, and living in the same area, was arrested and appeared in court accused of cheating people in fake marijuana deals. Abandoning the last of his scruples – if he still had any – the accused put on a performance that decided him on a life of crime. He simply talked his way out of it, baldly lying to the judge about what had happened, and doing so with such conviction that he walked free. The man who emerged from the courthouse was fearless, ruthless and utterly determined to feed off the weaknesses of others.

The hippie movement was beginning to fold, but Cohen, a member of the Free Love Association, hung on to his favourite aspect of it by making himself a part of the swinging community that quickly grew up in southern California. It eventually led him to start up a sex club in a well-to-do residential area of Los Angeles, to build one of the first ever sex chatrooms, and, of course, to take over sex.com. But back in the early 1970s his main priority was finding a new way to get cash.

And so Cohen became a "paperhanger" – a passer of bad cheques. At the time, long before electronic transfers of funds, many banks and even shops would happily cash cheques, especially if they had been charmed by the man handing them the worthless piece of paper. To Cohen, it was free money. He would open an account with a minimal amount of money, get a bundle of personal cheques, and then cash each one for an amount far exceeding the actual funds in the account. By the time the first cheque bounced, he had already cashed all the others at a number of different banks across California. Then he would open another account and do the same again.

"Cohen is a classic con man," explains one of the key attorneys in the sex.com case, Jim Wagstaffe. "I have had many dealings with conmen and they've sat there and looked me in the eye and told me the biggest load of rubbish and they could have had their mother there, be sitting on her knee."

In his rare moments of semi-honesty, Cohen admits to his criminal beginnings ("I had some misdemeanours when a young kid. I went through the judicial system. But I did not do jail time"), although on occasion these early forays are given the full treatment, and the one-man scam becomes an international multi-million-dollar laundering operation. For seven years, between 1972 and 1979, paperhanging was a good living for minimal effort. The problem was, while his charm was sufficient to get bank tellers to cash the cheques, his expertise wasn't sufficient to bypass the authorities.

Inevitably they caught up with him, and Cohen appeared in court a second time in March 1974 for cashing two cheques at two different beachfront Californian banks for $280 and $295 – the equivalent of around $1,000 today. Cohen's early court experience had left him with nothing but disdain for the law courts, however, and by the time he was finally sentenced in April 1975 and given five years' probation, he was already pulling the same scam. This time, however, he struck upon the idea of opening accounts under a slight variation of his own name – Stephen G. Cohen rather than Stephen M. Cohen. The hope was that cashiers wouldn't notice such a tiny change and they didn't – the scam worked beautifully.

Cohen was also learning to take greater risks. He would first cash a cheque for a small sum, and then return a week later to cash another one for a much larger amount. But the law caught up with him again. He appeared in court for grand theft and false impersonation in February 1977, this time relating to cheques for $1,000 and $2,500 – about $14,000 in today's money. It's impossible to know how many times Cohen followed the same routine, but he pleaded guilty to these two counts and then charmed the judge into giving him three years' probation plus a $10,000 fine.

A third court appearance served as a wake-up call. Not that he had any intention of going straight – crime was far too easy, profitable and fun to give up. But Cohen did decide he needed a less risky method: paperhanging was a good introduction to confidence tricks, but next time he would end up in jail. And so he started experimenting with other scams where the victims were less resourceful and less powerful than banks. Under the conditions of his first parole (which he had violated), Cohen was not allowed to own various possessions, including a car, without the permission of his parole officer. So he had started leasing cars to bypass the order – a habit that was to stay with him for the rest of his life. Impressive cars lend the driver an air of wealth and respectability that is invaluable when trying to separate people from their possessions. But Cohen stupidly fell back on his previous habit, and appeared in court twice more for writing rubber cheques to two different car leasing companies.

He was sentenced in April 1978 and then again in December 1978, and each time talked his way out of trouble, receiving nothing but small fines since his frauds concerned sums under $200. In the meantime, Cohen began testing and perfecting a range of new skills, including impersonating anyone from FBI agents to tax officials to delivery couriers, either to pull off a scam or scare people away. Ex-wife Susan Boydston tells of how he had a number of different phone lines coming into the house, including the bathroom. He would then use these different numbers to pretend to be different people, and some-times would even vouch for one of his other alter-egos.

But it was not all fun and games. Cohen's temper was as uncontrollable as his sexual appetite. Boydston would eventually divorce him when she caught him in bed with two other women, but not before he had pressured her into wife-swapping parties, used her name to get and then abuse credit lines, and thrown her down the stairs for letting one of his many creditors into the house. (Cohen used to simply leave the countless writs and subpoenas on the hall table and claim he never received them.)

By the 1980s, Cohen was already thinking up bigger and better scams, and soon realised that if he was to going to dive into the deeper end, he needed to know who he would be up against and how to work his way out. And so he signed up for law night classes at a local college to get an insight into the system that kept catching him out. He quit before completing the first year, but it was the start of an obsession with the law that henceforth would see Cohen misrepresent himself as an attorney. He took a job as a clerk with a local law firm where his boss, criminal counsel Roger Agajanian, tutored him on drawing up legal complaints.

Cohen certainly became adept at the specific areas of law that were of most financial advantage to him, but he wasn't prepared to put in the work past the point of immediate usefulness. Posing as an attorney Cohen could involve himself in deals but avoid being held responsible for them. He also found himself being drawn towards corporate law. The law surrounding companies, particularly in the United States, is designed to give people the best possible chance of turning their ideas into products and money. Individuals are encouraged to take risks, but at the same time the law allows for a business to go wrong and the person or people behind it not to be unduly punished by having to pay for the company's debts personally. US corporate law is a building block of capitalism.

When Cohen, aged 32, learnt this for the first time, his mind exploded with the possibilities. Most people see company law as an opportunity to make their dream come true, and at the same time as a safety cushion should things go wrong. Cohen could only see the cushion – plump with cash. He could effectively do the same as he had done with his personal chequebook and spend more than there was in the account, except that if he did it as a company, he could just declare bankruptcy, walk away, and it would all be perfectly legal. Stephen Cohen the individual could end up in court or jail, but a company run by Stephen Cohen could write thousands of bigger cheques and get away scot-free if the rules were carefully followed and then bent in the right places. And so, on 8 July 1980, he incorporated his first company, the Ynata Corporation. The name is strange but was particularly significant for Cohen. It was an acronym, and stood for "You'll Never Amount To Anything" – something his mother had repeatedly told him as an under-achieving teenager.

Over the course of the next twenty years, Stephen Cohen incorporated no fewer than 18 companies in the states of California and Nevada alone. More were incorporated in other states and in other countries, including Mexico, Costa Rica, Puerto Rico, Vanuatu, Israel and the British Virgin Islands. Several of the companies were declared bankrupt and then simply reincorporated with the exact same name once the creditors had given up on recovering what they were owed. Nearly all were shell companies – companies in no more than name. Many had shares in one another, some were subsidiaries of others, and most had names extremely similar to others, all of which aided Cohen in hiding assets and avoiding liabilities. On top of these incorporated companies came dozens of other company names that were owned by one of the registered companies. By "doing business as" one of these, Cohen made it even harder for people to track him down.

Cohen was obsessed with company law and bankruptcy, and in particular how he could hide transactions as well as his own role in carrying them out. Once he had mastered US company law, he then started attending seminars and conferences on offshore banking, learning how to set up and run bank accounts in countries across the world. His focus was on countries that prized the security of the accounts' holders as well as those that threw up institutional roadblocks for creditors. At one such meeting in Las Vegas, he met the man who would later nominally head the company through which he would filter tens of millions of dollars from sex.com. Originally called Ocean Fund International, Cohen would later change its name to the first company he had ever incorporated: Ynata. Except this Ynata was in the British Virgin Islands, very far from the prying eyes of the US legal system.

But back in 1980, aged 32, when Cohen founded his original Ynata corporation, he'd decided to stop the low-return, high-risk cheque fraud, but hadn't yet landed on his next line of business. The answer came through the California Department of Consumer Affairs' Bureau of Security & Investigative Services (BSIS). The BSIS is the branch of government that regulates the private security industry in California – everyone from private investigators to alarm companies. Cohen reasoned that if he was to branch off into other forms of fraud, it would be the private security industry rather than the police that would be after him. So he decided to learn about their workings from the inside.

He applied first for a repossessor's licence, sat a simple two-hour multiple-choice exam, paid a registration fee, and was relieved to find he had passed the checks into his criminal past. He then went through the same process to get hold of a private investigator's licence, and again for a locksmith's licence. Ynata became a repossession agency, turning up at people's houses and taking away their belongings if they hadn't paid their bills. Mostly the repossessions were cars, but once or twice they involved computers, which in those days were bulky metal machines that were still relatively rare even in California, home of the silicon revolution.

But Cohen's compulsion to break the law soon took hold. Clearing out one house, he came across a few software licences and decided to sell them on by advertising them in a local paper.

He was surprised by the demand and so simply made copies, reselling the same licence over and over again. It was only when the software company started receiving support calls from a number of people with the same licence that the scam was uncovered. Cohen avoided the purchasers' wrath by putting the company he was using through bankruptcy, but not before incorporating a second company, Repossessors Inc., under which he continued to run his business. The new name was a clever ploy to make it harder for people to chase him. If anyone complained that they had been conned by a repossession company called Repossessors Incorporated, Cohen could simply claim that they must have simply mistaken his company for the generic industry.

Not content with these two companies, Cohen was also "doing business as" another two – South County Towing, and Day & Nite Towing. Somewhat ironically Cohen's repossession business came to an end in 1988 when the tow trucks he had bought to do the job were themselves repossessed after Cohen persistently failed to make payments on them. With creditors and angry customers chasing him, Cohen decided it was time for another bankruptcy. Incidentally, the first ever Cohen bankruptcy had been in Colorado two years earlier when he as an individual declared himself bankrupt with debts of $4.87 million – just under the $5 million that would mean an examiner would automatically be put on the case. His personal wealth he stated as $8,450, plus "one dog, no value".

Although one of these bankruptcies put his beloved Ynata on the scrapheap, it wasn't for long. He simply reincorporated it two weeks later when he felt the heat was off. That wasn't the only thing that was suspicious. It turned out that Cohen had forged the signature of a former lawyer on the legal papers. The lawyer, Frank Butler, testified twelve months later that he hadn't worked for Cohen for over four years and hadn't spoken to him for two. Cohen's most recent skill – forgery – had come to light.

11

THE CLUB

During the software-licence selling scam, Cohen met two people who would have a big impact on his future – Barbara Cepinko, and her husband Steve Grande. Both of them worked for DEC (Digital Equipment Corporation), which at the time was the world's second largest computer company and at the peak of its powers. Cepinko had seen Cohen's ad and bought a licence from him. They hit it off.

Computers had already started to fascinate Cohen – there was a big buzz around them, yet few people had any real idea how they worked. He could smell the opportunities. And he found two ideal instructors in Barbara and Steve.

Barbara Cepinko was and remains a tough businesswoman. She started and runs an IT company called Midcom, which undertakes high-level corporate and classified government work for such clients as Bank of America, DEC, IBM, Lockheed, McDonnell Douglas, Silicon Graphics, Sun Microsystems, Xerox and Walt Disney.

Cepinko's husband Steve Grande is a technical whiz kid who in the early days of the Internet built the largest private network – known as a bulletin board system (BBS) – in the world. He later started an offshoot of Midcom called Medcom before starting and continuing to run the Net's largest website dedicated to trains – Trainweb.com.

Cohen became firm friends with both of them and they helped him back on his feet when he came out of jail years later, giving him a job and an address. But they were to fall out with

Cohen when they found how far he had abused their trust. Cohen persuaded Barbara to sit on the board of his Sporting Houses companies, using her as a patsy to cover his activities. He broke into Steve's email account (steve@liberty.com) and used it to steal sex.com. He sent the fake Dimmick letter to NSI from a fax machine in Midcom's offices. He posed as Steve Grande and ordered goods for himself. He showed people around the company's secure computer facility against the company's firm policy. And he installed his own server without their knowledge, and then broke the law countless times with his own BBS.

His future lawyer Bob Dorband remarked that the one thing that really struck him about Cohen was his optimism. "Even in the darkest moments, he's a very optimistic person. It's like you just can't keep him down. No matter what happens." Cohen is happy to admit it, and even reveals a little of the strange forces that drive him: "Even when things have been bad, they've never been *that* shitty. I have done more in my life than probably all my friends put together."

Cohen spent hours discussing and playing about with locks – a fascination of Grande's – in his guise as a locksmith. And he persuaded Barbara Cepinko to get involved in the more salacious aspects of his businesses, including the sex club, and the Los Angeles swinging scene.

Cepinko's involvement in the adult world became a source of some tension between Grande and Cohen, but nonetheless they let him start and run – with some help from Grande – his own bulletin board system (BBS). The French Connection BBS was one of the world's first efforts to combine the latest telecommunications technology with pornography. It also marked Cohen's first step into the world of online communications.

The setup, if not the actual technology, was simple: people would use their computer modems to dial and connect directly to the French Connection server at Midcom – it had its own telephone line. Once there, they could read messages left by others and leave their own messages on an electronic bulletin board. The real action though went on in subscriber-only parts of the BBS. To gain access to them, you had to supply your credit card details or send a cheque to one of the many PO boxes that Cohen operated. Once the fee had been collected, you received your own member number and password that gave you the level of access you had paid for: levels ranged from one (little) to six (everything). Level six cost $24 a month – the equivalent of around $40 today.

Cohen ran several different notice boards, a nudist board, a fetish board – he even ran a psychiatric board that was used exclusively by a group of doctors who had paid for the privilege. And while the bulletin boards were initially used for leaving messages for others to pick up – usually arranging or organizing swinging parties – advances in technology soon meant that pictures could be scanned and put into an electronic format that could then be downloaded by others. The number of subscribers soared as people joined the BBS to get hold of pornographic snaps of other members and scans of adult magazines.

But it wasn't only the virtual adult world that Cohen was interested in. On 2 July 1988, he opened The Club at 9881 Brier Lane in the exclusive Cowan Heights part of Tustin, five miles from his home.

Cowan Heights is a rich residential area in the hills southeast of Los Angeles. Made up of small windy lanes with very little street lighting and large comfortable houses, it is exceptionally peaceful. At night you can hear a pin drop. So it wasn't long before people started becoming concerned about their new neighbour. Brier Lane – which ends in a large circular turnaround – was jam-packed with upwards of fifty cars every Friday and Saturday night. As couples piled in and out of the house, often loudly and often drunk, the residents grew increasingly angry. To add to their suspicions that something untoward was going on, Cohen had blacked out the windows and raised the height of the fence at the front and side of the property so no one could see in.

The house itself – a spacious, nondescript, four-bedroom bungalow with a pool out the back – was owned by one Jackson C. Wang, who lived four miles away in Santa Ana and would later testify he had no idea what was going on. It didn't take residents long to figure out that Cohen was operating a sex club in their own street. They started holding meetings about what to do. A petition was quickly drawn up and enthusiastically signed.

The residents contacted the sheriff's department, but in the meantime The Club had started advertising itself in newspapers as "a social swing club for married and committed couples only", although bisexual and single women were, of course, exempted. A telephone answering machine described it as "a fun-loving group out for a good time … great food, good friends, wild lovers and the time of our life".

The problem was that it wasn't against the law to run a sex club – partner-swapping was protected under the right of free association – and so the sheriff was at a loss over what to do. At that time, there were at least half a dozen other swing clubs in Orange County alone, according to Bob McGinley, president of the North American Swing Club Association, who was interviewed by the local newspaper, the *Orange County Register*, soon after Cohen's escapades became public knowledge.

The sheriff's department discovered, however, that Cohen was in violation of zoning rules covering businesses in a residential area. Since he was charging entry, the sheriff believed he could pin zoning violation charges on Cohen, who didn't have, nor had applied for, a licence. Fire marshals and zoning regulators agreed, and in May 1990 – nearly two years after Cohen had opened The Club – charges were filed against him.

There were eight in total and all were misdemeanours,

meaning Cohen wouldn't get a jail sentence even if found guilty. But for the residents of Brier Lane, it would be enough just to have the club shut down. When the police arrived at his house in Anaheim, ten minutes drive from the club, to question him, Cohen savoured the experience. He was rich, he was in charge of a sex club, and the law couldn't find anything more than zoning violations to stop him. As he would reminisce years later when asked about The Club: "Man, that was a great deal – husbands paid me to fuck their wives." Cohen was supremely confident, he answered the door in his dressing grown and started cracking jokes with the police officers. He just knew everyone wished they were him.

A pre-trial hearing was scheduled for 28 December – seven months away – and a provisional trial date of 15 January 1991 was arranged. In the end, the court case didn't start until six months later, during which time The Club continued as before, although Cohen made sure the guests were better behaved and cars were parked neatly by the house. It wasn't until 20 March 1991 that The Club was finally shut down, following a court order pending the court case. Cohen had been running a swinging club in a quiet residential street, blatantly, for his own pleasure and for profit for nearly three years, but he finally admitted defeat and shut it down.

And then he started the exact same business, again called The Club, in another house in the same district – although he refused to tell the press where. He wasn't the most popular man in Tustin. In the final weeks before the Brier Lane closure, however, the sheriff's department sent two undercover officers, one male and one female, posing as a couple to the house to investigate exactly what was going on. What they reported from their visits on consecutive Saturdays made juicy listening at the trial.

Porn films were played endlessly on a wide-screen television in the living room. There was a dance floor in the dining room complete with disco lights, a Jacuzzi in the back garden and a

bar in the garage. The bedrooms contained padded bunk beds
and tunnels with cosy crawl spaces. Investigator Charles Daly
testified to seeing "a lot of shaking and dancing", and people
strolling about in lingerie, towels or nothing at all. "There was
dancing, drinking and one guy fell down drunk on the floor,"
he reported.

Daly went on to describe seeing people fondling one another in
the lounge, and men "performing sex acts" on a topless woman
on the dance floor. He also told the court he had witnessed group
sex in one bedroom, and wife-swapping in another.

But while all the salacious detail added to the scandal and
confirmed residents' worst fears, it was Cohen's money-making
that the prosecution focused on. Couples were charged $60 for
annual membership plus $30 on the door on Friday night, $40
for Saturdays and $10 for Sunday "pool parties". The authori-
ties estimated Cohen was making at least $100,000 a year.

Prosecutors had decided that under the law all they could get
Cohen on was running a business in the wrong area. "You can't
run a business out of a residential area, period," deputy district
attorney Kimberly Menninger told the *Orange County Register*.
"The fact that it's a sex club makes no difference." The state
was also delighted to discover an old county law shortly before
the case went to court that prohibited any "adult-entertainment
businesses" from operating "within 500 feet of any area zoned
for residential use". Even better, there was a precedent with a
swinging club called Sea Breeze in Los Angeles that had been
shut down and its owner sentenced to 75 hours community
service for just such a violation the year before.

As the prosecution played down the activities in the house
while letting jurors know exactly what went on inside, Cohen's
lawyer, Bill Kopeny, brazenly and cleverly put the sex issue in
the spotlight. Kopeny played on the adulterous behaviour at
the jury selection phase. Those who wouldn't be offended by
the notion of couples paying to enter a house so they could
have sex with complete strangers were almost by definition

going to have more open minds and so be more susceptible to his persuasion.

"Does anyone think it's wrong to have sex outside of marriage?" Kopeny asked the potential jurors. "My husband was a cheater, so I don't approve of it," said one middle-aged woman, who was then excused. Would the description of explicit sex acts make any of them feel uncomfortable, and so raise the question of their effectiveness to serve as jurors. "As a schoolteacher, I think I may have bias in this case," confessed one man. Judge Barbara Tam Nomoto excused him. Kopeny kept asking questions for another hour, and started again the next morning. Eventually, late in the morning of the next day, Friday 28 June 1991, the jury was decided, and Cohen's three-day trial began.

The prosecutors knew Cohen was not only comfortable and blasé about sex, but was also charming and amusing. Kopeny played on what he correctly judged would be the jurors' belief that what a man does in his own home is his own business. Prosecuting The Club was a violation of Cohen's right to privacy, he argued. Successfully. And so the trial concentrated on hard facts and the laws regarding running businesses. What the prosecutors were soon to realise, however, was that Cohen was a master at hiding money and profits. With staggering self-confidence considering the size of the lie, Cohen swore that The Club was not a business at all and that he was actually making a loss. It existed purely to promote the sexual lifestyle of swinging, he testified.

While there could be no doubt of Cohen's love of sexual adventurism, the idea that he would actually lose money promoting it was absurd to anyone who knew him. But, sure enough, bank records proved – or at least appeared to prove – that he had never made any money from the venture.

On the third and last day of the trial, the jury deadlocked at eight-to-four in favour of finding Cohen innocent. Cohen had moved the club the month before the trial started, but he left it until the end of the trial to make the dramatic announcement that no more parties would take place there. He was found not guilty, and a fortnight later the deputy district attorney was forced to concede that her office didn't have the evidence to bring a new trial.

"Everybody wants to put the emphasis on sex and on swinging," Cohen said disingenuously after walking free. "It's my position that as long as there are no laws being broken and it's lawful conduct, the police and the state should be stopped from interfering." He thanked the jurors: "I'm sure that in conservative Orange County, there are not too many people who condone this type of activity. These people went out of their way to give a fair and honest vote."

It was a virtuoso performance, and all the more incredible considering that Cohen's world was beginning to fall apart around his ears. As soon as the trial ended, the *Orange County Register* ran with what it had found out about Mr Cohen in the meantime.

On top of the sex club trial, the *Register* revealed, Cohen had also been sued by four of the biggest software companies in the world at that time – Microsoft, Ashton-Tate, WordPerfect and Lotus – for making their software freely available on his French Connection BBS. He had become one of the world's first software pirates.

He was also being investigated for bankruptcy fraud and pretending to be a lawyer in San Diego, the paper said, and he was fighting to keep his home after the government-created Resolution Trust Corporation won a hearing ordering Cohen out of his Trabuco Canyon house.

Unbelievably, in the middle of all this, and despite living on-and-off with his ex-wife Susan Boydston, Cohen married again. His new wife, whom he wed in August 1990, was Karon K. Brumfield, and the marriage was to last an even shorter time than the first, just over two years. But such was Cohen's manic confidence that he believed himself invincible, and his sheer audacity was enough to convince anyone he met – including the several women he asked to marry him – of the truth of what he told them.

12

THE WORLD'S FIRST
SOFTWARE PIRATE

Cohen had boosted the membership of his online bulletin board by offering free subscriptions to members of The Club. Reflecting a philosophy that was to become virtually universal during the dotcom boom a decade later, he believed that getting as many people connecting to his server as possible, even if he let them on free of charge, would pay dividends later on.

As a further enticement, he uploaded the latest and greatest computer software – word processing, databases, operating systems – which paid-up members were invited to download for free. Cohen assumed that the people he was taking money from would be unlikely to ruin the setup by reporting his copyright violations. But he bargained without Paul Curtis, who was president of an IBM PC user group in Orange County. Acting on a tip-off, Curtis set out to expose Cohen. He contacted the software manufacturers whose products were on the system and was asked to get proof. So he signed up to the French Connection BBS.

Cohen told him that access to the private boards would cost $18 a month. While there, though, he could download whatever software he wanted. He even showed him around Medcom and pointed out the server on which he stored all the software. Curtis signed up for two months and started recording which programs were available, downloading full copies of Microsoft's MS-DOS 4.0 operating system – the precursor to Windows – as well as copies of the most popular software of the time: Lotus 1-2-3, WordPerfect, and the dBASE IV database program.

Cohen was no fool, and had put a disclaimer on the site saying that people were not to download any commercial software because it was licensed and any infringement would see users reported to the district attorney. But it was so easy to get hold of the software that Curtis testified it was clear French Connection was in fact implicitly encouraging the unauthorised distribution of the software.

Cohen's defence was strangely prescient, given the battle being waged today by music and film companies against so-called peer-to-peer file-sharing networks on the Internet including, most famously, Napster. "I'm not a cop, and it's not my position to sit on my computer watching how people use the software," he argued. "If we become aware of illegal activity, we'll be the first ones to report it." However, messages on the BBS asking for certain versions of software or complaining about corrupted software that had been previously posted, undermined Cohen's position somewhat.

With the evidence provided by Curtis, the software manufacturers jointly sued Cohen on 5 July 1989 – around the same time the residents of Tustin were signing petitions against his swinging club. Eventually, however, the software companies called off their attack, for the simple reason that it was clear that Cohen was finally heading for a fall, with or without a conviction for copyright infringement. The lawyer acting for the software companies, Carl Blumenstein, explained at the time that the litigation had petered out. "We haven't been actively litigating it because of Cohen's other difficulties," he said.

Apparently, Cohen was the only person who couldn't see how badly things were going. Relentlessly optimistic and utterly convinced of his ability to talk his way out of any problem, he carried on regardless. So when he was finally informed by a judge that he was going to jail, he couldn't believe it.

On 21 October 1991 it was abruptly made clear to Cohen that his 17-year winning streak was over. It was the last day of a trial in which Cohen, alongside the elderly Robert and Helen Polvadore, was accused of two charges of committing bankruptcy fraud and one of conspiracy to commit bankruptcy fraud. Cohen was also charged with making false statements and obstruction of justice. He had told the Polvadores, who were unlucky enough to have met Cohen a few years earlier while they were facing bankruptcy and in a particularly vulnerable state, that he was a bankruptcy lawyer. He had introduced himself as Frank Butler, member of the State Bar of California, No. 79839. The real Frank Butler was sailing around the Pacific with his wife, blissfully unaware that his former client was borrowing his name.

The couple, having no reason to disbelieve him, hired Cohen, thereby providing him with access to their remaining funds, which he immediately set about embezzling. He disguised the funds by running them through a series of his own shell companies in a system that proved so complex that even an expert witness from the Inland Revenue Service confessed he was baffled.

Cohen managed to steal $200,000 before the deception came to light, and the federal government wasted no time in bringing charges against him and the hapless Polvadores. Both Robert and Helen were acquitted of all charges. Cohen, on the other hand, was convicted of bankruptcy fraud, making false statements and obstruction of justice.

The jury was excused at 9.10 a.m. on 21 October 1991 and the judge, the Honourable Judith N. Keep, turned to Cohen's lawyer Michael Mayock: "Now, as to Mr Cohen, I would like your comments, if any, Mr Mayock, as it's my belief that I should seriously consider remanding him at this time."

Mayock put up a good fight. Cohen had had every reason to believe he would be convicted, Mayock argued, and yet he had complied with all the court orders and had turned up. He asked that the court consider Cohen's "background and his appearance and his readiness to accept this verdict". Stephen Cohen should be allowed to remain on bail prior to sentencing.

But both Mayock and Cohen had reckoned without the extraordinary persistence and abilities of special assistant US attorney Elizabeth Hartwig, who had spent months researching the man she was prosecuting and had begun to piece together the real Stephen Cohen. "Your Honour, it's precisely Mr Cohen's background that leads the government to ask that this court exonerate his bond and remand him at this point in time," she countered. "He is no longer an accused; he is convicted. He has made his appearances, but there's a major change in his status at this point. And as was clear from his testimony from the stand, this man changes his identity, changes his occupation, changes his location at will.

"He drives on a Colorado driver's license. He recently lost his house – it was finally foreclosed on after a number of shell corporations that had been holding the house had gone bankrupt ... He doesn't drive a car that he owns. They're always leased. His business, at least one of his businesses, was recently moved ... He has no occupation at this point in time other than whatever his self-employed occupations might be, be they phoney law firms or whatever else kind of business he chooses to go into. He has lied in courts repeatedly, not just in the matters that came before this court in the course of this trial but over a period of 15 years or so ..."

The judge ordered that Cohen be remanded immediately. Three months later, he was sentenced to 46 months in jail plus three years' probation. The flamboyant, confident, arrogant con man had finally been nailed and jailed. He began life as prisoner 94912-012.

13

LIGHTS, CAMERAS, ACTIONS

"Plaintiffs Gary Kremen ('Kremen') and Online Classifieds, Inc. ('Online Classifieds') bring this action seeking money damages, a declaration of ownership and exclusive rights for Plaintiffs' Internet domain name 'sex.com' ('Sex.Com URL') and for a mandatory injunction ordering Defendants to return to Plaintiffs the Sex.Com URL misappropriated by Defendants." The 24-page complaint, filed on 10 July 1998, then outlined in plain terms what had happened.

Kremen had done his homework. The wording "Plaintiffs are informed and believe and on that basis allege ..." preceded each of 22 points that made up the case. Cohen lived in Mexico, was a US citizen and ran his businesses in the US, it stated. It alleged the five companies listed alongside Cohen as defendants were all shell corporations created by Cohen to confuse creditors and to move funds out of the US and into offshore accounts.

Ocean Fund International was based in the British Virgin Islands – a tax haven – and was "created to transfer assets outside the purview of the United States Court System". Sand Man Internacional Limited was based in Tijuana, Mexico and was a wholly owned subsidiary of Ocean Fund International. It was also created to transfer assets outside the US.

And then the three Sporting Houses companies – Sporting Houses Management, Sporting Houses of America and Sporting Houses General – they all operated from the same address in the neighbouring state of Nevada, but were doing business in California.

As Kremen would later discover, starting several different companies with almost exactly the same name was an old and extremely effective ploy used by Cohen to bamboozle officials, customers and creditors. If one company was approached for whatever reason – usually non-payment – it simply stated that it was not the right company and ignored the demand. Cohen could then shuffle assets, money and even contracts between the companies to keep them out of the way of creditors.

If one company was pinned down, Cohen had it declared bankrupt and continued trading with the other company names. From the outside it looked as though nothing had changed. As for making one company wholly owned by another company, this enabled Cohen to restructure companies at a moment's notice, and meant he could move funds invisibly from one to another while holding out only one company to the public. When the invisible company was based in a country with secretive banking laws, it's not too hard to see how Cohen managed to hide his money so effectively.

The final trick was to put friends and acquaintances on the boards of directors of his various companies while maintaining complete control of the business. Sometimes he persuaded people to be on the board; at other times he simply put their names down and never told them. Cohen knew from his company law that this approach afforded him a legal escape from debts and investigations – the equivalent of wiping his fingerprints off the weapon. Unfortunately his fellow directors made it clear in depositions later on in the case that not only did Cohen retain day-to-day control of each company but they had no idea what their responsibilities as directors were. Nonetheless, Kremen had managed to unravel this web of companies and clearly stated their true status in his complaint.

He also provided Cohen's history of fraud: "Cohen was convicted of Grand Theft in 1975 and convicted of, and incarcerated for, Bankruptcy Fraud, False Statements, and

Obstruction Of Justice in 1989, in which Cohen fraudulently signed documents proporting [sic] to be an attorney under both his name and the names of others."

The complaint listed the reasons why the letter sent to NSI was a fraud and a forgery (the forged, misspelt signature, the incorrect information, the incorrect grammar), and tied it to Cohen (Cohen had used the same unusual font he had used for all of his businesses and several other forged documents in the past – and he had faxed the letter from his business fax number).

Kremen included Cohen's phone call purporting to be from NSI, stated that Cohen had been found by the courts to have "repeatedly and illegally impersonated attorneys", and that his intention was "to mislead and intimidate Plaintiffs into not pursuing their legal rights". Kremen pointed out that Cohen's claim to have a trademark in "sex.com" since 1979 was false because the ".com" top-level domain didn't exist in 1979. And then he outlined Cohen's lawsuits against other holders of 'sex' domains.

Finally, Kremen's complaint gave a simple and concise explanation of how the domain name system works and the method by which domains are registered, and went on to detail how he, Gary Kremen, had registered the domain sex.com back in May 1994 "by both certified mail and electronic registration".

It was a damning, well-researched and provable series of facts that could only point in one direction: Cohen was a thief and had stolen sex.com. The complaint then went on to list no fewer than 13 claims for relief: fraud; conspiracy to commit fraud; conversion; deceit; racketeering; inducing breach of contract; violation of business code; unfair competition; trademark infringement; interference with contractual relations; interference with economic advantage; interference with business interests; and deprivation of property rights.

Kremen and his lawyers felt pretty pleased with themselves. The decision to sue had been hard, and they had made absolutely sure of their ground before filing. The information they had was solid, the case was clear. They had Cohen bang to rights.

A date of Thursday 12 November – four months away – was given for the case to be heard in court before Judge Ware, and Kremen started dreaming about what he was going to do with the domain once he had regained it.

It took two months and eleven days for the cold realities of the law to hit home.

14

SEX AND THREATS

Stephen Cohen had been in control of sex.com for nearly three years when Kremen finally sued him. He was now a big player in the adult industry, and getting bigger. He particularly enjoyed the opportunities to screw people, both literally and figuratively.

Cohen's whole way of life and his expanding empire depended entirely on his possession of sex.com. It was by far the most profitable website in the world, for the simple reason that millions of people typed the letters s-e-x-.-c-o-m into their Web browsers and hit return. Ownership of sex.com was also the basis by which Cohen was threatening other domain-name owners. Soon, he dreamed, he would own every dotcom domain with the word "sex" in it. The possibilities were staggering.

So it is hardly surprisingly that Cohen decided to throw everything he had against Kremen's attempts to get the domain back. He asked DuBoff & Ross – the firm chasing the "sex" domains – to take on the Kremen case. Partner Steven G. Ross agreed.

The response to Kremen's lawsuit was delivered a fortnight before the court deadline. It bore the title: "Notice of motion and motion to dismiss complaint pursuant to Fed.R.Civ.P.12(b)(6) for failure to state a claim upon which relief can be granted."

What reads like legal gobbledegook has it own very particular meaning in the US legal system. You can buy T-shirts that read: "Don't Make Me FRCP 12(b)(6) You!". You can even buy a thong with "12(b)(6)" printed on the front and tastefully pitched: "Whether you're taking home that guy from your

Torts class or sleeping your way to partner, nothing says 'grant my motion' like 12(b)(6) on your crotch." Cost: $9.99.

Reason 6, of sub-section B, under Rule 12 of the Federal Rules of Civil Procedure is infamous because it is the legal equivalent of laughing in your opponent's face. It says simply: You don't even have a reason to sue me. Go away.

It wasn't the last FRCP 12(b)(6) that Kremen was going to be faced with while trying to win back sex.com, but it was an early indication of how Cohen and his lawyers were going to play it. By the time the court case was closed nearly six years later (it has since been re-opened), the court had received just under 1,000 case dockets, amounting to tens of thousands of pages of legal argument. Lawyers call the technique "papering" – swamping the other side with so much information that you push their resources to the limit. And Kremen's resources were extremely limited.

Cohen's opposition motion quoted no fewer than 29 cases and eight statutes as providing the legal precedent for Kremen's case to be dismissed in its entirety. So involved, complex and precise were the legal arguments that it was nearly possible to miss the fact that the reply motion didn't actually refute any of the allegations made by Kremen about Cohen stealing the domain. It also ignored five of the thirteen claims for relief.

Incomplete though it was, Cohen's reply motion very nearly derailed Kremen's entire legal challenge. Most significant was the bold claim that Kremen's entire case was without merit because neither he personally nor his company Online Classifieds had a legitimate claim on sex.com. In what sounds like a ridiculous splitting of hairs, Cohen found a possible loophole for the whole case to slip through. Kremen had registered sex.com under the name "Online Classifieds Inc." because he thought – mistakenly as it turned out – that only companies or organizations were allowed to register domain names back in May 1994. However, Kremen had not actually incorporated the company until 23 June 1998, three weeks before he filed his lawsuit. Because of his long history of using corporate law to outfox creditors, Cohen noticed this omission almost immediately. "Neither Plaintiff can establish that it is a real party in interest with respect to the claims alleged in the Complaint," the response argued.

Cohen's response applied similar legal sleight of hand to the rest of Kremen's case. And – Cohen being only too well aware that the devil was in the detail – his response also demanded extremely precise detail from Kremen's side about what clauses in what contracts had been broken, the times and dates of offences, and so on.

The response also raised legal query after legal query, forcing Kremen to justify at every juncture his basis for making the claim. As the case progressed, this approach began to reach ludicrous heights, with Cohen and his lawyers making wild claims and assertions just to force Kremen to disprove them. That ate up Kremen's attorneys' time and had the beneficial effect of deflecting attention away from Cohen himself.

Unsurprisingly, Cohen fought particularly hard to have details of his criminal career and convictions removed from the case, filing a separate motion that argued they "occurred more than a decade ago" and so were "irrelevant and clearly included to prejudice the court". Of course, Cohen's criminal behaviour was not only directly related to the case but also vitally important – which is why Cohen was so determined to pull it out. His lawyers pressured Kremen's legal team at every opportunity to cut out the information, attempting to shame them into action by arguing that they were playing dirty. It worked, and the focus of the case gradually turned to the law surrounding the Internet and domain names rather than Cohen's criminal past. This was a massive strategic error on the part of Kremen's lawyers, since the Internet existed, and still does even a decade later, in a legal grey area.

On Kremen's team, it was Kathryn Diemer who was making the main strategic decisions. She saw the case as a unique legal matter. Domain names in 1998 were still undefined in law, but it was clear that they were becoming increasingly important. Through aggressive legal work, Network Solutions had managed to gain acceptance of its view that domain names were contracts with them but did not represent property. But the sex.com case was not only an opportunity to question Network Solutions' view of things, and so structure future law; it was also going to be high-profile – a winning combination for any ambitious lawyer.

And so the case began to stray away from nailing Cohen and getting Gary Kremen his domain back, and became instead a chance to redefine domain names in law while allowing the lawyers to make names for themselves. Since the case was being bankrolled by Levi and Warshavsky, the attorneys had free rein, and there was nothing Kremen could do about it. "They started to take over the case, and change it in ways Gary and I didn't feel comfortable with," Falco recalls. "He was starting to get rather disgruntled with the whole experience."

The lawyers had left Network Solutions out of the initial complaint (Kremen and Falco had heeded the company's warning that it would "take any action necessary to defend ourselves" if it was named as a defendant), but Diemer and her colleagues Joel Dichter and Sean Moynihan wanted to go after it, and legal history, and so took the opportunity of a first amended complaint to add the company to the lawsuit.

In this first amended complaint, some minor changes were made to the original, more information was added about Cohen's criminal actions, and greater detail was provided to back up the claims Cohen had scoffed at, but otherwise the same complaint emerged – except with two additional claims for relief solely against NSI: Breach of Contract, and Negligence. The complaint also named its parent company, the Science Applications International Corporation (SAIC). Kremen's legal team had decided to aim high. Far too high as it turned out. They had either not done their homework or were hopelessly optimistic about what would happen next.

Network Solutions *was* the Internet in 1998. It had won the contract to register domain names from the US government in 1993, and two years later, in what was to prove a defining moment in the history of the Internet, the government had allowed Network Solutions to define on what terms it sold domains. And NSI decided that it wouldn't in fact sell them. Instead, people would be allowed to rent a domain from them for a consideration – $50 per year for each name. The first person to apply would be granted the rights to rent a domain and would have first right of refusal to renew it, but that's as far as it went – Network Solutions would still retain overall control of all the names. It was an extraordinary act of calculated greed, effectively declaring that NSI owned all Internet real estate but would allow tenants to live there, but since NSI was the only show in town at the time, and because the US government no longer wanted to pick up the tab for the exploding computer network, it got its way. The approach stuck and continues to this day, informing the way that hundreds of millions of people and organizations interact with the Internet.

Picking a fight with NSI then, especially on its own turf, was not the wisest decision, even less so when you consider who its parent company was.

SAIC is, to all intents and purposes, the private arm of the US government's intelligence services. It retains very close ties to the US government at all levels, makes the vast majority of its money from government contracts, and its board of directors are a veritable *Who's Who* of top-ranking ex-government officials, including former heads of the National Security Agency (NSA), CIA, Pentagon and Department of Defense. In short, there is no more dangerous company to mess with in the United States of America.

SAIC is also the king of the Beltway Bandits – private companies located on the beltway around Washington DC that gather information about federal government plans in order to enrich themselves. SAIC learnt about Internet domain names and how the US government was planning to allow NSI to charge $50 per domain per year from September 1995, and so, in a most extraordinary coup, it bought the company – paying just $4.5 million in its own stock in March 1995. Two years later, in September 1997, SAIC took NSI public but retained 78 per cent of the company and, peculiarly, 97 per cent of the voting rights. A third of the $30 million raised went immediately into a dividend paid out to the owners of the privately held company. Investigations into this highly unusual chain of events – and blatant profiteering – never went anywhere.

With some of the country's most powerful and ruthless men personally profiting from NSI to the tune of millions of dollars, the company found it was afforded extraordinary protection. But the initial payday was nothing as compared to the eventual sale of NSI to VeriSign at the peak of the dotcom boom in March 2000 for an extraordinary $21 billion.

The NSI situation had not gone unnoticed by the White House. The US government was still in a position to dictate who ran the Internet and, worried that a private company was effectively in charge of a huge global network that the government itself had built and funded, the Clinton administration started developing a new organization called the Internet Corporation for Assigned Names and Numbers (ICANN). ICANN would be a non-profit organization to oversee the Internet – and NSI – with a brief to introduce competition on the Internet by adding more "top-level domains" like ".com" and by removing NSI's monopoly on selling domains (it was also needed to co-ordinate technical management of the Internet which was rapidly running out of control due to demand).

ICANN was created with a "memorandum of understanding" between it and the US government in November 1998, and the idea was that it would become autonomous within four years. Things didn't quite work out like that though. Network Solutions fought bitterly to retain as much power as it could – hardly surprising considering its monopoly and billions of dollars were at stake.

Since the US government retained overall control, the fight ended up in Washington, distorting an already complex situation. Network Solutions lost its monopoly on selling domains, but retained control over all dotcoms; and the model where people effectively lease domains from the company was kept in place, although the per-domain annual fee paid to Network Solutions was gradually reduced from $50 to $6. The company also applied heavy political, legal and financial pressure on ICANN to restrict the number of new top-level domains it approved so that the dotcom name remained – and still does remain – dominant.

This fight at the top of the Internet was only officially settled in 2006 when ICANN agreed to a new contract that gave VeriSign permanent control of the dotcom registry, and VeriSign agreed to recognise ICANN's authority. That deal was itself a matter of huge controversy, and led to a series of Congressional hearings. In the end, the deal was approved, but not before VeriSign pulled off another political coup by getting the US government itself – rather than ICANN – to award itself the right to decide who would run the dotcom registry in future.

But these battles lay in the future. When ICANN was created in November 1998, just before the dotcom boom kicked off, there were high hopes it would be able to bring some order to the Internet and, in particular, to wrestle the controls from NSI.

It was during this enormous power struggle, just one month before ICANN was created, that Gary Kremen filed his first amended complaint, in which he attempted to sue Network Solutions for fraud, deceit and negligence.

15

POLICY AND FORGERY

What NSI's reaction was when the first amended complaint arrived on its desk boldly stating the company had handed over control of sex.com "in violation of its own policies" is not recorded, but it is safe to assume that the people at NSI were not best pleased.

Within a month, NSI made it quite clear who the boss was when it came to domain names. Its legal reply was a blend of high-handedness, arrogance and aggression.

Kremen's complaint comprised 83 numbered paragraphs, and NSI took it upon itself to respond to every single one with the same line: "Network Solutions is currently without knowledge or information sufficient to form a belief as to the truth of the allegations of paragraph xx and, therefore, denies them." In a very few instances it deigned to recognise Kremen's allegation, and stated simply: "Network Solutions denies the allegations of paragraph xx." And NSI was to follow the exact same approach through every filing it was obliged to file with the court – utter disdain.

NSI did respond to one paragraph in detail, however. It was, predictably enough, to form the most controversial element of the fight. It was also startling in its audacity: "Network Solutions denies that any person or entity owns any domain name, including, without limitation, sex.com."

The company in charge of the vast majority of the Internet's property – including all dotcoms, dot-orgs and dot-nets – was stating in black and white that not only was Kremen wrong, but that he was so wrong that the company couldn't even be bothered to respond to his specific allegations.

It wasn't just idle talk either: NSI had built a legal philosophy based on its view of the Internet, and successfully applied it against inexperienced litigants. It may sound like common sense that if you buy a domain name, it is your property, but NSI could provide no fewer than 27 previous cases and five statutes that would tell you you were wrong.

NSI's response to Kremen came with no fewer than 37 defences – five times the number of claims against it. Many simply denied any form of wrongdoing; others came with exotic legal terminology, such as doctrine of laches, doctrine of estoppel, and doctrine of unclean hands. NSI's response accused Kremen of being personally negligent, and even borrowed Cohen's lack-of-standing argument that neither Kremen nor Online Classifieds were entitled to sue because sex.com had been registered to Online Classifieds but it didn't exist as a corporate entity until years later. Network Solutions had carefully reviewed everything Kremen had said – and dismissed every element of it. It hoped to intimidate Kremen's legal team and impress the court. And its strategy worked.

The vicious stuff came in the motion to dismiss from its parent company, SAIC, added a complainant and so entitled to file its own response.

16

THE HIGH ROAD

The decision to include SAIC in the complaint was a foolish non-starter, and it allowed Network Solutions to frame the dispute as a battle between two rather grubby men, both desperate to make money from online pornography.

The same lawyers represented SAIC and Network Solutions, but SAIC's inclusion allowed David Dolkas, of Gray Cary Ware & Freidenrich, and Philip Sbarbaro, of Hanson & Molloy, two bites at the same apple. While NSI's response was one of lofty disdain, SAIC's was pure muck-raking. It came, appropriately enough, in the guise of an FRCP 12(b)(6).

"SAIC is a complete stranger to this dispute and had no involvement, whatsoever, in the events which give rise to this lawsuit," it argued. And it was right, it had no place in Kremen's complaint. But for a company that claimed to have no interest in the case, it certainly had plenty to say. "The World Wide Web is a wonderful medium that enables users to access a wide array of valuable and enriching information," it began, bizarrely. But then it hit home: "The Web also enables access to a wide array of prurient and pornographic Web sites available through a simple click of a mouse."

While Kremen's team was trying to make the case about the legal nature of domain names, NSI decided it would push both Kremen and Cohen in the mud-pit. "This case involves a fight for the rights to the domain name —SEX.COM— which is apparently used as part of the World Wide Web address for a pornographic Web site," it stated, with "sex.com" rendered in capital letters and bold separated either side by a long dash.

"Plaintiffs allege that in October 1995, the —SEX.COM— domain name was fraudulently transferred to Stephen Michael Cohen, alleged to be a convicted felon and now residing in Mexico. Plaintiffs sue an intriguing cast of characters – e.g. an ex-felon and off-shore companies – and Plaintiffs plead a variety of eye-catching allegations against them – e.g. strong-arm tactics by the Defendants, fraud on the United States Patent and Trademark Office, forgery, and impersonating an attorney ... What is SAIC's involvement in this fight over —SEX.COM—? Absolutely nothing."

Despite SAIC stating it had "absolutely nothing" to do with the case, the motion then went on to list extensive legal arguments why it and Network Solutions were not liable in this case. And in a final *coup de grâce*, it announced that Network Solutions had put control and ownership of sex.com under the court's jurisdiction. It was for the court to decide what to do this with this domain name; NSI was washing its hands of the whole distasteful affair.

The judge got the message, and so did Kremen's team, who immediately dropped SAIC from the complaint.

17

DISMISSAL

This game of legal ping pong that was to last for two years began in earnest when Cohen's team filed their second response to Kremen's first amended complaint. There were 35 cases quoted (up from 29) to support Cohen's position; the number of statutes had actually fallen from eight to three, but had been beefed up with four federal procedure rules.

This system of amended complaints and opposing motions is quite common in US court cases – the idea being that the two sides thrash out precisely what it is they are arguing about before it appears in front of a judge. In the case of Cohen and his legal team, however, this amendment process was carefully and intentionally used to frustrate Kremen's case.

The central argument that neither Kremen nor Online Classifieds had sufficient legal standing remained, but it was clear that Stephen Cohen had personally had a hand in drafting the response because it came loaded with his particular blend of mockery and abuse.

The first amended complaint was, the response scoffed, "nothing more than a hodgepodge of general and conclusory allegations thrown together, with a generous portion of scandalous and irrelevant allegations directed primarily against defendant Cohen for good measure." The charge of racketeering was "pled in the most sloppy fashion and the most general and conclusory terms," the response continued. And details of Cohen's criminal activities were "redundant, immaterial, impertinent, scandalous and/or irrelevant" (but note that the word "false" never made its way in there).

While this legal chest-beating was going on, Kremen soon realised that his biggest problem was closer to home: Seth Warshavsky had stopped paying into the KVI joint company. "Seth was playing games with the money," Falco recalls, "and it got a little tense for a minute. No one was getting paid – Joel Dichter wasn't getting paid, Diemer wasn't getting paid, I wasn't getting paid. And I don't know if that was coming from Seth not doing it, or Ron. It's impossible to know, because they had one entity. But I know that ultimately none of the attorneys for a period of time – a few months – were getting their cash."

At the time, Seth Warshavsky was a big name, featured constantly in the media and reportedly pulling in more money than anyone save Stephen Cohen. But as with many things in Warshavsky's life and career, the image he projected was no more than a carefully constructed cardboard façade. Warshavsky was in dire financial straits. At only 25 years old, he was living fast, and appeared to have everything money could buy. But within a few years his empire had collapsed in on itself, and it turned out that everything had been hired, rented or based on a promissory note. To get cash, he had resorted to illegally double- or triple-charging his subscribers' credit cards; old member accounts were reactivated and charged; his "live webcams" were revealed as tapes on a loop; the 18-year-olds due to lose their virginity live on the Web (watch for $5) were not 18, not virgins, and weren't going to have sex; and a hyped stock-exchange float never happened. In fact nothing about Seth Warshavsky turned out to be what it appeared. And when the debt became impossible, he grabbed what possessions he could and fled to Thailand, where he lives still, occasionally chased by creditors, attorneys and ex-employees.

If anything, Seth Warshavsky was the first victim of the dotcom boom. His business appeared to be worth $500 million thanks to crazed calculations that assumed because anyone in the world *could* go to a particular website that they *would*. But the money wasn't tangible, it never rested in any bank account, and Warshavsky, himself deluded about his wealth, was spending cash he simply didn't have – and would never have. The multi-millionaire left the US with millions of dollars of debt.

Warshavsky's failure to pay what he had promised caused Kremen's attorneys to ease off. They lost track of dates, and then simply didn't turn up at the first scheduled court date. The dates had changed because of the amended complaint, but Diemer had failed to notify the court officially, so the hearing went ahead as planned. It was sloppy and unprofessional, and Judge James Ware was very far from impressed.

The first Kremen's lawyers knew about it was when they received a stern letter nearly a month later. A new court date was ordered for 8 March 1999. And a new case-management conference was ordered on 25 March. The judge made it clear they had got off to a bad start: "The Court admonishes Plaintiffs to abide by the applicable court procedures or risk dismissal of the action due to failure to prosecute."

The money eventually arrived for the attorneys, but already the case was looking like a lame duck. A response to Cohen's response was produced. It was distinctly aggressive and clearly frustrated. "Defendants' intent and malice is demonstrated, either explicitly or implicitly, in almost every paragraph of the pleading," the complaint complained. Of most interest though was an attached copy of the email – supplied by NSI now that it was part of the case – that Cohen had sent to seal control of sex.com.

With hindsight, if Kremen's team had concentrated on nothing else but this email, it could have walked away with the domain just a few weeks later. But amid the legal tussling the case had lost its focus. There were no fewer than thirteen different legal arguments in the complaint when it needed only two or three. In the heat of battle, the lawyers had ended up retaliating to every punch Cohen threw. It left the case exhausted and giddy. Each of Cohen's quoted 35 cases was tackled, sometimes to the point of tedium. It was the wrong approach, and it allowed Cohen to drag out the case still further. Which he did, making the same points all over again in his response to Kremen's response to his response to Kremen's amended complaint.

"Would Gary have won this case in six months if he had had me and Wagstaffe on it?" pondered one of Kremen's future lawyers, Richard Idell, years down the line. "Probably."

"Yeah," admitted Kremen when told of this, "that's probably true. But I couldn't afford him at the time."

18

LOST PROPERTY

The case finally had its first court date in front of Judge Ware. Kremen's lawyers, Cohen's lawyers and NSI's lawyers faced each other for the first time, ran through their arguments, and then waited for two weeks to find out what his decision would be. When at last it came, on 22 March 1999, it was an unmitigated disaster for Kremen.

Despite stressing that "motions to dismiss are viewed with disfavour and are rarely granted", Ware proceeded to do just that, annihilating Kremen's entire case. He agreed with Cohen's assertion that any fraud, had it happened, was between Cohen and NSI and had nothing to do with Kremen. The racketeering charge (that Cohen had formed a conspiratorial group to illegally profit from sex.com) was dropped because they had failed to satisfy the judge that Cohen and his various companies acted as a single enterprise.

The "interference with prospective economic advantage" was dismissed because it was a step too far (it was an odd conditional claim that meant that if Kremen had had sex.com he would have drawn up contracts with other parties, but since he had been denied possession he wasn't in a position to draw up those non-existent contracts). Under California law, the "interference with prospective business interests" was exactly the same as the prospective economic advantage claim that Ware had just dismissed, so that went too.

In fact, not a single claim that had been questioned by Cohen's legal team remained intact. At the end of the decision, only two were still standing at all, and even they were in bad shape. Cohen's team must have been kicking themselves that they didn't go all out and take on every aspect of Kremen's complaint. They could have walked out of the whole case that afternoon.

As it was, the five claims that Cohen hadn't tackled were still in the complaint: conversion (effectively, theft); trademark infringement; interference with contractual relations; and inducing breach of contract (the fifth was a claim for injunctive relief and so was dependent on all the others).

The two that had survived Ware's cull were deceptive and unfair trade practices, and unfair competition. But even so these were only granted on the proviso that Kremen's team came back with more detail. Ware did allow one ray of hope when he denied Cohen's attempt to strike out the details of his past criminal career.

As for Cohen's main legal argument that neither Kremen nor Online Classifieds was a legitimate party, Ware found that Online Classifieds was not but that Kremen personally was – but only in as far as the complaint claimed that he was.

The entire lawsuit was hanging from the barest of threads. While Cohen celebrated, Kremen's team was falling apart. The case they had been building for two years had been torn to pieces. Kremen had lost all faith in his legal team. And his legal team wasn't getting paid. The way Kremen saw it, his domain had been stolen, he had the indisputable evidence of that in his hand, and yet some smart lawyers had not listened to him, had gone their own route, and in the end had most of the case thrown out at the first hearing.

The legal team were not exactly in the best of moods either. They were ranged against a highly motivated and aggressive team from DuBoff & Ross, and had yet to even tackle the feared NSI attorneys. The glittering prize of writing new law for an exciting new medium was now further away than when they started, and to top it all off they were extremely uncertain if they would get paid for any more work on the case.

The second amended complaint was due in court just over a month later. When it arrived, much to Kremen's dismay and Cohen's delight, it was almost identical to the previous one. Sheri Falco's legwork in tracking down those individuals who had been threatened by Cohen was included to give the complaint greater authority. But that was pretty much it.

The demand that Cohen pay Kremen all profits from sex.com, plus damages and Kremen's legal costs, seemed, at best, wishful thinking. And just when no one thought it could get any worse, Gary Kremen nearly destroyed what little hope there was left in an official deposition with Cohen's new lawyer, Robert (Bob) Dorband.

Dorband cornered him into agreeing that Online Classifieds owned the name sex.com. Kathryn Diemer attempted to interject, but such was the level of distrust between Kremen and his lawyer at this stage that he talked over her and fell into the trap. Kremen hadn't grasped the fine legal point that the judge had decided only he as an individual rather than Online Classifieds as a corporation was entitled to sue Cohen and NSI. So by saying Online Classifieds owned sex.com, he was effectively ruling himself out of the case altogether.

The result was a triumphant FRCP 12(b)(6) response filed soon after by Dorband that called for each and every claim to be dismissed for "failure to state a claim upon which relief can be granted", along with a separate motion requesting that the entire complaint be dismissed for lack of standing. Attached to the complaint was, unbelievably, a copy of the letter Cohen had forged to get hold of sex.com – because it had "Online Classifieds" at the top of it and not "Gary Kremen". Cohen was using his own forgery to back up his case for keeping sex.com.

Drunk with confidence, the response cheekily suggested that it was Kremen, and not Cohen, who was up to no good, accusing him of "subterfuge behind the facade of inartful pleading". It then quoted 23 cases, of which an incredible 18 were new. Cohen's lawyers simply walked right back to their starting point in an effort to destroy the last of Kremen's resolve. And NSI? It simply threw back the same response it had written for the first amended complaint, and denied everything.

It is somewhat ironic then that on the same day that Cohen's motion to dismiss was filed, Match.com was sold by the company that had bought it off Kremen's Electric Classifieds for $50 million. Kremen had been right all along about the dating business he built from scratch. And he felt sure he was right to keep chasing Cohen for sex.com.

The whole case was crashing around his ears and he simply had no idea why. Kremen simply refused to accept that through clever legal games, one man could walk away with the biggest property on the Internet. He complained bitterly to his girlfriend, who told him she might know just the man to fix matters.

19

CHARLES CARREON

Charles Carreon recalls it was a beautiful Saturday morning in June the first time he met Gary Kremen. He had recently moved with his wife and kids from Oregon to Carpinteria in California, on the coast between Los Angeles and Santa Barbara.

Kremen and his girlfriend, Robin Kaufer, were driving from San Francisco to a party in nearby Santa Monica. Robin had been to law school with Carreon, and they arranged to meet up for lunch.

It was a month after Cohen's and NSI's responses, and Kremen was dismayed and angry. Carreon was not very impressed with Kremen's car – a beaten-up grey Honda Accord with wires poking out of the dashboard where the stereo should have been, but he found its occupant much more interesting. "He was overweight, kind of like a lump of clay that had been dropped from table-height and stuffed into a t-shirt," Carreon recalls. "Impish is the only word to describe him in those days. His constant mannerisms were emitting outrageous remarks punctuated by a malevolent smile and questioning eyes. It was impossible not to like him."

Kremen took to Carreon as well. When Kremen then told him over pizza the full details of the case, Carreon knew straight away it was his destiny to represent Kremen. This was the case he had been waiting for – an exciting, high-level challenge that was a million miles from his normal bread-and-butter legal work.

He told Kremen he was interested in taking on the case right there, and so they agreed that Kremen would send him the most relevant files, Carreon would read them, and they would arrange to meet up at the next available opportunity at Kremen's flat in San Francisco. And that's exactly what happened. Carreon was dismayed to read some of Kremen's deposition testimony, but nonetheless was certain that he was looking at a once-in-a-lifetime opportunity. With his mind bubbling with ideas, Carreon took the train up to San Francisco, where he and Kremen spent the day, evening and then the early hours discussing the case and how to win it. Carreon eventually collapsed on Kremen's couch. A friendship had been forged.

That friendship started off as it went on – intensely. Kremen was desperate to get Carreon up to speed and to test his dedication, so he flooded him with dozens of emails and phonecalls every day, covering every aspect of the case. That wasn't the only reason – time was rapidly running out. Kremen and Carreon had devised an entirely new approach to the case. Unless this was introduced to the court before Kremen's existing lawyers got much further, the window of opportunity would close and it would be dismissed by the judge.

In fact, there was a very good chance that the judge would dismiss it anyway – there had already been three different versions of the complaint and the case was clearly foundering. An entirely new complaint with an entirely new lawyer was going to be a hard sell. But Kremen was determined; Carreon even more so. The new, improved Carreon plan was to go in all guns blazing and paint Cohen as a thief, a villain and a liar. Carreon had also decided to go for NSI as well by refuting the idea that Kremen had anything sleazy about his character. It wasn't a fight between two pornographers; it was a battle between a respected businessman and an out-and-out con man – and NSI had taken sides against the businessman.

The modesty affected by Kremen's previous lawyers

(sex.com for example was always referred to as "the domain name") had the unfortunate effect of making Kremen look sleazy – and embarrassed about it. Carreon decided the case should acknowledge the fact that they were fighting over sex.com – and do so proudly and unashamedly. After all, sex is the most natural thing in the world. And Gary Kremen never said he intended to post *pornography* on sex.com.

But what Kremen hadn't done yet was to tell any of the existing lawyers working on the case what his plans were. Communication between Kremen and the legal team had broken down, and the lawyers' belief in the case was almost non-existent, to the extent that Kathryn Diemer failed to file a response to Cohen's motion to dismiss the case. The deadline was 28 May 1999 and Diemer missed it completely.

The case could have collapsed there and then had it not been for a press release put out by Cohen on behalf of his Ocean Fund International company claiming to have bid $3.6 billion for Caesars Palace (except the illiterate Cohen had misspelled Caesars as "Ceasars" and referred to the Nevada Gamming, rather than Gaming, Commission). The whole thing was phoney, and Cohen had even created a fictional company chairman for the occasion, Sir William Douglas. Within hours of the announcement, a spokesman for Starwood Hotels was telling reporters that not only had the company not received an offer from Ocean Fund International but he had never even heard of it. Sir William Douglas, it turned out, was a former chief justice of Barbados and high commissioner to London, and he had even less idea what was going on.

It didn't stop newspapers across the world from reporting the "bid" as fact, however. Douglas ended up forcing an apology out of one UK newspaper ("we wish to make it clear that the article 'Save the City from Sex.com insanity' contained allegations in relation to Sir William Douglas which were wholly untrue ..."). And Cohen was caught posing as his lawyer Bob Meredith on the phone. And yet, despite it all,

Cohen claims, years later: "The difference between me and Kremen is that everything we publish, we verify."

The press release reminded everyone on Kremen's side that they were fighting a common enemy. Here was irrefutable evidence that Cohen was a confidence trickster, a man prepared to fashion and promote the most outrageous lies for personal gain. It was also the perfect time for Kremen and Carreon to put their plan into action – they would go for Cohen's jugular and force the court to recognise that here was a thief and a charlatan, a forger and a fraudster. The only difficulty was that Kremen hadn't actually told his current lawyers about Carreon, or that he was going to tear up the current complaint and start again.

What happened next is opaque at best, further complicated by the fact that Levi and Warshavsky stopped paying the legal bills altogether. Carreon's sudden appearance caused consternation and led to a flurry of paper between Kremen's various lawyers and the court, with the judge offering secret meetings so Cohen wouldn't know Kremen's legal team had descended into civil war.

To add to the drama, Kremen's lawyer Joel Dichter received $150,000 in a wire transfer from Stephen Cohen's bagman, Jordan Levinson, around the same time. Charles Carreon believes this is evidence that Cohen found out about the funding problem and picked up Warshavsky's tab in order to undermine Kremen's legal battle. How else could an experienced legal team have completely missed a vital filing deadline? Did his lawyers throw the case? Asked straight out, Kremen gives a long thoughtful pause before answering. "I don't know. I didn't find out about [the $150,000 payment from Levinson] until a long time later."

The court then heard of an extraordinary series of coincidences. According to Diemer's declaration, which appeared three days after the press release, she had "inadvertently calendared the briefing schedule according to state court rules ... rather than the correct Northern District deadline".

The story grew more incredible. While playing ice hockey on 25 May, Ms Diemer "sustained a concussion which caused some short term memory deficit". The next day (two days before the real court deadline), Ms Diemer then "believes she discussed the possibility of filing an amended complaint with Cohen's attorney, Mr Dorband". What this amended complaint was going to contain is anyone's guess, especially since no one had discussed any changes to the second amended complaint. The court deadline came and went.

It was only a fortnight later, according to Diemer, that she suddenly realised she had made a mistake. And despite valiant efforts, none of which were recorded, she only reached Bob Dorband on the same day that Cohen put out his press release – a dramatic coincidence if there ever was one.

It would seem that Cohen's approach to problems – throwing as many interrelating facts at the situation as possible in the hope of strolling through the fog unscathed – had become contagious.

What did Kremen make of this strange turn of events? Even years later he is careful: "All the lawyers I know have these case-management systems and elaborate diaries. These guys have to know deadlines and it pops up three days before their deadline. That's one of their most important jobs." But he won't say any more than that – perhaps just as well because Judge Ware was well within his rights to kill case 98-20718 right there.

But, by some miracle, four days later Ware agreed to grant an extension, which brought Carreon into the case and gave him just three weeks to rebuild the case. It was, Ware said, "in the interests of justice", but he wisely chose not to go into too much detail.

20

CIVIL WAR

True to his word, Carreon came charging into the case throwing around allegations not only against Cohen but also against Kremen's previous lawyers.

He asked to be allowed to file a third amended complaint, and as justification was scathing about Diemer, complaining that she was "bedevilled by a conflict of interest that apparently dulled the edge of her zealous advocacy" and had "omitted many facts of importance to the action". He should be allowed to put in a new complaint "so that justice can be done". It was stirring stuff, but Carreon risked pushing it too far by attempting to re-introduce a racketeering claim that had been specifically dumped by Judge Ware months earlier. "I mean no disrespect to the court's ruling," he kowtowed, going on to explain that it was his "sense of ethical responsibility to zealously advocate every claim that appears to have a meritorious basis in fact and law ..." It was a foolish gesture and, predictably, Ware dismissed it.

Carreon had a wild streak that added an element of danger to Kremen's case. It worried Cohen and his legal team. Carreon wasn't driven by high ideals and a determination to assign domain names their proper place in law: he wanted to nail Cohen's lies and get sex.com off him. In pursuit of these aims, Carreon would go off on unpredictable but often startling tangents, such as adding supposed sex.com chairman Sir William Douglas as a defendant to the complaint. Carreon was determined that every time a motion was filed, the judge should be reminded that Cohen was a liar.

Carreon was also planning to correct a major failing in Kremen's case up to then: discovery. Kremen's interview with Cohen's lawyer had nearly wiped out the case, but Kremen's team had yet to grab a single formal interview with one of the defendants. Cohen may well have been able to buy the finest legal delaying tactics in the country, but it is a different matter when it comes to being sat in a room with a microphone and a trained lawyer asking questions. Besides which, Carreon was itching to get at Cohen, and Cohen knew it.

Kremen also added to Carreon's hunger by cutting a deal with him that made his stake more than just professional pride. Kremen still couldn't afford a full legal defence, so he offered a 15 per cent cut in return for a reduced per-hour rate. "From the time I met him in June until November, December, he didn't really have much money," Carreon explains. "He was always way behind: I was doing five times as much work as he was paying me for, even at the $100-an-hour rate, and I was even advancing costs and stuff, because I really loved the case. I believed in it. I liked Gary very much, too."

It was a deal that enabled two friends, despite all the odds, to take on Cohen, his millions, and his killer legal team, and win back sex.com. But the same deal, signed in a drug haze months down the line, also ultimately led to the ugly and rancorous destruction of that friendship.

21

THE TAC

Carreon made a thorough case for allowing his third amended complaint. There was only one problem: he handed it in a day late.

Cohen's team had a field day. To Dorband's mind, this was it – the end of the case. Kremen's lawsuit was gasping on the ground, and even as Carreon pumped away on its chest, Dorband was preparing to deliver the news that the ambulance wasn't coming. The news was delivered in three documents totalling 58 pages, and it is hard to imagine how Kremen's lawsuit made it through.

Carreon's failure to meet the deadline was professional incompetence, Dorband roared. Besides, with Carreon now on board, Kremen had no fewer than four lawyers working on the case – how come not one of them managed to meet the court deadlines, asked Dorband. Even if one of them had suffered a "head injury", the "excuses" to explain the missed dates were "frankly, insulting". Dorband asked what if there was any point in continuing with the case at all.

Delivering the killer blow, Dorband attached a number of letters from Carreon to him in which Carreon was sharply critical of Diemer. She was, said one, inept. And she had virtually abandoned the case. In another, Carreon accused Diemer of being unprofessional and incompetent. Also attached was Gary Kremen's "business plan" for sex.com, which was in reality no more than a few scribbled words on an A4 piece of paper.

Network Solutions lodged a similar but more restrained motion. The case was going nowhere and NSI didn't want to waste its time any further, it argued. It was also clear that Cohen's and NSI's legal teams had been conferring on how best to bring an end to the case. Any normal attorney would have advised Kremen to walk away at the earliest opportunity. But then Kremen's new counsel was very far from your average attorney.

Born of Native American and Mexican parents, Charles Carreon is a ponytailed hippy with a Joey Ramone fixation. A loose cannon with a passionate heart and wandering eyes, he was irresistibly drawn to the case. The very thought of winning sex.com – the epitome of sex on the Internet – sent a shiver down his spine. Plus Charles Carreon was up against the very people he had become a lawyer to bring down: a smug, powerful corporation that knew it had done wrong but also knew it could get away with it; and a con man, a bedazzler, a two-faced crook who lived off other people's weaknesses. The bonus was that Kremen was a brilliant, sharp, if slightly fanatical geek who was equally determined to stick it to The Man. Carreon was drunk on the idea of winning against all the odds, and then walking into the sunset with a beautiful woman on each arm.

"Kremen and Carreon were probably not the best combination," reflects Jim Wagstaffe, the man who finally won the case for Kremen. "They're like two Roman candles when you get them together: they make a lot of light – or maybe I should say heat." Even Kremen recognises that their personality traits may not have helped: "Charles was bad on focus – he'd jumped around a lot – but that's okay, I'm not good on focus either. Actually it was bad. Bad because we're both bad at focus."

Kremen and Carreon became firm friends, but work soon strayed into their personal lives. "I'm not good with boundaries," Kremen confesses "We started doing a lot of drugs together, that was one of the bad things."

The fact was that it was the fall of 1999 and the air in San Francisco was so full of opportunity you could taste it. Anything was possible. A short drive out of town in Silicon Valley, a whole new generation of companies were popping up – eBay, Google, Yahoo – young, wide-eyed kids thinking up the future as dozens of venture capitalists who had been dreaming of a return to the boom days threw enormous sums of money at anyone with half an idea. Gary Kremen had been investing small sums in interesting start-ups since the early 1990s, and suddenly, after years of not even being able to pay his lawyers' fees, it started paying off – to the tune of millions of dollars. He was sitting in the cauldron of a technological revolution, had more money than he knew what do with (one day he paid for his whole building in cash – "I must have had some liquidity"), and what's more he was going to be the owner of sex.com – the biggest, baddest domain name in existence.

As Kremen cashed in his shares, putting half the proceeds up his nose and the remainder in Carreon's pocket (which then went up *his* nose), the one thing that bound them – the fight for sex.com – became sacrosanct. Death before dishonour. You would have had to be high to continue fighting the case when it was clear that Cohen and NSI would fight to the death and equally clear that they commanded vastly greater resources. Fortunately for their case, that's exactly what Kremen and Carreon were: high, riding the dotcom wave, and brimming with bravado.

Not that it was easy. Carreon confessed to being scared of Cohen's lawyer, Bob Dorband. "Bob is a very, very scary attorney," he admits. "He has the sense of commitment, and a shark-like edge to him, that is just hard to deal with. He's not mean, he's not nasty; but you can tell in his voice that he means to have you leave the table with nothing. You can feel that. And that is really powerful."

Fortunately Carreon had an answer: "In litigation, I have

always decided that bullying tactics should be responded to with a hard return blow." And so his responses were "an orgy of breast-beating, filled with fiery promises of future tenacious combat."

In fact, Dorband was surprised and slightly unsettled by the furious exchange of letters, and hoped to turn it back on Carreon by attaching several of them to his court filings to embarrass and belittle Carreon in front of the judge. Carreon at first tried to have them removed from the record; when Ware refused, he calmly wrote them off as "letting off steam".

Carreon's passion brought new life to the case. He pointed out that the area of law that was being dealt with was new and evolving. Internet domain names had appeared in the real world in vast numbers, but they had not been created by statute or by legislation, so in a legal sense they were in a no-man's-land. By stressing the amorphous states of law regarding the Internet and domain names, Carreon also cleverly made excusable the sudden change of course in the Kremen case. How could you expect otherwise, when the law itself was in such flux? He also, rightly, stressed the importance of the current case in building up the foundation of Internet law. It was a case, he argued, that would dictate how the whole medium was approached by the courts in the future.

There was no doubt that domain names had enormous intrinsic value, some being traded for literally millions of dollars. A large number of court cases over domain ownership had also recently starting appearing. Something very significant was happening with these "unique identifiers" on this invisible computer network. And Carreon's argument – to be his lead in the whole case – was that a domain name was personal property. His client had owned property, it was wrongly taken away from him, and so under the law it was "conversion" – a legal term that defines the injury that occurs when someone takes or uses your property without permission.

Carreon also went in strong on Cohen's past: something that both he and Kremen were convinced was vital if they were to persuade the judge that this was more than a sleazy dispute in a grey area of law. Nor was it a misunderstanding: Cohen's acts were criminal, Carreon pointed out, and he argued that the case was a matter of public good. The theft of sex.com wasn't just harming Gary Kremen, it was an act against the whole Internet-using public. It was vital that such behaviour be punished as a lesson to others.

It was a bold and passionate appeal and, incredibly, it worked. Judge Ware reprieved the case, but in his ten-page judgement made it clear just how close to the brink Kremen's case was. A few weeks later, Judge Ware then approved the introduction of Carreon's third amended complaint (TAC).

It could hardly have been more timely. At the same time that the TAC appeared in court, the country was plunged into the state of irrational euphoria we now call the "dotcom boom". The rest of the world had finally realised what Gary Kremen and Stephen Cohen had understood five years earlier: that domains were the shop fronts for the biggest market the world had ever known. Kremen had long waited for the dotcom wave to appear on the horizon, and as a result saw it earlier than most. By the summer of 1999, it was impossible to miss. But this seemingly universal explosion of energy all around caused Kremen to reflect on whether he was really doing the right thing. Having a proven track record of Internet businesses, he was in high demand, and was turning down dozens of exciting opportunities. He had enough money to do anything and go anywhere – why risk everything on a court case that was very far from a safe bet?

Kremen agonised about the decision for twelve straight hours. It was an enormous gamble. All or nothing. If he lost, he would have squandered the biggest opportunity of his life – everything from building his first computer aged twelve, to his engineering degree, to his Stanford MBA had been leading up to this point in this city (San Francisco) at this time. And here he was, planning to blow it all on a crusade with a very limited chance of success. Was it just hurt pride? Did he really stand any chance of beating this Cohen character? Could he and Carreon really scare Network Solutions – a company that was used to fighting running battles with the US government? In the end, it was the very fear of failure that made up his mind. "I hate people who call themselves entrepreneurs and they sit in cocoons and they don't make hard decisions, and scary decisions," Kremen explains. "I think that's what separates the men from the boys: are you willing to bet it all on red if needed? And that was it. It was the defining moment."

From that point on, Kremen's commitment to the case was unwavering. He read every piece of paper, followed every detail, tracked every movement in the case. Every lawyer since then has confessed that they have never had a client like him. "Gary is full of adrenaline. He's really involved in the case. I've had lots of clients involved in their cases, but not as much as Gary is," says Wagstaffe. Richard Idell, who now acts as Kremen's general attorney, says the same. Another, Tim Dillon, adds his name to the list. Even Kremen admits he's a difficult client. "I call them all the time. I call them at home. I call their wife's friends to call their gynaecologist to call their wife to get them on the phone. Whatever they're doing. There's a US saying, it's called 'high touch' – it's like high maintenance but different. Because it's not like I'm asking dumb questions – I'm reading the stuff, I'm actually going in and reading and editing it and going line by line by line. I think that's not usual for clients to do that – they tell me it's not usual for clients to do that." And it all began with Carreon.

Kremen sold his stake in Interwoven, a company started by his old Match.com colleague, Peng Ong, which had just gone public (at one point, Ong was – nominally – worth a cool $1 billion). It made him $3 million from a $5,000 investment. He also had several million more from other investments in, among others, Multiplex, Tut Systems and Resonate. And he went for broke, putting the entire sum behind Carreon in his bid to beat Stephen Michael Cohen.

His entire fortune now rested on a 33-page document of new and largely untested legal theories presented by an attorney with limited experience of Internet law and of prosecuting cases, with whom Kremen shared a heavy drug habit. Considering who the lawsuit was pitched against, it was, by all accounts, sheer madness.

22

SEX AND PUBLIC SERVICE

Much like the very first complaint written by Kremen and Falco, the third amended complaint was a sharp and persuasive document that outlined exactly what had happened and why Cohen couldn't be trusted.

Carreon had also reviewed Cohen and Dorband's methods, and designed the complaint around them. He cut one of their tried and trusted lines of attack by providing extensive and precise information, down to precise dates and names, for every accusation. Details about Cohen's convictions and criminal conduct before he stole sex.com were kept pretty thin. Instead, Carreon concentrated on what Cohen had been up to since he had taken control of sex.com, using Cohen's own press releases to damn him.

Carreon boldly stated that the Caesars Palace press release "was an utter lie" and amounted to "a pattern of deceptive conduct". He then went into some depth about the unpleasant realities of sex.com and pornography on the Internet, slapping on the sleaze: "Sex.com charges approximately $25/month for the privilege of viewing primarily women in various states of undress and simulated sexual excitation, as well as explicit images of heterosexual and homosexual activity."

But it wasn't just pornography that Cohen was putting out there – he was also ripping off his own customers, Carreon asserted. "The Defendants ... promise 'new users' the opportunity to 'browse' archives of sexual imagery at no monetary charge ... however, once the Internet user submits the requested credit card information ... it is resold to marketing companies. This true purpose is not disclosed to the Internet consumer."

Carreon accused Cohen of overcharging customers, lying about the true number of visitors to sex.com, and under-paying other website operators. In contrast, Kremen was painted as the exact opposite of this sleazy porn baron. He was "a well-established Internet entrepreneur featured in the January 3, 1996 issue of *MicroTimes* magazines as one of the nation's top 100 computer entrepreneurs, and has been the subject of feature articles in the March 3, 1997 issue of *Fortune*, the September, 1995 issue of *Wired* magazine, the August 14, 1995 issue of *Interactive Week*, and the July 3, 1995 issue of *Forbes*. A substantial portion of his business activity involves the creation of business plans utilizing the Internet's commercial potential."

Carreon then pushed the argument he had dreamed up while first reviewing Kremen's case: that of Kremen as public-health guru. "Kremen created the 'sex.com' domain name as an item of personal property," the complaint read. "Kremen did not intend for this domain name to be used as a world online pornography distribution centre; rather, his plan focused on a completely different level of market interest: the wholesome aspect of sex and personal relations; public-health issues such as sexually transmitted disease education, underage pregnancy, and women's health; and many other issues which are of great importance and interest to many persons, and indeed, to persons who constitute a very desirable market for online advertising."

This was all bunkum, as Carreon would later admit, but it put useful space between Kremen and Cohen as the case went forward. What had Kremen really intended to do with sex.com? His answers have varied over the years. He told this author that he had planned to create "a sluttier version of Match.com". Other answers over the years have ranged from the pure public-health response to an admission of maybe some soft porn. The truth is that Kremen hadn't come up with a plan at all. He obtained sex.com for free along with a range of other domains but decided to focus on Match.com. The "business plan" that Cohen's team had submitted in evidence was a lucky find more than anything else, and comprised a one-page list of loose handwritten ideas.

Carreon also went for NSI: "It has become fully obvious to NSI that the transfer to Cohen was wrongful. NSI nevertheless refused to transfer the domain name back to Kremen, and has attempted to assume the role of a disinterested stakeholder." As for the real business of listing the legal claims against Cohen and NSI, Carreon pulled out three of the original thirteen claims, and added seven of his own: conversion by bailee; breach of trust; negligent representation; breach of contract; breach of third-party beneficiary contract; Lanham Act violations; and slander of title.

The ball was back in Cohen's court. Dorband's approach was to start papering the case all over again. Dorband's response came complete with a whole new range of quoted legal precedents (26 this time). It was an exhaustive, nitpicking and carefully manufactured response: page after page of argument. It was aggressive, smart and expensive lawyering, something that Cohen was more than happy to pay for, and Dorband's response was fired back at Carreon along with the usual complement of insults and wild assertions. Cohen could play this game for years.

NSI's response to the TAC could, to all intents and purposes, have been a photocopy of every opposition it had yet filed. It had 24 defences.

23

THOU SHALT NOT STEAL

Carreon's response to this latest round of legal tennis was inspired. He decided to go in for plain speaking. Under a heading "Thou Shalt Not Steal", he wrote: "Cohen has blatantly stolen one of the most valuable items of personal property in the world, and refuses to return it."

Kremen was the original and only legal registrant of sex.com. Cohen was not. Cohen had not approached NSI and pointed out that he had more right than Kremen to sex.com, and he had not approached Kremen either. He simply took it. So a legal debate about the nature of rights was pointless, Carreon argued, because no matter which way you looked at it, Kremen had more right than Cohen to sex.com.

Cohen, who from day one had followed the case with the same intensity as Kremen now possessed, didn't like the new approach. He was far more comfortable with the lawyerly language than clearly stated bald facts. And so he fired back a response that was, in turn, sarcastic, derisory, contemptuous and in its best parts, unspeakably rude. At one point, Kremen became a cybersquatter "who gobbled up marks with only the intent of selling it back to the trademark owner ... In defendant Cohen, plaintiff believed he had an easy victim."

In response to Carreon's "Thou Shalt Not Steal" came "Thou Shalt Not Lie". "Plaintiff once again resorts to personal attacks on defendant Cohen, going so far as to quote God. While defendant Cohen has tried to refrain from giving these attacks the dignity of a response, the court should note that not only do these attacks have absolutely no bearing on the *legal* issues that are before the court, they are intended to deflect attention from the outrageousness and audacity of plaintiff's own actions."

Cohen then launched into an extraordinary rant, which Dorband wisely decided to demote to a footnote in the finished filing: it accused Kremen of "indiscriminate and intentional 'cybersquatting', intending to extort value from obtaining control over names in which trademark rights are already attached; misrepresentations and lies to the domain registrar in an attempt to hide his scheme; outright lies and falsehoods regarding his 'plan' to establish the SEX.COM domain for commercial use; lies and falsehoods regarding transfers and assignments of his 'interest' in the SEX.COM domain in an attempt to commit a fraud; blatant and knowing violation of California law regarding business registration and attempts to cover up his illegal acts; and mysteriously disappearing books and records of shady business entities, and lies to cover up their disappearance.

"All this from a man who claims to have an MBA from Stanford University but who has a checkered employment background and less than visible means of support. All this from a man who claims to be worth seven million dollars but can't afford to pay his attorney's fees. Just who is the 'con man' in this drama?"

It was an extraordinary outburst and it strongly suggested that Cohen had been investigating why Diemer and Dichter had been pulled off the case. He learnt that they weren't getting paid, but also that they had been paid by a limited liability company called KVI, instead of Kremen's own company. Cohen smelt a rat. He was certain that Kremen had limited funds, so who had been putting in the money? Had they now pulled out? Who was paying Carreon?

Cohen and Dorband's game plan had always been two-pronged: one, drag out the case beyond the legal cut-off point, at which point they would file to have it dismissed under the statute of limitations; and two, dry up Kremen's funds. But the complaints were still coming in, and the case that had been on its last legs now had a fresh, confident approach – and the opposition had just stated for the first time in black and white exactly what Cohen had done: he had stolen sex.com.

So Cohen decided to test the water, and through Dorband offered Kremen $20,000 to drop the case. It was a classic piece of Cohen reverse-psychology: the sum was far too small, and by offering it he hoped to panic Kremen into thinking Cohen was supremely confident of winning, and thereby undermine Kremen's confidence in the strength of his own case. Carreon rejected the offer out-of-hand, assuming it was intended as an insult. That was when Cohen started worrying.

He started crawling all over the issue of who was paying the attorneys and shortly afterwards his sales director, Jordan Levinson, wired Joel Dichter $150,000 – the amount he was owed for the legal work he had done for Kremen. Soon after that, Cohen suddenly learnt it had been Ron Levi and Seth Warshavsky behind Kremen's legal fight.

It is possible this information came from Dichter, but it is far more likely it came from Warshavsky himself. Dichter had represented Warshavsky previously – Warshavsky was sued no fewer than 14 times between 1998 and 2000 – and the former "prince of porn" was in serious financial trouble. It is not too difficult to see him cutting a deal with Cohen. How do we know Cohen found out who had stumped up the money? Because almost immediately afterwards Ron Levi found himself on the receiving end of the first of a series of Cohen lawsuits. Warshavsky was left alone.

Cohen was beginning to realise that this chump Kremen from whom he had stolen sex.com might not be as simple and stupid as he had always assumed. "The court should not be fooled nor swayed by plaintiff's improper and persistent appeal to the court's conscience," Cohen finished his court filing, kicking himself for not realising Kremen was just as sharp as he. "There are no 'saints' in this tawdry drama."

24

THE WORLD DEPOSITION TOUR

Just a fortnight after Cohen's rant, Judge Ware decided the future of the case by granting in part and denying in part Cohen's motion to dismiss it.

After all the fire and bluster, it finally became clear what the legal battleground for the case would be. The charges left against Cohen were: conversion, unfair competition, and declaratory relief. Since NSI had simply denied outright any connection to the six claims against them, they all remained in.

It was clear that Judge Ware was growing impatient. "This case has already gone through an inordinate amount of motion practice," he complained, "and the parties are more than familiar with the allegations." It was 12 October 1999, and the court drew up three hearings for March, April and May with a planned trial date of 5 June 2000. And so the case moved onto the next step – interviewing all those involved in the case to prepare the evidence for trial.

Carreon had three months. But if he thought the going would be any easier, he was sorely mistaken. Cohen simply didn't turn up for his depositions. Furthermore, he failed to supply contact details for people that Carreon needed to interview, and then – from nowhere – Cohen and Dorband produced a deposition world tour.

Carreon was already rushed off his feet, and so, on 12 November, with extravagant malice, Cohen provided a list of depositions that his legal team would be carrying out during December 1999. At these depositions, the named people would provide evidence proving that Cohen's claims – the most significant of which was that he had used the term "sex.com" since 1979 on his French Connection BBS – were true.

First on the list was Thanin Sacchasiri, who would make his deposition on Friday 3 December 1999 at the Marriott Hotel, located at 4 Sukhumvit Sol 2 in Bangkok, Thailand. The deposition would start at eleven a.m. but Dorband offered no estimate as to how long it might go on, simply stating that it would continue "from day to day until completed." "Defendants intend to cause proceedings to be recorded stenographically. Plaintiff and plaintiff's counsel are invited to attend and cross-examine."

Carreon had no idea who Thanin Sacchasiri was, what relation he had to Cohen, what he was likely to say, or what he knew about the case; nor could he get any of that information from Mr Sacchasiri, since Cohen had supplied no contact details of any kind for him. All Carreon knew was that Cohen's team was planning for him to make a deposition in Bangkok in 21 days' time.

But that wasn't all. Six days after that, another deposition was going to take place. This time, the subject was one Joseph Steele – although no one, except perhaps Cohen, knew who *he* was, either. Mr Steele lived in Moscow, Russia, and he would be at the Sheraton Hotel, at 1 Tverskaya, 19 Yamskaya Street from ten a.m. on 9 December 1999. Once again, Mr Carreon was invited.

Carreon informed the court in a subsequent filing that it would cost him between $924.45 and $1,918.45, and take 48 hours and 45 minutes, to get to Bangkok to attend Thanin Sacchasiri's deposition. Travelling to Moscow to meet Joseph Steele would cost between $6,000 and $8,000 in air fares and take a mere 45 hours and 35 minutes from California – although this trip might be more worthwhile, since Ivan Schvartz would also be available at the same place on the same day. Whoever he was.

Assuming Carreon had recovered from his jetlag, he was invited to attend the deposition of Chris Ott four days later, this time in Geneva, Switzerland. At the Hotel D'Angleterre, no less. Eleven a.m. sharp. Three days after that, Eliyahue Roussos would be available for cross-examination at the Sheraton in Tel Aviv, Israel, starting at nine a.m. Assuming Roussos didn't have too much to say, Carreon might just be able to catch the beginning of Ami Dvash's deposition at one p.m. in Haifa, 40 miles to the north.

And finally, assuming Carreon had picked up a taste for criss-crossing the globe interviewing people he had never heard of, he could finish off five days later on 22 December 1999 with three depositions in the same day at the Park Hotel, 10 Alexandras Avenue in Athens, Greece. Anli Eliezer would be there for nine a.m., Salvo Amarillo at one p.m., and finally Jacki Solomon at four p.m.

Before he headed off to Athens though, Carreon really didn't want to miss one deposition being held rather closer to home, in San Francisco on 21 December: the deposition of Stephen Michael Cohen.

This deposition world tour was clearly a nonsense. If the names weren't simply made up by Cohen, they were most likely randomly selected sex.com customers and unwitting participants. It was just Cohen's way of mocking and infuriating Carreon.

The trouble was that Carreon could not afford to simply ignore the list of depositions: the danger was that Cohen might slip in a real witness among all the phoney ones. Carreon was pretty sure the people on the list were fictitious characters, but if just one was real, and Carreon was not in attendance, Dorband would have the opportunity to lead the witness into saying exactly what he wanted him to, without the hindrance of cross-examination by Carreon.

That wasn't all. Dorband then requested depositions with people close to Kremen that he knew full well would refuse, and who in some cases the court would refuse – in the case of previous attorneys and Kremen's former psychiatrist. It was all just to pile another layer of work on Carreon and to get up Kremen's nose. Cohen also served Ron Levi with a subpoena for "any and all documents relating or referring in any way to the acquisition or transfer of any interest in the internet domain SEX.COM."

This legal jousting became increasingly hostile and bitter. Carreon was desperate to get the interviews and the information he needed, yet Dorband consistently stymied him with unwarranted legal queries. Dorband also agreed to deposition dates and then cancelled at the last minute. More than fifty motions, replies, answers and declarations were handed in to the court. Every one added delay and cost. And as they fought back and forth, the allegations grew larger, wider and more damaging. It grew so ugly that the last few filings are held under seal where not even the lawyers themselves are now entitled to review them.

Carreon was having similar trouble with NSI. He wanted details concerning similar cases that NSI was involved with in the past. In the course of investigations, Carreon had found that when a number of big companies, including Yahoo, had had their domain names taken by a third party NSI had behaved quite differently.

When Kremen provided NSI with evidence that the Dimmick letter was a fake and demanded sex.com back, NSI refused, stating it would do nothing unless there was a lawsuit. When Kremen did finally sue, the company simply deposited the ownership of sex.com with the court, but let Cohen continue to use the domain. On previous occasions involving larger companies however, NSI had returned the domain immediately to the correct owners. But proof of this could only come from NSI.

But NSI refused to provide a single piece of paper for eight of Carreon's 25 requests for documents, two of which were crucial because they covered NSI's behaviour towards other companies that had been in the same situation as Kremen. The refusal came with a letter in which David Dolkas, one of the lawyers for NSI, haughtily stated that his client had no need to hand over the documents under dispute because the company would soon file a motion for summary judgment that would remove NSI from the case entirely. When the judge granted that motion "this entire issue becomes moot", it crowed.

25

VIRGIN(IA) TERRITORY

Network Solutions' motion for summary judgment – formally asking the judge to remove it from the case altogether – proved to be the second most important document in Kremen's entire ten-year court battle, the first being the forged Dimmick letter.

The NSI motion was immaculately produced. Clear, concise, firm, professional and ruthless, it quoted no fewer than 19 federal cases (of which NSI was a party in six), 25 state cases, four federal statutes and five state statutes. And every one of them told Judge Ware to let NSI out of the case.

The company's chief litigation counsel, Philip Sbarbaro, had effectively been honing the document for five years. NSI's legal team had faced and dealt with virtually every legal angle thrown at domain names. They were also in the useful position of knowing more about the system than any of their opponents ever would, thanks to NSI's unique role as overseer of the Internet's infrastructure. When it came to domain names, whatever NSI said, went, unless you could prove otherwise. Which of course you couldn't, because the company wouldn't provide anyone with the information to do so.

Even the US government had failed in its effort to control Network Solutions. Its creation, ICANN (the Internet Corporation for Assigned Names and Numbers), fought a pitched battle against NSI for years before the two sides eventually signed a three-way contract with the Department of Commerce in which NSI got to retain nearly all its power in return for allowing competition to run underneath it. If all that wasn't enough reason to take NSI seriously, there was the fact that the company appeared to be no more than a third party in a controversial and distasteful legal fight over a pornographic website.

Online pornography was on a lot of people's radars at the time. Not only had explicit sexual imagery become readily available to anyone with a phone line and a computer, but the Internet made it both cheap and simple for people to bypass existing laws and post whatever they wanted. Many feared, with some justification, an epidemic of people gaining easy access to illegal and disturbing content. NSI wanted no part of this high-profile fight. And who could blame them?

The case had already dragged on for 18 months and got nowhere, besides which NSI had already handed the court complete control of sex.com. It had refused to be drawn into any argument, and pointed out that the item in question was but a single domain among the millions it had dealt with, and the millions more it continued to deal with every day.

Kremen had redrawn the legal complaint three times, and in the latest complaint the claims against NSI were largely experimental. Network Solutions' arguments, on the other hand, were precise, coated in existing law and coherently pled. You can't blame Judge Ware for the decision he was to reach a few months later: every arrow pointed him in the same direction.

The only problem was that Network Solutions' entire philosophical position on the nature of domain names was not only flawed but flew in the face of what everyone else on the Internet knew to be true. NSI held that domain names were equivalent to telephone numbers – despite the fact that all the evidence pointed to the fact that domains had become intrinsically valuable in themselves.

In the days when only academics and entrepreneurs like Gary Kremen registered domain names, NSI's concept of what they were and what interaction they should have with society and the law was logical and acceptable. But the simple fact

was that Network Solutions, like any monopolistic organization, had grown so attached to the status quo – itself – that it
saw only risk, damage and conspiracy in any attempt to
change it. Where everyone else in the world saw many varied
and colourful possibilities in the exponential growth of the
Internet, Network Solutions saw only two things: greater
profit and greater risk. Every domain name registered or
renewed was another fee directly into NSI's coffers, but at the
same time it represented another potential lawsuit. This fear
made the company aggressively defensive. The more people
who railed against its outdated philosophy, the more aggressive NSI became.

Except, of course, it wasn't that simple. Network Solutions
was, and remains, at the forefront of the Internet, and it knew
only too well what was happening to domain names in the real
world. The company also hired a very large number of very
smart people to make sure it didn't trip up over its own legal
arguments. So, starting in 1995 and continuing to the present
day, it has produced and continually revised a series of legal
contracts that new and renewing domain-name owners automatically sign up to, contracts that provide a bridge between
what NSI used to say and what NSI currently believes.

There was also another element in NSI's favour: location.
Network Solutions is headquartered on the east coast of the
United States, in Herndon, Virginia, just south of the seat of
power in Washington, and the other side of the country from
Kremen in California. Virginia contains the headquarters of
the CIA, NSA, the Pentagon, a major arm of the FBI, and
countless other governmental organizations, and this federal
government influence has led to a different legal approach and
structure than those found in other US states.

In the previous five years, NSI had persuaded a number of
Virginia judges, in particular those in the Eastern District of
Virginia where it was based, that its phone-number philosophy
was correct, logical and true. According to NSI, all someone

who registers a domain gets in return for their money is "the right to continued registration services for a period of time".

The Virginia courts had good cause to view things from NSI's perspective: a huge number of Internet disputes, not only in the US but also internationally, were fought and decided in Virginia thanks to NSI's role. That has made Virginia the first stop for Internet law – even if some of the decisions made by Virginia courts have subsequently faced ridicule. A knock-on effect of this was that hundreds of Internet companies were drawn to the state, complete with jobs and hundreds of millions of dollars in investment, profits and taxes.

The huge stumbling block that sex.com presented was that Kremen had registered the domain in 1994, when NSI didn't charge for domains nor have contracts, and it had been stolen in 1995, just when Network Solutions became a commercial organization. The case had virtually been designed to strike NSI on its Achilles heel.

The decision taken at the time, for whatever reason, was to ignore Kremen in the hope that he would disappear. But now, in 1999, Kremen had somehow reared up again. The company feared that if it was to move even a step away from its stance, there was a risk that its whole legal infrastructure – assembled from a series of previous legal victories – would fall in ruins around its ears.

NSI's motion for summary judgement can be summarised in three points: Kremen had taken too long to sue, he had no contract with the company and domain names were not property.

In Virginia, a number of legal situations are governed by a two-year statute of limitations, whereas in Kremen's California it is three or four years. If you don't file a lawsuit within that time from the date you were wronged, it is not valid. NSI argued that Kremen's claims should be decided under Virginian rather than Californian law, which meant Kremen had not pled them in the required period of time, so they should be struck down.

The issue of a contract between Kremen and Network Solutions was fundamental. There were two underlying facts that Kremen, despite a number of legal sidesteps, couldn't avoid: he hadn't paid a dime for the name sex.com, and he had never put a website up at the domain sex.com.

"Network Solutions is caught in the middle of the fight," it complained, maintaining that Kremen and Cohen "should be left to fight over sex.com themselves". It had no reason to believe the Dimmick letter was a forgery, the company claimed, before belittling the case as "a myriad of law firms asserting a myriad of claims against a myriad of defendants".

"Network Solutions never received anything of value from the plaintiff," the company went on. "Nor did it expect to receive anything of value from the plaintiff."

But despite the company quoting extensively from several lawsuits it had won in the past, the fact was that domain-name law was rapidly changing, even while NSI was typing out the motion. It had just recently lost its first case that it was appealing, and this led to a last-minute addition to its motion in the Kremen case. "Even if, *arguendo*, plaintiff could establish the existence of a contract pertaining to the registration of sex.com, any such purported contract was terminable at will by either Network Solutions or the plaintiff," it stated.

This rather startling addition led to an even odder conclusion: "Network Solutions' deletion of the domain name was a permissible termination of an at will contract." Effectively, NSI was saying that it could do exactly as it wished with any domain whenever it chose to – something, no doubt, that the rest of the Internet community would have something to say about. Especially companies like Amazon, eBay and Yahoo.

The NSI motion continued along similar lines for another ten pages, pointing out its legal victories and espousing its view of the status of domain names. Unfortunately, if its logic were accepted, it meant that the entire foundation of the domain-name system – the only visible part of the Internet for the majority of its millions of users – existed in a legal no-man's-land. Despite having complete control of the domain-name system, NSI was not legally responsible for anything that went wrong with it. So you've had your domain name stolen – tough luck, kid. NSI *might* return it to you – and it most certainly would if you were a big company like Microsoft or Amazon – but then again it might not. Only NSI would decide, and do so apparently arbitrarily. And it was getting $50 a year per domain for providing this service. It's no wonder the company fought so hard to retain the status quo.

26

PRESENTATION

In his next filing to court, Carreon came out fighting. He dismissed the previous legal cases that NSI had won, arguing that times had changed and that Kremen had "a right to develop his own factual record in this case".

NSI knew "or should have known" about security problems with its registration process, Carreon said, alleging that it had knowingly misrepresented the situation to Kremen. Kremen had got his hands on an internal NSI document that discussed how security in the registration process needed to be improved.

He also outlined his frustration with the tactics used by both Cohen and NSI in the case. "These defendants have been engaging in outrageous discovery misconduct," Carreon complained, pointing out Cohen's deposition world tour and his requests against Kremen's former lawyers and his psychiatrist. "The evident purpose of this strategy is to 'bury' plaintiff's attorney in a mountain of paper, and to unduly delay the proceedings by requiring a motion to obtain every single thing plaintiff wants. NSI appears more than happy to join in the strategy ... NSI's lawyers never return plaintiff's phone calls, and initiate communications only to set forth demands and seek concessions."

While Cohen was doing everything in his power to run Carreon ragged, NSI was simply refusing to have anything to do with him. Carreon outlined how the law surrounding domain names was changing all the time, and how NSI's arguments were already outdated.

Carreon also showed that domain names had suddenly become big business, hitting the news headlines. He attached press clippings reporting that "wallstreet.com" had just been sold for $1.03 million. "Business.com" had gone for many times more – it had been sold for an incredible $7.5 million. The domain "liberty.com" (run by Steve Grande, whose "steve@liberty.com" email address Cohen had used to steal sex.com) was being offered for lease – not even for sale – for $100,000 a year. And according to a website that had been set up just to sell other domain names, the *bidding* for "woman.com" currently stood at $2 million. It was quite clear that domains were very far from the phone-number model that NSI insisted upon. After all, who had ever heard of people bidding $2 million for a phone number?

The second piece of evidence put forward was the NSI internal report that Kremen had dug up. Its conclusion intriguingly suggested that NSI knew of security holes in its own systems. Was it possible that NSI *knew* that its own systems were to blame for people losing their domains?

With relations between the opposing attorneys spilling over from hostility into open threats, Carreon, Dorband and Dolkas were pulled in front of the case's magistrate, Judge Patricia Trumbull, in order to get the case back on the track and heading toward Ware's courtroom.

The hearing was a messy affair, and Judge Trumbull frequently indicated her irritation. But of far greater importance was that the hearing revealed for the first time a fundamental problem in the entire prosecution of Kremen's case: Charles Carreon was powerful on the page but weak in person.

During the hearing, and nearly all the subsequent hearings, he floundered. While concise, precise and direct in court filings, he had a tendency to beat around the bush in person and under pressure. When up against lawyers of the calibre of Dorband and Dolkas, the problem was only compounded. And this did not enamour him to either Judge Trumbull or Judge Ware.

Kremen felt there was also an element of prejudice. Carreon had spent his entire professional life up until that point defending common criminals – and it showed in his performance. "He hurt where it mattered, in the courtroom: the judge didn't take him seriously. It's unfair to Charles. But going in with a ponytail, you're a defence lawyer – you defend criminals: that's like strike one and two, to any serious judge. I found out later that it's the *Animal Farm* syndrome – all animals are equal but some animals are more equal than others. There's a certain kind of establishment lawyer that gets treated differently to the non-establishment lawyer."

And Carreon certainly got treated differently. When he tackled Dorband over the patently ridiculous deposition world tour, Carreon was stunned to find Judge Trumbull giving him a hard time. Carreon explained – or, at least, tried to explain – that it would require him to fly around the world (five countries and nine depositions in just 20 days) to interview a series of people whom Cohen had identified only a week before, of whom he had never heard, for whom he had no contact details. Furthermore, he had no idea who they were, or what they would testify to.

Incredibly, Trumbull was inclined to let the depositions go ahead. Why couldn't they be done over the phone, she asked Carreon. "I have grave concerns about extending Mr Cohen and his attorney even the slightest degree of trust," argued Carreon. "This gentlemen's history is one of deception and fraud. It has been pled and it is the case that he has a career of being a bankruptcy defrauder."

She was unpersuaded. What was actually at issue here? "If I am taking these depositions by telephone, I have no means of verifying who this person is," Carreon pleaded. Trumbull continued: what difference would it make if he was actually there? "I could compare his driver's licence with his face, his passport with his face," Carreon explained, thinking on his feet. "I could seek additional people in the place to ascertain who they are. I could hire a private investigator ..." With something very close to disdain, Trumbull simply suggested a teleconference.

Dorband gave Cohen's side of things. "These are trademark issues – my client owns the trademark in sex.com. It was purloined by a fictitious entity, presumably Mr Kremen, from my client. My client ultimately gained control of it. There is still the underlying issue of who owns the trademark rights and my client contends that he does. And if he does, and if we can establish that, it is our contention there was no conversion – there could be no conversion for something my client already owned."

Trumbull ordered that the world deposition tour go ahead, but that it be done by teleconference and at Cohen's expense. Three weeks later, Dorband informed Carreon that they had decided not to do it after all.

This treatment of Carreon, and the off-hand dismissal of his legal argument in court threatened to derail Kremen's entire case. Even Trumbull refused to buy Dolkas' extraordinary claim that NSI wasn't able to provide documents relating to sex.com and similar cases that Carreon had requested because there were too many documents to be sifted through. But at the same time, she also refused Carreon's reasonable request to move court dates because of the delay tactics, which gave him just thirteen days to prepare, and just three days with the material that Trumbull had ordered NSI to hand over. He was then going to have to go through the whole thing again in front of Judge Ware when the latter heard NSI's motion for summary judgement.

While Kremen was taking a battering in the courtroom, he was already two rounds up in the court of public opinion. There was no denying that the fight for sex.com was a great story, so Kremen had already provided *Wired* reporter Craig Bicknell with a wealth of information about Cohen.

The first of many hundreds of articles on the sex.com battle appeared on 19 April 1999. It included full details of Cohen's criminal past, his sex club, the Dimmick letter, Cohen's trademark claims and his threatening of other "sex" domain holders. Bicknell did his job and called both Cohen and NSI for their responses. Cohen was not at his friendliest, and Bicknell reported as much: "'Anything that's of a legal nature has to go through the attorneys,' he snarled. 'I thought that I made that real clear to you.' His lawyers also declined comment."

Wired followed this article up with another just two months later, after Cohen released his phoney press release about the purchase of Caesars Palace. Sex.com was also featured in *Internet Magazine* as the world's number-one desirable domain name, complete with a brief summary of the theft and ongoing fight.

Cohen starting facing awkward questions from advertisers on sex.com, and NSI delayed transferring Cohen's latest domain victory – hot-sex.com. The actual ownership of sex.com also came under continual attack, presumably by readers of the magazine articles, many of whom started sending fake faxes and emails to NSI trying to shift ownership back to Kremen (and, in some cases, to themselves). And so the battle for sex.com turned personal.

The case up to that point for Cohen had been interesting, even intriguing. He loved watching Kremen and his lawyer try twenty different ways to get the domain off him, and relished writing mocking responses to their amended complaints – but the case had started getting serious. It should have been finished off four months before, but instead Gary Kremen was appearing in the newspapers telling everyone that he, Cohen, was a liar, a thief and a con man. And people started walking away. What was even more unbearable was that people in the adult industry started to mock him, in online forums and off. He absolutely *loathed* being laughed at. And what's more, every time someone laughed at him, he knew Gary Kremen would be smiling to himself. That thought ate away at Cohen and made him all the more determined to screw Kremen over.

27

POOR HEARING

Predictably, NSI simply failed to provide the discovery material that it had been ordered by Trumbull to produce within ten days – which would have given Carreon just three days with it before appearing in front of Judge Ware to argue why NSI shouldn't be allowed out of the case altogether.

Carreon knew they would fail to provide the information, so he had already prepared a court filing slamming the company for stonewalling. He filed as soon as he was able to: first thing on Friday morning (the documents were due Thursday). But NSI couldn't care less: it was due in Judge Ware's court at nine a.m. on the Monday, and there it would ask to be excused from the case entirely.

Come Monday morning, even the gods were against Kremen and Carreon. On the Sunday evening a storm had started brewing on the west coast of America, grounding aircraft and bringing traffic chaos across California. Carreon arrived late, having had his flight from Portland cancelled the night before.

To add to the general disarray, there were two new attorneys in the courtroom. "Good morning. Richard Diestel on behalf of counterclaimant Gary Kremen," one of them addressed the court, before pausing. "I'm in a little bit of an awkward position. My office was contacted last week to represent and defend Mr Kremen on the counterclaim that has recently been filed." Without Carreon there, he was at a loss as to what to do. He had not even met Carreon or Kremen, and had only been handed the enormous stack of case files on the Friday.

Fortunately, Carreon turned up soon afterwards, praising a "heroic cab driver". Judge Ware was intrigued by the latest twist in the case. "Now, tell me a little bit about the counterclaim. What has happened?" he asked.

What had happened was that Cohen had decided to up the ante by suing Kremen for defamation and, unbelievably, cybersquatting. (In fact, the full list of counterclaims was: defamation, intentional interference with contractual relations, intentional interference with prospective business advantage, civil conspiracy, trademark infringement, cybersquatting, and unfair competition.)

Ironically, this aggressive move gave Cohen no escape from the one thing Dorband had spent over a year cleverly avoiding: Cohen's deposition by Carreon.

Cohen lived, or claimed to live, in Mexico, and so was outside the US court's jurisdiction. It gave Dorband the opportunity to provide a deposition date several months away, and then cancel it at the last minute, with no legal repercussions. But, as Ware pointed out to Dorband, now that Cohen had filed a counterclaim, he had availed himself of the US courts and so Ware was thus empowered to demand Cohen's deposition. Cohen had shot himself in the foot.

And so onboard came Richard Diestel, as Kremen's insurance lawyer, who would to take over one side of the legal fight and provide Kremen with an unexpected boost of resources, leaving Carreon to concentrate on nailing Cohen. But before that happened Carreon had to defend himself against a Network Solutions brimming with confidence and insisting it be pulled out of the case altogether. Within five minutes of Ware's hearing, it was clear that NSI's confidence was well founded.

Judge Ware's very first question addressed the standing issue that both Cohen and NSI had been fighting so hard to raise (that neither Kremen nor Online Classifieds was entitled to sue). And then he raised the issue of the Dimmick letter. Carreon was on uncertain ground and was forced to throw in the best information he had about NSI (especially since he hadn't had the documents from NSI). "I have interviewed one witness personally, a gentleman who told me that he personally heard Mr Cohen brag that he had a girlfriend at NSI, and therefore, he could obtain any domain name he wanted. It could be just tinfoil on the radar, your Honour. It might be true. I really don't know."

Ware was uncertain: "All right. The court is disposed to grant this motion for summary judgment, but I'll give you a brief window of opportunity to present to me a basis not to. As I understand what you've just told me, you might have evidence that someone at Network Solutions had some inside informa-tion with respect to the operations of Online Classified, knew of the fraud and ignored it?"

Carreon outlined the flimsy evidence: he had had a phone call with an old Midcom employee who had worked with Stephen Cohen at the time (soon after he stole sex.com) and he said Cohen had someone inside NSI. Ware wasn't reassured. But Carreon was desperate not to allow NSI out of the case. With NSI involved, the complaint was more legitimate and, oddly, safer. Without the company it was just him and Kremen against Cohen - a man who was willing to do almost anything to win the case.

Carreon pulled out an explanation he had recently grown attached to in order to explain why NSI should be kept in the game. It was to prove crucial to the entire case, but, while it was a clean analogy, Carreon fluffed it with a rather stumbling and confused delivery: "If I can indulge your Honour with an analogy. I would take my automobile and I would leave it at the car parking lot and somebody comes and they – I have lost my wallet and they find my claim check and they go and give it to the Auto Park place and they get the keys and they drive my car away. I come back and I inform the car parking lot about them. I inform the car parking lot what happened, that they have been defrauded into giving away my car, and I say to them you have some possible responsibility to get it back if you know the identity of that person. And they say, oh yeah, we do. We can identify him. We can locate him, but we have no responsibility to you, Mr Carreon, it is now between you and the thief."

Judge Ware had clearly already decided that NSI should be let out of the case, but he gave Carreon one last shot, asking him what evidence he had that Network Solutions could have known that the Dimmick letter was a forgery before they were informed by Kremen.

Carreon argued that NSI had a legal duty to check whether requests to change ownership of domain were legitimate. And he argued that Cohen's claim that he had used the mark "sex.com" since 1979 was clearly ludicrous, as the dotcom registry had not even been created until October 1984 – something NSI would have known as the world's expert on domain names. But Ware simply pointed to a previous case that had decided NSI had no duty to investigate changes in domain names.

Dolkas, for NSI, chose his moment to step in and finish the job off. "We, frankly, don't care [who owns sex.com]," he told Ware. "If Kremen gets a judgment against the purported thief, Cohen – and the lawsuit should be just between those two guys – we will abide by the judgment. You know, God bless them, go get them, get a judgment and just direct us what to do with the registration." Ware was already there. "I doubt if I'll have you back," he told Dolkas. "It wouldn't be the end of the lawsuit. We would have a different kind of case."

Carreon wasn't ready to let go of NSI, and he tried to press on the discovery issue. He still wanted evidence of prior cases. But Ware wasn't having it. "You say it's a forgery. That's pretty strong language. This was not an accident. This was not someone who was authorised to do it. They received a forged letter saying 'release this name,' and they released it. And whose deposition do you need to take? They're admitting they released. What is the fact that you need to take a deposition?" Carreon continued to press the point until Ware flatly refused his request: "I won't permit you," Ware told him, "to go to Network Solutions and ask the question 'Who could Mr Cohen possibly have slept with here?'"

Carreon pleaded for the release of NSI documents that showed the company had behaved very differently when it came to big business. Again, the answer was no. "I won't let you go after that. If this is a forgery situation, negligence won't help you." Instead, Carreon was given just two weeks to prove a case that could easily take two years. It was a disaster, and NSI already had one foot out the door.

The other new lawyer in court that day was Robert Selvidge, who was also late thanks to the bad weather. Dorband was out of the country and Selvidge was the new man brought in to advise on the case, owing to his lengthy experience in Californian courts. He agreed to extend the discovery deadlines and to produce Cohen – finally – for a deposition.

Ware named the date. Stephen Michael Cohen was ordered to appear for deposition on 3 February 2000 in San Diego, California, starting at ten a.m.

28

CARREON VS. COHEN

Carreon had been under immense pressure and a monstrous workload for months. But in that time he had managed to compile a huge dossier on Cohen, and was itching to confront him with it.

Despite Kremen having already made four depositions – quotes from which were used extensively in NSI's and Cohen's legal motions – Dorband's stalling had managed to keep Cohen away from deposition for an incredible ten months. Now, thanks to Ware's order, there was no escape.

Carreon intended to make Cohen squirm and he was hyped up when he arrived at 1202 Kettner Boulevard, Suite 6100 in San Diego at ten o'clock on the morning of 3 February 2000. It had been little more than a week since Judge Ware effectively threw the whole case against NSI out. In the days running up to the deposition, he had been in a pitched battle with both Dorband and Dolkas, firing off emails and faxes, making countless phone calls, arranging dozens of subpoenas, and having to write – and respond to – court filings. What's more, Kremen was starting to give his friend grief for not doing a good enough job. The whole case was unravelling, and Carreon grew more and more tired, frustrated and on edge.

He knew the deposition was absolutely vital. It was the first time he had confronted Cohen face-to-face, and it was unlikely he would have another chance, as Dorband was certain to embark on yet more stalling tactics as soon as it was finished.

But it just wasn't Carreon's day. His opening gambit set an unfocused tone that was to haunt the whole deposition until it finally ended at 6.35 p.m.

Carreon: Okay. Mr Cohen. You're under oath. You've been under oath before, right?

Cohen: Yes, I have.

Carreon: And let's see. Were you under oath in any civil proceeding at any time?

Cohen: Yes.

Carreon: And what civil proceedings were those?

Cohen: I don't recall.

Carreon: You have taken the oath so many times that you don't recall where?

Dorband: Objection. Mischaracterises his testimony, leading, suggestive. You can answer.

Cohen: I've been under oath many times.

Carreon: And in civil proceedings many times?

Cohen: Yes.

Carreon: And – so you know what the oath is about?

Cohen: Yes.

Carreon: Does it constrain you in any way?

Dorband: Objection. Ambiguous.

Carreon: Does the oath constrain you in any way?

Dorband: You can answer.

Cohen: No.

Carreon: You mean you can say whatever you want under oath? Did you understand my question?

Cohen: I understand your question.

Carreon: Okay. So …

Dorband: Do you know what he means by "constraint"?

Cohen: I'm here to tell the truth.

Carreon: Ah. That's constraint from my point of view. Okay. Let's try to stick with words that we both understand. Does the oath bind you in any way, the oath that you just took?

Cohen: Yes, it does.

Carreon: And what does it bind you to?

Cohen: I'm here to tell the truth without exception.

Carreon: You're here to tell me all the facts you know in response to the questions that I ask?

Cohen: That is correct.

Carreon: And you will do that?

Cohen: That's correct.

Presumably Carreon was going somewhere with this, but he had lost the thread on the way. The whole day, his questioning followed the same pattern: it was as if he had run the whole meeting through in his head but was thrown when reality failed to match up to it. He would stubbornly try to get the answer he wanted from Cohen before progressing, but each question grew increasingly garbled as Carreon tried to rephrase it without giving away where he was headed. In short, it was a shoddy performance, helped only by the fact that Cohen's web of lies had grown so complex that merely forcing him to answer questions threw up dozens of contradictions.

Cohen had no choice but to claim repeatedly that he could not remember exact details. And yet this image of a vague and forgetful personality was undermined by Cohen himself. Whenever he was on safe ground, such as talking about the French Connection bulletin-board system, Cohen could recall extensive and obscure details, only to be struck by a severe case of amnesia as soon as the conversation turned to stickier matters. But over the course of the deposition it became clear how Cohen operated. His basic approach to getting away with scams is to confuse matters as far as humanly possible. And his most frequent, almost habitual, tactic was to use the same name for several different entities, both companies and people.

There were, for example, the three Sporting Houses companies: Sporting Houses Management, Sporting Houses of America, and Sporting Houses General. There were two

Ynatas: one in California (shut down and later reincorporated) and another in the British Virgin Islands. There was even a Yanta Inc. – note the switched "a" and "n" – created for no other purpose than to confuse people. There were two Omnitec Internationals, one in California (which was formed three times – in 1982, 1995 and 2000) and another in Nevada – which themselves were confusingly similar to Omnitec, a large corporation whose permission Cohen has forged in order to register the name Omnitec International.

There was a weak point to this method of obfuscation, however: individuals. If you had the name of an individual, then playing around with company names was pointless. Fortunately for Stephen Cohen, however, he had been born with an incredibly common name – especially in California. There are 18 Stephen Cohens registered as attorneys in the State of California alone, ten of them active. And we know that Stephen Cohen stole the identity of at least three of them at some point to misrepresent himself as legal counsel. It's unknown how many other Stephen Cohens were dragged in. Stephen Cohen would also make out that he was great friends with the casino giant Steve Wynn. Billionaire Steve Wynn is certainly good friends with *a* Stephen Cohen, but *that* Stephen Cohen is the hedge-fund manager, not the con-artist. Sometimes just the Cohen surname was enough to sow sufficient confusion.

Cohen even went so far as to hire people *because* of their name. When Carreon inquired about Cohen's finances and who his accountants were, Cohen testified that for a number of years his father, David Cohen, was his accountant. After his father's death, Cohen hired a new accountant who, oddly enough, was also called David Cohen, of San Diego firm Hockman and Cohen. From the second David Cohen's deposition, it became clear that Stephen Cohen had very little interaction with him, and frequently ignored his requests for information. David Cohen had simply served as one of Cohen's many smokescreens.

Cohen also hired several people for the same job, and then claimed he couldn't recall who had done what. On top of the two David Cohens, he also had a Mexican accountant called Morales who was himself chosen because it was the same name as an old business associate, and a New York accountant. When all else failed, Cohen claimed that one or other of his ex-wives had done whatever it was that he was being accused of.

By these means, Cohen was able to confuse most issues, especially to do with his financial records. That Cohen's father was dead was particularly convenient. In fact, a suspiciously large number of the people with vital information on Stephen Cohen subsequently shuffled off this mortal coil.

Cohen's chief partner in crime for nearly a decade was also a big fan of using other people's names. Unfortunately for him, he had been christened Marshall Zolp, so namesakes were not quite so plentiful. Instead, Zolp used pseudonyms: James Powell, Werner Wassler, Alex Seagrove, Frank Williams. Cohen was careful never to mention Zolp by his real name, since a quick check on the name immediately threw up an extensive criminal record for multi-million-dollar scams. However, Cohen felt no compunction about laying responsibility for a number of matters that incriminated him personally at the feet of Mr James Powell.

The apotheosis of this stunningly effective ruse came when Cohen simply created a completely fictitious character in order to keep himself one step removed from any wrongdoing. This invisible friend made his first appearance at the deposition, and was attributed a crucial role in one of the central issues of the case, the forged Sharyn Dimmick letter. Cohen christened his manufactured scapegoat Vito Franco.

Carreon suspected almost immediately that Franco was not a real person, and that Cohen was simply making it up as he went along. When Carreon started to focus on Mr Franco, within seconds the whole thing descended into farce. What was Franco's area of expertise, Carreon inquired. "He's an ex-police officer. He was a movie producer," Cohen explained. Which police agency, asked Carreon. "I'm not sure. I think it was somewhere in Hawaii. That was before he moved to California, where he was a movie producer – quite distinguished – and he was also ... he also did building."

It would appear that Cohen had suddenly realised that Carreon was going to ask him why a crime-fighting Hollywood producer would be working for him, so he quickly attributed some construction experience to Vito Franco – a wholly uncommon name in Hawaii, it should be noted. Right on cue, Carreon posed the question. Cohen explained that Franco was helping to oversee the construction of some new buildings for him in Mexico.

The reality is that Cohen probably saw an episode of the 1970s US cop show *Hawaii Five-O* the night before while in his hotel room and remembered the show's lead character – the head of an elite organised-crime unit – because they shared the same first name. Detective Steve McGarrett, meet compulsive liar Steve Cohen. Cohen gets a thrill from taking risks, especially when it involves inventing people and stories. As such, concocting an entire persona on the hoof, while being deposed by a lawyer trying to take away his most valuable possession, was pure adrenaline.

He especially enjoyed toying with Carreon because Carreon was clearly so determined to nail him. "Did Mr Franco tell you that Ms Dimmick had told him that Online Classifieds had fired Mr Kremen?" "Yes." "He did not make a tape of their conversation?" "I don't know." "He located Sharon Dimmick by what method?" "I don't know how he located her. I honestly don't know." "Mr Franco is still an employee of Sand Man Internacional?" "No." "Is he his own freelance person?" "No." "Who does he work for?" "He doesn't." "He's just chilling, huh?" "You could say that."

Carreon should have seen it coming. But he was too busy chasing. "Where is he?" "He's in heaven." "He's in heaven? He's in heaven?" "He's in heaven. He just recently passed away." "I see. Where are his records?" "I don't know."

Carreon paused and gave a wry smile. "I'm not going to pass away, am I?" he asked Cohen. "I hope not," Cohen replied. The two sparred for ten minutes, with Cohen leading the way and Carreon following with a mixture of irritation, disbelief and derision. Months later, Carreon managed to obtain a statement from the hospital where Cohen said Vito Franco had died confirming that no such person had ever been admitted there. But by then Cohen had already let the cat out the bag.

It seems that Cohen wasn't only a fan of *Hawaii Five-O*, he also enjoyed *The Godfather*. Later on in the case, while ascribing yet more activities to the dead Mr Franco, he slipped up and accidentally referred to him as Vito Corleone. Kremen's lawyers instantly seized upon it and referred to Vito Franco as Vito Corleone from that point on. The appearance of Marlon Brando's famous Mafia boss also helped explain Vito's middle name, which Cohen decided at some point was Anthony. Anthony was the name of Vito Corleone's grandson, born in the first film.

The Corleone slip was rare, however, and Cohen took great pride in his method of confusing people and companies, and often places and dates, to create an impenetrable fog of "facts". Despite constantly pleading that his memory wasn't good, he had the entire network of lies carefully mapped out in his brain and carefully tied in with real-world events. He also took great delight in correcting Carreon when he made an error, simply stating "incorrect".

Most crucial and most complicated was the web of shell companies that Cohen had built around himself. He had it all clearly logged in his head, but trying to recreate the same model by asking short questions of the architect was an almost impossible task.

Here is a quick rundown of one thread. Cohen was the current president of Sand Man Internacional. He had been a vice president of Omnitec International, and of Ynata, but was now only an officer of both. He was also an officer of First City Financial. He *had* had an ownership interest in Ocean Fund International - but then he sold it back to one of the other companies, which at some point became a subsidiary of one of the other companies. But he couldn't remember when exactly he sold that interest, or for how much. There was also a confidentiality contract governing another sale of stock, so he couldn't talk about that. Or it could even have been the same sale.

This fantastically, hopelessly tangled chain of events was all baloney: Cohen had incorporated each and every company, and he personally ran each one. But he knew that under the law a complaint would have to identify who was responsible and then prove their involvement. Cohen's carefully created corporate model was a reflection in water: touch it, and it disappeared.

Whenever Carreon did get close to pinning Cohen down on something, Cohen simply claimed ignorance. Detail that he didn't want to give – such as the name of his New Work accountant – he characterised as "crazy". "You can't remember that gentleman's name?" asked Carreon incredulously. "It was a crazy name," replied Cohen, "Radonovich or Ranonovich or something of that nature." "Who had the confidentiality agreement on the sale of Ocean Fund stock?" "The officers in Costa Rica." "Who are the officers in Costa Rica?" "I've already testified to that." "You did?" "Yes, I did." "What's the address in Costa Rica?" "It's a crazy address ... I'll supply it to you."

Carreon got Cohen worried when he started asking about the suit brought by Microsoft and others against Cohen for allowing software to be illegally downloaded from his French Connection BBS. Carreon had done his homework. "Are you aware that Susan Boydston [Cohen's ex-wife] filed a declaration on behalf of the Ashton-Tate attorneys saying that all the papers sat on your nightstand for weeks while you were claiming that you had never been served?"

Cohen was caught off-guard: "For the record, this was filed under seal of a protective order." Carreon had anticipated this objection: "I've got the order unsealing it right here." Cohen recovered quickly: "Can I finish my comment? For the record, this was filed under a protective order and this is the very first time that I've ever seen this document."

Carreon also had a declaration from Cohen's former lawyer Frank Butler stating that he had not represented Cohen for years prior to the case. And yet a Frank Butler had appeared as legal representative in the case: it was Cohen impersonating him, and not for the first time. Carreon confronted Cohen with the declarations. Cohen quickly slipped into another of his personas, that of the affable, entertaining story-teller. "This case had a very unusual thing happen in the middle of the case," Cohen explained on an unrelated tangent, "and the case fell apart after that happened, and I'm not quite sure I remember exactly what happened in that particular case because of what happened that was crazy." Cohen's co-defendant in that case was one John Cook. John Cook, it turned out, had also died.

But every now and again, Carreon's curiosity got the better of him and he chased Cohen around a tall tale. Such as when Cohen claimed he was a legal adviser to the Panamanian dictator General Manuel Noriega.

Noriega had been a CIA informant from the late 1950s, and came to power in Panama in 1983, but eventually the US turned against him, and in 1989 invaded Panama and deposed him.

Stephen Cohen claimed to have met this general "several times" in 1976 – the same year that Noriega was the personal guest of then CIA director George Bush in Washington. It is certainly possible that Cohen visited Panama at that time, possibly to get away from the Californian authorities, who were after him for passing bad cheques. But any further than that, well …

Carreon, despite himself, was intrigued: "What were you doing in Panama in 1976 to 1977?" "Visiting Manuel Antonio Noriega." "Were you really?" "Yes." "Had he invited you there or what were you doing there with Manuel?" "I went to apply for membership to the Bar." "Were you just pulling my leg about visiting Antonio?" "No." "No? Okay. So did you actually meet with General Noriega?" "Several times."

And on it went. Clearly it was a story that played well, which makes it all the more likely that Cohen had simply made it up. The Panama story was also a fundamental lynchpin of Cohen's entrenched fantasy about being a lawyer. Cohen had certainly attempted to study law. He went to evening classes at the Southern California School of Law about 30 miles from his home in Irvine. But Cohen dropped out in the first year. He also claimed to have gone to Western State University – the only university in the county where he lived that had an accredited law school at that time. But there are no records of him ever attending. He also claimed to have passed an equivalency exam in San Francisco, but was unable to provide any details more than "I believe it was on Market Street."

The fact is that Stephen Cohen has no legal qualifications whatsoever. What he does possess is an extremely sharp mind capable of storing and applying whatever information is useful to him. For a while he worked with criminal defence lawyer Michael Mayock, who would later defend Cohen on numerous occasions. But if he was asked to learn for learning's sake, to cover a curriculum, Cohen was hopeless.

It is highly probable that he wanted to become a lawyer to prove something to his accountant father, but when Cohen failed, at least once, to qualify as a lawyer it was a powerful blow to his ego. And so he slipped into a fantasy world, a world where he not only met Manuel Noriega, but was asked by him to take the Bar exam in Panama – which he of course passed. The fantasy was then extended to include the CIA. All this made Cohen feel important at a time when he was no more than an illiterate, ill-educated kid reduced to petty fraud to survive. The fantasy took root and Cohen introduced himself as an attorney from that point on. Even close friends were amazed when told nearly twenty years later that Stephen Cohen had never passed a single law exam.

Cohen married his first wife soon after he supposedly visited Panama, and persuaded her he did occasional work for the CIA. His pretence of being a proper attorney and also a government secret agent, became too important to Cohen for him to ever let it drop, and he carried it through to his second marriage and beyond.

At his trial in 1992, when he was convicted for impersonating an attorney, Cohen even went so far as to obtain authorisation from the court in California to travel to Panama to obtain the records that showed he was registered there. When he got back, he confidently handed them to the judge. But he had failed to get the documents authorised by the US consulate in Panama, as demanded. He had an explanation, of course: he had turned up at the consulate but the officer that signed off such documents had left for the day. And because he was under a court order to return the next day, he was forced to leave without the documents being authorised.

That wasn't the only time that Stephen Michael Cohen provided a US court with documents from a foreign government supporting his case, as Kremen would soon find out. Fortunately for Kremen, Judge James Ware lent them just as much credence as Judge Judith Keep had given the documents purportedly from the Panama Supreme Court back in 1992. Nevertheless, when questioned about the whole Panama business twenty-four years later by Charles Carreon, Cohen's eyes lit up, and he wallowed in comforting excitement.

The fact was that Cohen knew nothing about Panama or Noriega or the CIA beyond what he had read in newspapers and magazines. Of course, the advantage of posing as a CIA agent was that he could just tap his nose and explain he couldn't say any more.

Carreon became more and more frustrated as he questioned Cohen, and his frustration spilt out into arguments with Dorband – who kept breaking his flow with objections. Carreon knew he had blown it, and was getting increasingly aggressive, to the extent that even David Dolkas – there to question Cohen on behalf of NSI – asked Carreon to calm down. Eventually Dorband threatened to leave unless Carreon stopped raising his voice.

Carreon was furious with himself and with Cohen over how the deposition had gone. His examination finally ended with Cohen denying that the signature on a legal filing from an earlier court case was actually his, at which point Carreon ceded the floor to David Dolkas, who was growing impatient because it was past five p.m.

Dolkas dampened down the combustible atmosphere in the room with simple, precise and clear questioning. Had Cohen ever personally met an employee of Network Solutions? No. Had Cohen ever had an intimate relationship with someone at NSI? No. Did Cohen ever pay anyone at NSI to get them to transfer sex.com to him? No. Did he ever promise something to someone at NSI to transfer sex.com? No. Did he believe Sharyn Dimmick was authorised to sign the letter? Yes. Did he believe the letter was in fact signed by Sharyn Dimmick? Yes. Did he ever suggest otherwise at any point to NSI? Absolutely not. Dolkas had no interest in tackling Cohen, he simply wanted enough just cause to remove NSI from the case altogether – and he got it.

Cohen left the deposition room just before seven p.m. in an excellent mood. He had sized up the lawyer determined to bring him down, given NSI everything it needed to get out of the case, and cheered himself up by insulting Gary Kremen several times.

But he was also troubled by Carreon's zeal. Carreon was very fast to spot Cohen's lies, and he didn't like it, so he decided to pull Carreon into the game as well. Less than a fort-night after the deposition, Cohen brought a second defamation lawsuit against Carreon in his home state of Oregon, with Kremen named as a co-defendant. If Carreon was going to get in Cohen's face, Cohen would return the compliment.

The two wouldn't meet again until six months later, thanks to Dorband's stalling tactics. That occasion would be marked by a far more significant meeting: Gary Kremen and Stephen Cohen, face to face for the first time.

29

PANZERS AND TOES

Back in February 2000, Carreon and Kremen's main priority at that point was to keep NSI in the case. If NSI was out of the case, then Carreon and Kremen would be left chasing Cohen around and around the table. Both Kremen and Carreon knew the case had much wider implications. NSI was stating in filings that Kremen had no right to the domain – in fact it was saying that no one had any right to any domain, and it could do with them whatever it wished.

This was so clearly and categorically incorrect that the two friends knew they could win the case. And when they did, they would not only have sex.com, but would also have set a vital precedent for the future of the Internet. This was the big one. Of course it would also have crossed their minds that if NSI admitted guilt, it would have to pay compensation, and even at this stage Kremen and Carreon knew that the chances of getting any money out of Cohen ranged from slim to non-existent.

The problem was that Carreon didn't have a lot to work with. Months of legal work became effectively worthless after Ware refused to order NSI to hand over the documents Carreon wanted. Ware wanted to know if Carreon had evidence that NSI *knew* the Dimmick letter was forged, or if he could prove that Cohen was sleeping with someone in NSI and had used them as an inside man (or, rather, woman) to push domain transfers through the system.

Carreon knew the chances of him being able to prove either, even if he had more time, were remote. But he was determined to try to get Ware to see the bigger picture. NSI *should have known* that the Dimmick letter was a forgery. If he could prove that, Judge Ware might just start listening to his other arguments.

NSI was certain it was home and dry, but even so it didn't underestimate Carreon's drive and cunning. There remained a risk that he would somehow dig something up that made the company liable not just for sex.com but also for hundreds, maybe thousands, maybe tens of thousands of other domains. And sure enough, its fears were realised when Carreon struck gold and persuaded Ellen Rony to testify on Kremen's behalf.

Outside of Network Solutions' own staff, Ellen Rony was perhaps the most knowledgeable person on the planet about how the domain-name system worked in reality and how NSI interacted with it. Not only was she one of the people there from the very earliest days of the Internet, but she had decided to build an historical resource about its formation and its policies over time. In many ways, she knew more than NSI about the company's approach to domains.

Rony had already written the definitive book on Internet domains, *The Domain Name Handbook: High Stakes and Strategies in Cyberspace*; she had worked alongside Network Solutions for years; and she had been asked by the US government, the World Intellectual Property Organization, and numerous other international bodies to present her expert views. In short, she was the perfect witness.

NSI's team were already congratulating themselves on a job well done, and another legal victory in its pocket, when they learnt Rony was giving evidence for Kremen. When they then read her declaration, they nearly had a collective heart attack.

Rony used NSI's own procedures and rules to knock down each argument the company had used against Kremen. Regarding the standing issue, she had this to say: "According to NSI's internal procedures described in Version 2.0, Section 5 of the Domain Name Registration Template with attached

Registration Agreement adopted by NSI in September 1995, the domain name is considered to be registered to an 'organisation', even if the organization is individual."

Regarding the question as to whether Kremen had any contract with NSI: "On July 28, 1995 Network Solutions introduced a new Domain Name Dispute Policy ... Network Solutions applied the Domain Name Dispute Policy as binding upon all existing registrants in the WHOIS database, not just those registered after July 28, 1995."

Regarding the question as to whether NSI was obligated to contact Kremen before it made changes: "According to NSI's own stated procedures, any request to delete a registered domain name from the database should have been initiated by Kremen or by the host provider, netcom.com. Kremen did not initiate a delete request for the sex.com registration, nor was Kremen queried to see whether he concurred with the delete request. According to NSI's own stated procedure, any notification of the deletion and the approximate time it would take effect should have been sent to the requester as well as to Kremen and the technical contact at netcom.com. Neither Kremen nor netcom.com were notified of the impending deletion of the sex.com domain name registration." Ouch. But Rony had more.

NSI knew the value of domain names because of the large number of domain disputes it had to deal with. Between 28 July 1995 and the end of that year, NSI's dispute policy was invoked 166 times. By October 1995 – when the company handed over sex.com to Cohen – "a domain name such as sex.com was extremely marketable and not likely to be abandoned", said the world expert in domains and NSI policy.

Rony then went into great depth over how the transfer of sex.com would have worked, should have worked and all the reasons why the Dimmick letter didn't meet the criteria necessary to make that transfer. "The letter's content is internally inconsistent ... The letter is questionable ... The letter is inappropriate ... The letter is dubious ... This was a suspect admission ... should have triggered further investigation ... nothing in NSI's normal registration business practices at the time would justify changing the domain name registration."

"Had NSI followed its own notification procedures ... it would have quickly learned the true nature of the facts," Rony concluded. "A letter like the forged letter was a complete procedural anomaly that should have been rejected out of hand."

It was devastating. And NSI realised straight off that it could be enough to change Judge Ware's appraisal of the situation completely. And so on the afternoon of 23 February 2000, NSI's legal frontman Philip Sbarbaro, with a second lawyer listening in, took an extraordinary risk and called up Ellen Rony at home to warn her off the case. She wasn't there at the time, so Sbarbaro left a number with her son and she called back shortly afterwards.

Not only was it highly irregular that opposing counsel would call up the other side's witness in the middle of a case, but Sbarbaro's behaviour when he spoke to her was quite extraordinary and wholly unethical. He had known Ms Rony for several years and clearly felt that an aggressive approach would yield the best results. He started off by telling Rony that Charles Carreon was a "loony", unpredictable and untrustworthy, and warned that she was "going against NSI", for which she would suffer the consequences.

"Mr Sbarbaro told me he had received word I was an expert witness opposing NSI, and he seemed quite surprised," Rony later told the court. He had in fact already read her declaration and decided to scare her into recanting the most damaging parts. "He said if I thought I knew anything about NSI's processes, I was wrong. He said that while we were friends, this was litigation, and he would try to get me removed as an expert witness because my name had not been submitted in a timely manner. He said if he was unsuccessful in doing that, he would depose me, and I would find that to be a very unpleasant experience."

And then, incredibly, Sbarbaro began to threaten Rony physically. He said he would "let out the Panzers" on her, and then grew even more explicit. "He told me that if I remained an expert witness in the case, he would discredit me, my expertise and my testimony. Then he said he would 'cut off my toes'," Rony testified. "While Mr Sbarbaro declares that he 'joked' about how aggressive he would be in deposing me, I assure the court that no one was laughing," Rony declared. "He engaged in considerable sabre rattling and threatened me with bodily harm, which, given his tone, was clearly meant to alarm."

Sbarbaro then announced that another attorney, Kevin Golden, was on the line listening in, before probing her about what she had seen with regard to the case: which testimony, which documents, which judgments, and so on. He then threatened to cut Rony off from any future help or support from NSI in regard to her professional work. Rony confessed that the phone call left her "feeling very unsettled". She told the court: "His comment about cutting off my toes was particularly distressing, and I felt it was both personally and professionally inappropriate for him to make that threat."

Once she had composed herself, Rony called Carreon to tell him what had happened. Carreon hit the roof, dropped everything else and immediately wrote and printed a court motion demanding that Sbarbaro, Golden and their firm, Hanson & Molloy, be prevented from representing NSI any further, that NSI's motion for summary judgment be put on hold, and that sanctions be brought against all four for unlawful contact with a witness.

The next day, Carreon received a series of urgent calls from Dolkas, but ignored them until he had finished the first draft of the complaint. He then called Dolkas back. Dolkas was on the offensive: he had a "very upset client" he told Carreon, because Ellen Rony had read a deposition of NSI's director of business affairs David Graves that was under seal – and so Carreon had no right to show it to her. It's a classic move: if you have no defences and are about to be attacked, rush forward and attack first.

Graves' deposition wasn't in fact protected in any way. It was readily available for purchase if you were so inclined, as Carreon was to prove shortly afterwards. But it was all NSI had to go on at the moment, with its lead lawyer having physically threatened Kremen's main witness.

Still furious, Carreon typed up a letter and faxed it to Sbarbaro, copying in both Rony and Kremen. "Dear Mr Sbarbaro: This letter is to advise that I will be moving for sanctions against you personally for calling Ellen Rony and threatening her with Nazi images and threats of dismemberment ... Your behaviour is bizarre. My motion for sanctions will follow."

Sbarbaro fired one right back. "Dear Mr Carreon, You file motions out of time, using undisclosed 'expert' witnesses never previously designated, provide that witness with material designed 'attorney's eyes only', and believe it your right to criticise other counsel. Ellen Rony and I have been friends for a number of years. I am permitted to call her any time ..."

Carreon added Sbarbaro's comments to his complaint, printed it out, put it in an envelope addressed to the court and posted it. When he got back to his house, there was another fax, this time from Dolkas. "The purpose of this letter is to address the problem you caused which, hopefully, we can immediately remedy," it began. "Apparently, you provided to Ellen Rony most, if not all, of the documents I previously produced to you from Network Solutions on an 'Attorneys' Eyes Only' basis."

Carreon ignored it. The weekend came and went, Carreon's complaint was filed with the court, and battle resumed. Sbarbaro realised that his plan had backfired dramatically, and came to the conclusion that the best thing he could do was withdraw from the case. When he then did in a carefully worded fax.

They were weasel words, and prompted another round of aggressive and threatening court motions, faxes, emails and phone calls between the attorneys. The court date for NSI's summary judgment hearing was set back. And set back again. Eventually, Ware decided the matter was getting out of hand and stepped in, insisting on a date for an oral hearing at which all pending motions would be decided.

Despite Carreon's relentless pursuit, the truth of the matter was that he was out of his depth. Not only did he have to contend with NSI, but at the same time Cohen and Dorband were doing everything in their power to bury him under paper. Carreon didn't have the backing of a big law firm – he was a lone practitioner, and stubbornly tried to do it all. When the workload became impossible, he hired his wife and his daughter as para-legals, but neither of them were trained, and soon they were swamped as well. Kremen recalls visiting the office one day and being amazed at the total disorder and chaos. Charles was his close friend, but he was paying him a small fortune and he was not getting the service he thought he deserved.

It was during this period that Cohen outlined yet again how far he was prepared to go to prevent others from learning anything about his financial affairs. In response to a discovery request for full tax returns from 1979 to 1999, Cohen provided precisely two sheets: each a page-long summary of the French Connection BBS business, showing that it had made a loss of $1,319 in 1984, and a profit of $87 in 1988.

They were, naturally enough, forgeries. But Cohen hadn't been able to resist adding a little twist, typing in the business name as "THE FRENCH CONNECTION & IT'S SERVICE KNOWN AS SEX.COM". It was patently ridiculous that a business would call itself that on a tax filing, and if anyone remained in any doubt about its genuineness, the illiterate Cohen had included an incorrect apostrophe in "its", in much the same way he had written "ad's" in the forged Dimmick letter.

When Judge Ware finally stepped into the all-out warfare and set a hearing date for Monday, 1 May 2000, ten a.m. sharp for all these things to be decided, there were a few more shots fired over the barricades before it suddenly went quiet. Then, for two whole weeks, there was not a peep.

30

EXIT 1

In the build-up to the big day in court everyone in the case finally had time to take stock of what had happened in this fight for sex.com.

The importance of it all began to sink in. When sex.com was first registered in 1994, it was no more than a geek getting hold of a fun address on an obscure computer network in California. All the people in the world even aware of domain names could fit inside a large hall. When Cohen stole sex.com in September 1995, the Internet and domain names had a fun, cultish buzz around them, and people were coming up with wild predictions about what might be done. As the network grew, the constant influx of new people with new ideas became difficult and then impossible to follow. Suddenly you would stumble across an entire area of the Internet you hadn't even known about before. It was like walking down the street one day and suddenly realising a new building had appeared from nowhere. You stick your head in, and to your utter amazement inside is an enormous foyer with hundreds of people milling about, chatting. Where did all these people come from?

You leave and then notice that there is another building across the road that you've never seen before either. So you stick your head in there as well. A week later, there are so many new buildings you have to decide which one to check out next. And before you know it, you are asking complete strangers which buildings they have been in and if there is anything interesting inside. They gladly tell you and then ask you the same. And then, as you stand there, you feel the ground shake as a new building begins to appear, fully formed, from the ground. It eventually comes to a halt, workmen appear from nowhere to remove and tidy up the broken concrete and tarmac at its base, a huge fluorescent sign flickers on and the doors open ...

This was the strange, fascinating world of the dotcom boom. People with eyes full of wonder and creative ideas bubbling up through their brains. All of a sudden, getting back to work after lunch was not as important.

The wild predictions of just a few years earlier started to look oddly realistic. By the time Kremen finally filed his lawsuit in July 1998, Yahoo – a company that did little more than tell people what they could find in these buildings – had already been listed on the stock exchange for two years. The year before it launched itself on the stock exchange in 1996, the company had lost $643,000, on a measly turnover of $1.4 million. If it was any other company at any other time in history the company would have been put into receivership. As it was, its shares rocketed and by the end of the first day it was worth $1 billion.

When Carreon filed the third amended complaint in October 1999, the entire world was in the grip of Internet fever: billions of dollars were being thrown at businesses with patently ridiculous business plans; millions of domain names were being registered, bought and sold; tens of thousands of consultants, visionaries, gurus were painting spectacularly rosy futures. A website offering cheap flights, among other things – Priceline.com – was suddenly valued at more than the entire US airline industry. Of course the crazy valuations were soon to collapse in on themselves, but that didn't detract from the fact that something monumental was happening.

We now know that Kremen's court showdown on May Day 2000 occurred at the absolute peak of the dotcom boom. The Internet was already a multi-billion-dollar medium of seemingly limitless potential, and right at its heart stood dotcom domain names and their owner, Network Solutions.

It wasn't only Kremen that had been through the wringer recently; Network Solutions itself had had a tumultuous few months. The US Justice Department had just ended an in-depth anti-trust investigation into the company. The European Union had also been investigating it for six months (although in the end it called off the dogs). NSI had just been cleared by the US Supreme Court for domain charging, and found not liable by an appeals court for violating yet more US laws. It had also reached agreement with ICANN, and had managed to keep control of the dotcom registry.

The dust was settling, but there remained one big, vitally important battle left: sex.com. If NSI beat its way out of the case with its legal arguments intact, it was home free. But if the judge rejected its arguments and NSI was forced into court with Kremen, there was a very real risk that the company would be crushed as dozens of other lawsuits rained down upon it. The world was watching, and the stakes were very, very high.

Nonetheless, NSI was extremely confident. Ware had already made it plain that unless Carreon pulled something spectacular out of the bag, he was going to rule the company out of the case. Carreon fought hard. He fought hard and he fought well, but he just didn't cut it. Judge Ware wasn't going to take anybody's word – let alone the word of a ponytailed defence lawyer fighting for a pornography website – over that of a company that had recently been given the all-clear by the US government and the European Union.

Ware signed the order four days later – six years and one day since Kremen had registered sex.com – and on Monday, 8 May 2000, his order granting Network Solutions' motion for summary judgement was made public. The Internet giant was out of the case.

Kremen winces even now. "Oh that was a horrible day. A horrible, horrible day. I had done a lot of research. I read

Charles' pleadings, read his previous cases, read other cases, read books on law – and eventually I understood it was a process. There's hardly anything in the world that is not understandable eventually as a process. And once I understood the process, I realised this was bad."

It was worse than bad – a lot worse. To even get NSI back in the case Kremen would have to go to the Court of Appeals. That meant a different, specialist, extremely expensive lawyer. The case would then have to be rebuilt in order to jump a much higher legal hurdle than the one it had just failed to clear. And if by some fluke it made it that far, after several years of work, the case would be right back to where it had been 20 minutes before Ware granted NSI's motion.

As the full weight of the failure landed on Kremen and Carreon's shoulders, they realised exactly what they had to do. They went out, bought all the cocaine they could find and flew their way over the wreckage. The drug and each other's company restored their bravado, and the pair vowed that they would win, they would get back sex.com, and they would have the last laugh. And just to prove it, Carreon drew up an agreement right there and then in which he promised to get Kremen sex.com, and in return Kremen promised him that when he did he would give him 15 per cent. They signed it, threw the pen down, and it was as if the deed was already done. Kremen would have sex.com. That was decided. They then both passed out.

Anyone close to an NSI executive that same day could have been mistaken for thinking that they were also on drugs. Network Solutions was on cloud nine. Not only was it out of a case that had become worryingly ominous, but its legal argument that it only provided a "service" had been given strong legal backup at an absolutely crucial moment.

So significant was the decision that within hours the company had rewritten its own terms and conditions to include the term "service". The case with Kremen was the final match of the season for NSI, and it had walked it to take the title. The company that rarely commented even on its successes had executives queuing up to talk to the press.

Official spokesman Brian O'Shaughnessy was succinct: "We provide a service. This is not a property, per se." Phillip Sbarbaro, the same man that had threatened to cut the toes off Kremen's lead witness a few weeks earlier, provided the same message: "A domain name is not property, it's a service. To say people buy and sell domain names is the vernacular, but it's not accurate."

Even Network Solutions' CEO Jim Rutt wanted a piece of the action: "The Court's decision is a clear win for Network Solutions and domain name registrars. By succinctly denying the conversion claim by the plaintiff, the Court has clarified the rights and responsibilities between the registrar and registrant."

Ware's ruling was an intriguing read. There was of course lengthy legal explanation and justification for dismissing each of Kremen's six counts, but Ware also made it plain that it wasn't NSI's argument that won the day – it was the fact that he didn't want to be the judge who decided what domain names were and were not in law in May 2000. With hindsight, it was the right decision: the Internet was little more than an infant that had just started to walk. It was simply too much of a legal gamble to go against the prevailing philosophy of the time – even when it was clear that change was needed. And he didn't want another judge to be faced with the same problem either. So he stated quite explicitly in his judgment that he felt the decision about what domain names were was something for the government to deal with through the normal democratic process of law-making.

"The Court believes there are methods better suited to regulate the vagaries of domain names. The Court leaves it to the legislature to fashion an appropriate statutory scheme to regulate the vagaries of domain names. The Court leaves it to the legislature to fashion an appropriate statutory system to protect dormant domain names unprotected by trademark law."

Ware ruled there was no contract between Kremen and NSI because Kremen hadn't paid the company any money when he registered the domain. And he warned that to hold NSI responsible would stifle the domain-registration system by "requiring further regulations by NSI and potential increases in fees".

Kremen summed it up neatly for reporters: "It's ridiculous. If you follow the logic here, it's open season for stealing domains. If I go hijack your domain and use it for a year, you have absolutely no recourse."

Of course, it is easy to say in retrospect that Ware should not have accepted NSI's legal arguments, but at the time there were plenty of lawyers who agreed with his cautious stance. Trademark lawyer Sally Abel told *Wired*: "The court points out, rightly, that the law has yet to catch up with the Internet, and it would be overreaching if it ruled for the plaintiff. The judge is right – at this time."

Massachusetts attorney Maury Ringel agreed: "We are in the wild, wild West stages of Internet law. Keep in mind that we have many Federal Circuit Courts in the US, and one Circuit can rule completely differently than any other."

But others took exception. "Domains have many of the attributes of property," intellectual property lawyer Rob Phillips commented. "People pay a lot of money for them, they create a huge amount of value, and they exist, albeit in computer form. If they're not property, what are they?" What was noticeable, however, was that the only people who agreed with NSI that domains were not property but "a service" were NSI employees.

Not that it mattered. NSI was out of the case. It was now just Kremen and Cohen, head to head. Judge Ware had extended discovery to 6 October and set a trial date of 13 March 2001. "Nothing has changed against Cohen," Kremen stated grimly.

31

JAMES WAGSTAFFE

Cohen couldn't help but create mischief. Annoyed at what was being written about the case and about him in the press and on internet forums, he decided to send an electronic card claiming to be from Gary Kremen to Luke Ford, the Californian adult industry's unofficial news hound and gossip columnist.

Ford's website was read by most in the industry, and Ford himself operated an open-door policy in the notoriously back-biting industry: he would write up almost anything that anyone told him. The con man in Stephen Cohen couldn't resist plying Ford with acres of twaddle about Kremen and the case.

The e-card, which Cohen sent Ford on the same day as the NSI left the case, read: "The United States District Court in Kremen v Cohen rulled [sic] against Gary Kremen yesterday and dismissed Network Solutions on Summary Judgement. After talking with the Court Yesterday, it looks like Cohen will win based upon the fact that this is in-tanagble [sic] property and there is no conversion – Gary Kremen." It claimed to come from Kremen's email address.

The message was, of course, nonsense, and Cohen's poor literacy ("rulled" instead of "ruled"; "in-tanagble" for "intangible") gave the game away. Ford emailed Kremen, telling him about the e-card and asking him how he felt about being impersonated by Cohen. It gave Kremen an opportunity to vent his anger in, yes, yet another court motion. "I am outraged that Mr Cohen would engage yet again in the misuse of my name," Kremen fumed. "First, he stole my domain name by slandering me and claiming that I had been fired by my own company, now he steals my name again and puts words in my mouth that I do not agree with. If the rule of law means anything, it means that when such things are brought to the notice of the Court, that the Court will act to prevent the recommission of such criminal acts."

The card was harmless enough, but it marked the start of an escalation of the increasingly bitter and personal fight between the two men. Kremen continued to attack Cohen in the press, and Cohen threatened to sue anyone who repeated what Kremen said. Slowly, more and more of the dispute between the two took place outside the court: in emails, phone calls, on public forums, through proxies. The case was starting to eat away at Kremen; every day it became more important that he won back sex.com and with it enough money to at least cover the cost of his legal bills. But as Kremen grew more determined, Cohen became more tenacious. It was now just the two of them locked into the fight. There was no way Kremen was going to lose, and there was no way Cohen was going to be beaten.

On top of that the relationship between Kremen and Carreon had started to fracture, and in less than a year it would end in a painful lawsuit between the two former allies. The long hours, the enormous workload and the pressure had started setting them against one another, and Carreon's consistently poor performance in oral argument had put doubts in Kremen's mind. NSI being allowed to leave the case was the final wake-up call. It was clear that Carreon would not be able to pull NSI back into the case and win. He had already been badly knocked down by Ware, but more than that, he simply didn't have enough time to appeal Ware's decision, and simultaneously fight the case against Cohen.

The alternative came courtesy of another of Kremen's lawyers, Richard Idell, who had been brought in just to work on the trademark side of the case. He had warned Kremen that

Carreon was not going to play well in court. Kremen didn't understand what he was talking about at first. "I thought maybe he had a bad experience with a hippy with a ponytail once, I don't know." Kremen also hadn't been to the magistrate hearings so he hadn't seen just how bad Carreon's court performances were. Idell told him he knew the perfect man for the job of getting NSI back in the case – a star attorney called James Wagstaffe. Kremen decided to take Idell's advice.

It nearly didn't happen, however. "Our company is very straight-laced," Wagstaffe explains. "And my partner [Rod Kerr] was very unsure about the whole case." Even Wagstaffe wasn't sure: "I was raised a Catholic and I don't know what my mom would think of me doing a case for a porn site. I don't think I've ever actually looked at sex.com." Wagstaffe and Kerr nevertheless arranged to go out for a meal with Kremen to discuss the case. According to Wagstaffe, Kremen "was really out of it that evening. And straight away afterward Kerr said to me 'We have to drop this client.'" But Wagstaffe persuaded him that the case was worth doing. "At the time, it was just to appeal the NSI part of the case, and the case was *very* interesting," he explains.

Kremen didn't realise it at the time, but he had just landed on his feet: Wagstaffe is one of the most sought-after First Amendment attorneys in the US, having successfully defended numerous newspapers, magazines and broadcasters on the grounds of free speech. He is also an authority on federal civil procedure, and as a result an instructor on court procedure to newly appointed judges. In addition, he has written several books covering legal ethics and public speaking. Put simply, Jim Wagstaffe not only knew most of the judges in California personally, but came with an impeccable reputation and a talent for talking.

"He's no bulldog like Idell," recalls Kremen. "He won't just keep grinding away. And Carreon has this ability to do a little punch, and then go over here and do little punches, like a little ninja doing drugs ... But when you saw Wagstaffe perform in court ... well, there's no comparison."

Wagstaffe had a similar view of his two fellow attorneys. "Richard [Idell] and I are very old friends. It fact it's odd that we get on so well because he is much more willing to take risks with the crazy stuff. Carreon has the kind of mind that would come up with ten crazy ideas, one of which was great. You just had to filter it out. Good lawyering is like juggling, it's all about keeping your eye on the ball – and Carreon didn't do that."

There was something of a clash of personalities between Wagstaffe and Kremen. Wagstaffe relates one incident: "There was one late-night meeting where we were all in the office trying to work out the best strategy. And in the end we had to put Kremen in a room by himself to get it done because he had rewritten parts of the response and made it worse. And the next day, my secretary came to me and said, 'Did you have Gary Kremen here last night?' So I said yes, and she took me into the room and showed me a chair – and there on the chair were his initials. I don't know whether he did it on purpose or absent-mindedly, but it's fair to say that Gary always leaves his mark wherever he goes." Wagstaffe adds: "We thought my partner would notice straight away and go nuts, but it's been there years now and he still hasn't noticed."

Kremen may have bagged a top-notch attorney, but Wagstaffe did not come cheap. "Jesus Christ. And I had to pay him up front and I had to pay him cash. But I decided to take this last million dollars I had, which I didn't even pay taxes due on yet, and say, okay, I'm going to give it to Idell and Wagstaffe, 'cos Carreon is not doing the job and I see this heading to zero. Charles was doing more and more drugs. It was a train wreck. And Wagstaffe saved the train wreck."

It was not a decision Kremen took lightly. He knew he was committing every last penny of what was once a fortune to hiring the best attorneys to chase down NSI, the Internet's biggest company, with absolutely no guarantee that in a year's time the judge wouldn't just dismiss the whole case and leave him penniless.

Kremen now had four attorneys working on the case: Carreon was chasing the main case and Cohen; Diestel was chasing Cohen's counterclaims; Idell was following the key trademark issue that was still bubbling away; and now Jim Wagstaffe was appealing the NSI decision.

Kremen's war chest was dwindling very rapidly, and there was still an enormous distance to cover. But then, slowly, something began to dawn on all those involved: with NSI out of the case, for the first time Kremen's team had room to breathe. And for the first time, Kremen was outgunning Cohen. Dorband's papering technique was turned 180 degrees back on him. Suddenly it was he who was under pressure, trying to keep up with Kremen's attorneys. Carreon had been chasing Cohen for so long he had learnt all his tricks, and Diestel had got to grips with Dorband's delay tactics: Diestel would no longer be relying on Dorband's word, he would simply send letters and then file into court.

The case was still semi-conscious, but Cohen was no longer able to keep kicking it. And it wouldn't be long before it was strong enough to get to its feet and give the bully a bit of his own medicine.

32

UNITED FRONT

With a court date set and Ware extremely unlikely to move it, the two-year court case stepped up another gear. Wagstaffe officially entered the case on 7 June. A week later, he had entered the fray with a request for more time to respond to Cohen's motion for summary judgment.

Wagstaffe took the opportunity to fire a warning shot across Dorband's and Dolkas' bows. He outlined in precise detail the efforts that his associates had made to contact both Dorband and Dolkas, including the names of secretaries, assistants, times of call, result and so on. The message was clear: don't mess around because we are highly organized and we are playing this by the book.

The Kremen versus Cohen battle was now being fought on several different fronts. In the main case, discovery had been reopened, so Carreon was busy serving a new batch of subpoenas on both individuals and companies, either for documents or to give them notice of deposition. In response, Dorband was doing the same to Kremen, and also disputing every deposition Carreon tried to take, including an ex-wife, an ex-boss and an ex-work colleague of Cohen's.

Wagstaffe was working on the appeal against the judge's NSI decision, which had the effect of dragging him into the main case when Cohen started using the fact that NSI had been removed from the case as a main argument in his motion to dismiss the complaint.

Then there was an ongoing fight over the trademark for

sex.com. Cohen's claimed trademark was his axe against those in the adult industry who tried to use the word "sex" in their domain names, but Kremen's opposition had blunted it, and Kremen's own attempts to then register sex.com as a trademark pulled it out of Cohen's hands altogether. An Oregon judge had put three of Cohen's trademark cases against "sex" dotcom domain owners on hold as a result of Kremen's action, effectively putting a stop to Cohen's successful crusade against his competitors.

And then there were the defamation lawsuits. The one brought in California against Kremen was still ongoing, and Richard Diestel, who was handling the defamation cases, was asking the court to compel Cohen and his lawyer Michael Mayock for deposition. The Oregon case brought against Carreon had its own parallel game of legal-motion ping pong, with Carreon hitting most of the best shots. Eventually common sense prevailed when Judge Janice Stewart ordered that the case be put on hold. She concluded: "It appears that Cohen may be simply harassing Kremen and his attorney."

Cohen was beginning to panic, especially regarding the relentless press interest in the case. Kremen and Carreon had been providing details to a number of newspapers and magazines in order to level the playing field with Cohen. In particular, Carreon wrote an in-depth six-page press release outlining the case, as well as Cohen's criminal past and his conduct in the case. It was used as the basis of stories by journalists at *Wired*, *Red Herring* and *Forbes*, and much to Cohen's horror resulted in them calling him up and asking difficult questions. When an aggressive refusal to comment failed to stem the stories, he fell back on his tried-and-tested skills.

Cohen had good reason to fear the press: not only are journalists trained truth-seekers, they are also backed up by organisations that believe it is their duty to defend published stories. The journalists had given Cohen the opportunity to respond, and so they were on safe legal ground. Cohen's only hope was to scare people off with legal threats. There was little chance of that tactic working: this was sex.com, after all – the story virtually wrote itself, and it was irresistible to journalists. Ware's decision to allow NSI out of the case was also eminently newsworthy, because of the legal questions raised around domain names. The result was that even more people heard the story of sex.com. It had entered the media's consciousness, and there was no escaping its attention from that point on.

And so Cohen responded by filing another defamation lawsuit, this time against the one person he could strike with ease: Luke Ford. Ford is a self-employed and self-proclaimed chronicler of the Californian adult industry. A prolific writer, he knows everyone in the business, and has an unusual, rambling and often confusing writing style that involves repeating verbatim everything he has heard. If someone feels aggrieved at something that has appeared on his website, they need only email or call him and complain – and he will post that as well.

Occasionally, however, Ford embarks on some investigative work and posts the results of what he finds, complete with wild assertions and harsh criticisms. Most journalists would regard this as just the raw material for a story, but Ford simply posts all the material without going to the trouble of turning it into a story. Unlike many of the people in the industry he covers, Ford earns very little money, and has been living for years in a converted garage in the suburbs of Los Angeles.

As such, Ford was a perfect target for Cohen. He didn't have the money, or the company back-up of other journalists, and he had a high profile in the adult industry. By bringing a lawsuit against Ford, Cohen effectively warned the rest of the adult industry not to mess with him, and he did so by demanding a ridiculous $50 million in damages for libel while also naming as co-defendants between one and ten "Does", meaning that he was as yet unable to identify other people ("John Does") who had libelled him. It was a crystal clear warning to people who might be tempted to talk to the press that if they did, Cohen would come after them.

In the main case, at another hearing in front of Trumbull, things were going badly for Carreon. His determined efforts to cut through the crap were constantly stymied by Judge Trumbull, who mixed contempt and feigned ignorance in equal measure when dealing with him. For whatever reason, her dislike of Carreon was starting to hold the case back. And Carreon was getting increasingly angry, which only made matters worse.

Diestel, working on the defamation suits, was more successful. He is eloquent and precise under pressure, and more focused than Carreon. Diestel wanted three things: Cohen's continued deposition, Cohen's attorney Michael Mayock's deposition, and full details from Dorband of Cohen's witnesses. Dorband and Cohen had pulled exactly the same trick on Diestel as they had on Carreon, providing a long list of unknown individuals, with incomplete details, who stretched right around the globe – this time including Buenos Aires and Tehran.

Dorband had also pulled his customary ruse of appearing to agree to what the other side wanted just days – sometimes even minutes – before they were due to enter the court to argue it out. He would then tell the judge everything had been sorted out, undermining the other side, but without giving any detail – so immediately after the hearing was over he could break the very promise he had just given. Diestel, however, was an insurance attorney and that meant he had seen it all before.

Diestel refused to accept Dorband's terms in court, and read out Judge Ware's various rulings. After some argument and bartering Trumbull finally ruled that Kremen's side was to get another 18 hours of deposition – three days of six hours – with Cohen, on dates between 11 and 21 July. And that ruling – in which Diestel was very careful to make sure that Trumbull stated there would be no restrictions on topics, questions or attorneys – was the one that broke the case for Kremen because it gave Carreon, Diestel and Wagstaffe the chance to pin Cohen down. A con man's tricks are never less effective than when he is under direct questioning. Dorband immediately set about trying to minimise the problem.

But what was most remarkable about the hearing was the way in which Trumbull's demeanour instantly changed the moment Wagstaffe very briefly entered discussions. Wagstaffe was still getting up to speed with the case, and so had sat in the court without saying a word. Wagstaffe was an unknown quantity to Dorband, but he knew of his impeccable reputation. So Dorband tried to argue that only Carreon and Diestel should be allowed to depose his client, at which point Wagstaffe stood up and turned on the charm.

It's hard to explain what it is about some individuals that immediately conveys to others precisely who they are. Some exude charisma, others danger; some give off an air of intimidation, others draw people to them straight away. Carreon admitted to feeling intimidated by Dorband's powerful aura of confidence. The other attorneys (on both sides) were unsettled by Carreon's passion and unpredictability. But what Jim Wagstaffe has is better than fear: he exudes an air of subtle yet unmistakable authority. Dorband's confidence comes from having beaten so many people; Wagstaffe's from having beaten so many Dorbands.

"Your honour, just so the record is clear," Wagstaffe offered. "I'm representing Mr Kremen. I'm neither representing him on only the counter-claim or only the plaintiff's side."

"Well, it's an unusual case, you must admit, Mr Wagstaffe," Trumbull responded.

"I do, your honour."

"When I have lawyers representing the same person for different positions in the lawsuit ..."

"I understand. When there's insurance involved, that's frequently the case. But I will say, your honour, since I'm coming in simply to advise Mr Kremen, just so the record is clear, I'm coming in to represent him on *all* aspects of the case."

Trumbull finally capitulated, and granted Wagstaffe permission to question Cohen at his deposition:

"Well, I don't care who ... It can't be beyond these three lawyers. These three lawyers for the 18 hours, and you have to divide it up."

Carreon chipped in: "May Mr Kremen be present? I anticipate an objection should he appear."

"He has a right to be present, unless there's some problem," replied Trumbull.

33

THE THREE-DAY DEPOSITION

And so it was that three weeks later, on Tuesday 11 July 2000, Cohen returned to 1202 Kettner Boulevard, Suite 6100, San Diego, California to begin his second deposition.

Carreon, Diestel and Wagstaffe had agreed between them to take one day each, with Diestel first, followed by Wagstaffe, and then Carreon. Between them they hoped to cut enough holes in Cohen's cloak of deception – his claims, alibis and explanations – that anyone, and particularly Judge Ware, would be able to see through it.

It wasn't all smooth sailing though. As Wagstaffe had made it quite clear in Trumbull's hearing, he was there to represent Kremen "on all aspects of the case". Since that hearing, he had also filed a statement of facts in opposition to Cohen's judgment motion that strayed heavily into the main case. Carreon was feeling resentful, especially since Trumbull had virtually fallen over Wagstaffe only minutes after she had treated Carreon himself with such disdain. Wagstaffe was only supposed to be dealing with the NSI appeal, but was increasingly encroaching on the case Carreon had spent a year of his life fighting, at reduced rates.

The real pressure was on Cohen and Dorband, however. Cohen's life was absolutely littered with events that undermined his credibility, and while he had formulated a consistent story about what had happened with sex.com, the simple fact was that 80 per cent of it was untrue and he would have to rely on his wits to get through the three days.

Analysing Cohen's approach now, it is easy to pick out a number of ruses that he had clearly found to be effective over the years, and which he threw in, tailored to the occasion, whenever the questions grew too close for comfort.

These are his favourites:

The Grim Reaper. Anyone from Cohen's past who was likely to give a very different version of events to his usually found themselves deceased, frequently from a dreadful disease and with a distracting story attached. Some were reborn only to die again soon after.

John Cook, for instance – who ran Cohen's bulletin-board system – died shortly after Cohen came out of jail in 1995, and then again in 1997, possibly from cancer.

Dave Hapgood – who took over from John Cook and so possessed all the computer equipment that could prove or destroy Cohen's claim to have used "sex.com" since 1979 – died from "sugar diabetes" in 1997, the same year as Cook's second death. Cohen apparently never met him, but he was, "completely disfigured".

Gino Steffe – who Cohen may well have met in jail, and who was on the board of one of Cohen's shell companies and was unhappy with the stock scam Cohen tried to pull – died "subsequently".

Vito Franco – Cohen's famous Hawaiian ex-policeman-movie-producer-builder, who also created the Sharyn Dimmick letter, got Sharyn's signature even though she didn't live at the address he didn't go to, and who drew up Cohen's list of "witnesses" without any contact details – died in October 1999 from both a heart attack and diabetes in a hospital that had never heard of him.

David Joseph Cohen – Cohen's father, who was, according to Cohen, his accountant for most of his life – died and took the secret of his son's accounts to his grave.

Renee Cohen – Cohen's mother, who is still answering her

telephone to this day – turned out to have died sometime between 1997 and 2000 when Cohen was asked for contact details.

No entiendo. Despite living in Mexico for most of his life, marrying a Mexican woman, arguing in Spanish with his Mexican employees (according to witnesses) and starting up several companies in Mexico, Cohen claimed he only spoke "about three words of Spanish" and was unable to read any of the language. This had not stopped him from signing numerous legal documents written in Spanish – but it did prevent him from being able to understand a word of them when they were put in front of him by Kremen's lawyers.

The Russian dolls. Every company under scrutiny existed within another company, all of which Cohen had incorporated. However, he was unable to supply even the most basic details about any of them. He didn't know who was on the board of directors for any of them because he was not a company officer. Although he was an officer of some of them, but only an officer with limited authority. He had no stock in any of the companies, except for those that he did, but he may have sold that stock for an unknown amount to one of the other companies at some point, although he could never remember when. That company was a subsidiary of one of the other companies anyway.

Cardiac arrest and amnesia. The former was usually reserved for legal filings, and the latter for depositions. Cohen had his first heart attack in 1987, which explained why he missed a filing date. In 1988 Cohen, while impersonating Frank Butler, had another heart attack, which explained why he missed a filing date. Another heart attack somewhere around 2000 meant that his memory failed him. But his memory had been failing long before then. He couldn't remember when he was married, or divorced, any of the four times, or when he left school, or went to university, or pretty much anything in fact. Date amnesia was also only the tip of the memory-loss iceberg: people, places, deals, documents, just about anything that *can* be stored in the human mind consistently wasn't. But, intriguingly, only when the information was potentially incriminating.

The promise. Using a technique favoured by many company press officers, Cohen would avoid difficult areas by failing to recall details but instead would promise hand-on-heart to go away and provide the information as soon as possible. Of course, the information would never be forthcoming.

*

While Cohen has his numerous methods for deflecting questions, he was ably assisted by Dorband, who, just prior to Cohen's second deposition, pulled a trademark last-minute announcement out of the hat. Due to previous engagements, both Dorband and Cohen were unable to appear at any deposition the following week, so – since the court had ordered three days of depositions to be carried out before 21 June – all three would have to be done that week.

Dorband explained he was lead counsel in a case back in Oregon, and Cohen claimed that he had a business meeting in Europe that he wasn't able to get out of. But the reality was that it was clever damage limitation. By holding the depositions back-to-back, the opposition lawyers would have virtually no time to fact-check what Cohen said and throw it back at him in a later session. It also removed the opportunity for studied reflection – a vital tool at the best of times, but especially important in Cohen's case, because he threw out so much chaff.

Dorband and Cohen had also failed to produce a number of discovery documents that the order had specified be there for the deposition. Cohen was "working on it", Kremen's team were told. It was clear that Dorband and Cohen were planning to play dirty. Even Wagstaffe became angry when Cohen announced he hadn't brought his glasses with him and so would have difficulty reading any of the documents in front of him. Cohen had pulled exactly the same trick at his first deposition.

And so it was that Gary Kremen, facing Stephen Cohen, entered his case for the first time by suggesting they go downtown and buy some eyeglasses. It turned out it would probably be okay and Cohen should be able to read what he was handed.

34

FANTASY AND TRAGEDY

A number of intriguing facts came out of the three days of questions. For one, Cohen had two social security numbers – and so effectively possessed two entirely valid but completely separate personas. Who knows how many scams this enabled him to pull off.

The full extent of Cohen's lawyer fantasy was also revealed. Cohen claimed to have attended at least five universities, some to study law, some to study programming, but was unable to provide a single document as proof. He had also worked with three law firms as a clerk, but never progressed any further. This didn't stop him from claiming to be an attorney, however, impersonating at various times his ex-boss Roger Agajanian and his ex-attorneys Frank Butler and Bob Meredith, as well as several Stephen Cohens licensed to practice law.

As the questioning went through his life, the twisted wreckage of his emotional life came out. His sisters used to visit him in the 1980s, but now he said he didn't see them anymore and wasn't sure where they lived. His marriage with Susan Boydston broke down amid drug addiction; his marriage to Karon Poer collapsed when he went to jail and then sued her, sending people round to her house to seize equipment; he has several kids whom he never sees. The teenage Cohen had never grown up, and the adult Cohen had never had a fulfilling emotional relationship. He was in his late 50s and he still boasted, unconvincingly, about getting lots of sex.

Cohen's complex web of companies also started to unravel. He claimed he was being paid by one company but working for another. He claimed to have sold all rights to sex.com to one company, but later on exercised a sub-clause that enabled him to take back all those rights. He laughably stated that his salary was only $12,000 a year but that he was given a limitless expense account – somewhere between one and seven million dollars. It was all nonsense, and Cohen wasn't able to produce a single contract or receipt that backed up the fantasy deals he concocted between his own companies.

The tension in the room, as Cohen continued to evade and lie, was building. Kremen in particular was seething. The man that had caused him so much grief was sitting there blithely lying while every hour it cost Kremen tens of thousands of dollars to get at the truth. The only person not making money while sitting in that room was Kremen himself.

Cohen stopped halfway through a sentence. "Would you please stop," he said looking at Kremen directly before turning to Diestel. "Ask your client not to give me looks when I'm testifying. I know he's got a drug problem and it bothers me." Dorband jumped in: "Mr Diestel, I've noticed Mr Kremen has been making faces at my client for just about the whole deposition. If it does continue, I'll ask that he leave or else we'll terminate the deposition."

Diestel and Dorband then started arguing with one another until Wagstaffe stepped in. "This is all very interesting and juvenile. Let's continue with the questions, please." An hour later, Cohen picked it up again. "I'm having a problem with your client, you know, smiling." Again the proceedings degenerated into petty argument and again Wagstaffe provided the authority to get things back on track. "Let's get on with the questions and quit the commentary about whether someone has smiled, unless your lawyer wants to stop the deposition. There's no harassment going on here. Let's go forward."

As Diestel went through Cohen's criminal history and

convictions, Cohen grew increasingly irritated and started to make veiled threats. Diestel was having none of it: "It's inappropriate to use this deposition as a forum, either to make litigation threats or to intimidate or to, frankly, waste time." There was no denying that Cohen was a dangerous man to corner. He was immensely wealthy, and capable of just about anything if he felt it served his needs.

The first day ended. Diestel picked up the thread again the next morning. The subject matter was a little more colourful on the second day: multi-million-dollar stock scams, and Cohen's plan to build the biggest, most luxurious brothel in the world.

35

WANALEIYA

It was to be every red-blooded American man's fantasy land: a 300-acre resort featuring state-of-the-art sports facilities, including skeet shooting, championship golf and Indy car racing, but with a special kick – 500 female companions to be shared among the 300 guests.

Just $7,000 would buy you unlimited all-inclusive weekend access to Wanaleiya, described in promotional material as "the ultimate full-frill sports/fantasy play world ever constructed in North America." The Polynesian-style resort would have 300 separate houses, four restaurants, night clubs, a health spa, a conference centre, an 18-hole golf course, swimming pools and botanical gardens. And it was to be built on the site of Las Vegas' most famous brothel, Sheri's Ranch. That's where the female companions come in.

Wanaleiya's (pronounced, yes, "wanna lay her") glossy sales brochure featured a wet, bikini-clad torso on the front. Inside, it promised you would be able to "browse the resort in search of the lady that you'd like to accompany you to dinner on your first night. The 500 companions are friendly and experienced – they will not hesitate to see to your comfort with pleasure and spare no time in making you feel at home." These same ladies would "live to serve your every desire" and you would be able to "select as many companions as can be indulged in a weekend". Just in case there remained any doubt, the brochure assured the reader that "there is no request that can be denied you at Wanaleiya".

If all this sounds like a middle-aged man's fantasy that's because that's exactly what it was. Stephen Cohen's, in fact. Diestel asked about it, and Cohen continued outlining his fantasy vision. "It's a place like Eden where people can engage in wild and crazy sex. It was going to have a section for married people, an area for swingers, an area for gays, an area for lesbians. It was going to be a five-star resort, something with the class that you would find at the Ritz Hotel."

But beyond the steamy visions, there was a reason why Cohen had produced the brochure, and why he had appeared on the radio to talk about the project, given interviews to local papers, and paid Sheri's Ranch $25,000 as a down-payment on an intended $7 million purchase. The reason was that Wanaleiya was a million-dollar stock scam, designed by former cellmate Marshall Zolp and executed by Cohen, the master salesman. "People go on expensive singles trips to Club Med all the time in hopes they will meet someone," Cohen told the *Rocky Mountain News*. "Here, it's a guarantee."

Anyone who looked at the details of the project for longer than five minutes would have recognized it was a scam – there is no way, for example, that even if such a place were to exist, it would cost $7,000 for a weekend. Even $70,000 a weekend would have been under-pricing it. But Cohen was counting on people – men – to use something other than their brains when it came to investing in Wanaleiya. There were to be one million shares at $1 each, and the sales pitch wasn't subtle. "Purchase stock in a REAL WHOREHOUSE!" screamed the resort's own website next to various pictures of attractive naked women. Then a sign flashing "You will have sex soon!" came up, followed by the company's prospectus. It's not impossible to imagine 100,000 men spending $10 each on such a fantasy. Hell, Stephen Cohen knew it was a virtual certainty.

The actual scam appeared in black and white in the report Cohen was obliged to file with the State of Nevada's Securities Division to allow the company – Sporting Houses

Management – to float. But then who out of Cohen's planned investors was going to read a securities report? And even if they did, how many would understand the details? It made illuminating reading.

The first alarm bell came in the warning that Nevada only provides brothel licences to individuals and not companies, so each director would be required to apply for, and be awarded, a licence. Quite aside from the fact that no one in the company had any experience of running a brothel, at least one director – Barbara Cepinko – was completely unaware at the time that the company was even considering opening a brothel. Another, Jo-Ann Bauer, was appalled when she discovered what was being done in her name.

"Any investment in the company is highly speculative and could result in the loss of the investment," the report accurately warned. In fact, due to the system that Zolp had invented, the very second you bought your one dollar share, it would instantly collapse in value to 23 cents, with 73 cents going immediately to the "present stockholders" and the remaining four cents paid to brokers. The company had no income or revenue, it hadn't carried out any business, and was entirely dependent on the float to begin business, it warned. What's more, even the $1 million might be "insufficient to permit the company to realise any or all of its objectives". The report also noted that "the offering price for the shares offered hereby bears no relationship to the assets". And in the small print, it turned out that Sporting Houses Management was in fact a subsidiary of Sporting Houses General, a company in which James Powell – aka Marshall Zolp – and T.H. Armstrong – aka Stephen Cohen – owned all the shares. It had scam written all over it, but the point was that by listing it honestly in the filing to the Securities Division, Zolp and Cohen were complying with the law. If people were stupid enough to invest, that was their lookout.

The whole Wanaleiya scheme was the first fruit of Zolp and Cohen's partnership. They met one another in Lompoc jail in

1994, 100 miles north of Los Angeles, where Cohen was serving three years for bankruptcy fraud in the Polvadore case and Zolp six and a half years for an attempt to defraud America's largest pension fund, the California Public Employee Retirement System, of $100 million. Zolp had already been sentenced to twelve years a few years earlier for running a stock scam surrounding a self-cooling beer can. The can didn't exist but Zolp had achieved massive press coverage and boosted worthless shares in a shell company to $3.50 before finally being caught. He made $3.6 million. Zolp would be caught and jailed again for six years in 2003 for running yet another stock scam.

They were destined to be friends. Cohen had become an expert in company and bankruptcy law; Zolp in financial law. At Lompoc they taught one another what they knew and formed a dangerous alliance. "You are the consummate racketeer," Judge Alfred J. Lechner had told Zolp back in 1991 during sentencing. "There is no doubt in my mind that at this very moment you are conjuring up another scheme and that, as soon as you get the opportunity, you will perpetrate that scheme." He could just as easily have been talking about Stephen Cohen.

The Wanaleiya scam fell through. Cohen claims it was because their broker became embroiled in an FBI investigation focusing on a different company whose stock it was selling. The truth is much simpler: Cohen screwed up. The owner of Sheri's Ranch, James Miltenberger, pulled out of the agreement to sell his brothel because Cohen failed to produce any more of the agreed payments. Out of habit, Cohen had offered a series of his usual excuses as to why no more money was forth-coming – he was going on holiday, he was going into hospital next week, and so on. But without the Sheri's Ranch sale, the whole project was transparently worthless. As soon as Miltenberger cancelled the purchase option, the press picked up the story, and that led in turn to the Nevada authorities looking a little more closely at the intended stock flotation of

Sporting Houses Management. If Cohen had kept Miltenberger sweet with another $25,000, it is possible that the whole scam might have gone ahead, with an immediate $730,000 to be shared between him and Zolp, and possibly $750,000 more if they were able to off-load the other three million shares they had kept in reserve. As it was, Cohen simply put Sporting Houses through bankruptcy and then re-incorporated it a few months later.

The failure of the scheme didn't prevent Zolp and Cohen from working on numerous other stock scams, some of which have been discovered and some not. One of these scams involved the fake press release from Ocean Fund International in which Cohen claimed to have bid $3.6 billion for Caesars Palace just weeks after a bid from another company had been accepted. Cohen's fake bid received a lot of press coverage, and the hope was that it would cause the shares of the buying company to dip, at which point Cohen and Zolp would buy thousands of them and then sell them again when the story was revealed as untrue and the share price rose again.

Most recently, Cohen was named as the website administrator for a company called Red Sea Management which ran a number of huge stock scams in 2002. Corrupt FBI special agent Jeffrey Royer supplied Red Sea Management boss Anthony Elgindy with insider information on companies, and this information was dispersed through the website to its 300 members, who paid between $200 and $600 a month each. The members then organised the release of the negative information, mostly through Internet notice boards, so they could profit to the greatest degree possible from the subsequent drop in share prices. Elgindy and Royer were found guilty in January 2005 of racketeering, conspiracy and securities fraud, and Elgindy was sentenced to eleven years and three months in June 2006. Royer and a number of other people tied in with the fraud are yet to be sentenced.

As well as meeting Zolp in jail, Cohen also encountered a

legendary figure in the financial world, Michael Milken. Milken made billions in the 1980s through a clever manipulation of the markets whereby high-yield but high-risk bonds (called junk bonds) were used by small companies to buy out larger companies. In 1989, Milken was found guilty of 98 counts of racketeering and fraud, but avoided a recommended ten-year jail sentence, serving only 22 months. With those three brains – Cohen, Milken and Zolp – in one jail, it was inevitable that something would result. For Cohen, Wanaleiya was the first in a series of international scams over the next decade.

But Cohen's heart always lay in the adult industry, and he revelled in his ownership of the most desirable Internet domain in the world, sex.com. The scams provided the buzz, the money was the pay-off, but sex on the Internet was his real passion.

36

STEAKS AND SETTLEMENT

Unfortunately for Stephen Cohen, he was just about to confront for the first time the lawyer who would eventually take sex.com back off him and end his five-year reign at the top of the Internet sex industry.

"Mr Cohen, sex.com is an asset, isn't it?" was the first question that Jim Wagstaffe posed to Stephen Cohen on the second day of his three-day deposition in San Diego. "I don't know how to characterise it," Cohen replied.

Cohen was extremely wary of Wagstaffe – and for good reason. Where Carreon aggressively played along with Cohen, and Diestel asked simple factual questions in order to build his case, Wagstaffe's style was a confusing blend of the two. He maintained a calm disposition and asked apparently simple questions but with the unnerving chess-move confidence that the best attorneys possess.

Wagstaffe described his own technique thus: "When giving depositions I have this method of not listening to the tone, I just listen to the answers. And Cohen's answers just weren't believable. If you listen to *him*, you believe what he has to say."

Wagstaffe picked up where Diestel had left off – talking about Cohen's three Sporting Houses companies and the brothel stock scam. Cohen had also put ownership of sex.com under one of his Sporting Houses companies and then created an elaborate sale process to confuse who owned it when, and where the money made from it had gone. But as Wagstaffe was to reveal, the sale was no more than a figment of Cohen's imagination. And while Cohen was smart enough not to contradict himself directly, his constant lapses of memory, the convenient appearance of confidentiality contracts, and his endless attempts to steer the conversation away from difficult areas, made it quite clear that Cohen was personally behind sex.com and all the shell companies circling it.

Cohen had complicated the situation by pulling into his web of companies a number of foreign companies, again all of them started and run by him: Sand Man Internacional in Mexico; Ocean Fund International (later renamed Ynata) in the British Virgin Islands; and then several "corporate headquarters" in countries such as Costa Rica and Puerto Rico. In the United States, company information is easily and cheaply obtained, but elsewhere in the world it was a different matter. Cohen knew this all too well.

By the end of the second day, it was clear that Cohen wasn't going to crack under questioning. He had discovered several excuses to fall back on and used them whenever cornered. But the most interesting part of the day was still to come, when Cohen, Dorband, Kremen and Carreon went out for dinner together.

Despite the obvious risk that the meal would descend into a shouting match, everyone remembers the evening fondly. "We had drinks with Barbara, the court reporter," Carreon recalls. "Then we met up with Cohen and Dorband at this little restaurant in San Diego and had dinner – steaks and red wine. I had a really great time, we had a lot of wine and a good laugh." Kremen remembers it similarly: "We all had a really pleasant dinner. Cohen talked a mile a minute and was so convincing that I almost believed I had stolen sex.com from *him*." Talk turned to a possible settlement. After two years of vicious fighting, it was perhaps too much to expect that all the rancour could be forgotten over one restaurant meal; nevertheless, during the course of the evening Cohen and Carreon stepped outside, leaving Kremen and Dorband chatting. Under a street-light, a pivotal moment in the fight for sex.com unfolded.

Cohen gave Carreon a final settlement offer: $700,000 for Kremen to walk away.

Carreon said no. It was too low. Not only had Kremen already spent the best part of $700,000 getting the case this far, but Cohen was making millions every month from sex.com. Carreon had shaken hands with Kremen over a year earlier and vowed to get the domain back, and of course he also had a 15 per cent interest in sex.com if he won – something Cohen didn't know at the time.

Cohen was surprised. The last time he'd tried to settle and offered $20,000, he thought Kremen was on his knees. This time, $700,000 was good money. "My legal fees were in the millions; every week, $30,000 to $40,000. He should have settled early on. He should have settled," Cohen despaired.

Kremen had learned to trust Carreon on negotiations. "Well, Charles had a better instinct than me. You know, lawyers do that for a living – they negotiate. How many negotiations have you been in? I mean, now I've been in more, but back then I hadn't been in many. So to me sometimes taking the money and running makes a lot of sense."

Whatever the previous games they'd played, everyone knew that night counted. Even though it was a relaxed and convivial night out, it was the last time they would all meet outside the courtroom, and they knew it. They were entering the great unknown. The Internet revolution was rumbling its way forward, and the attorneys who just a month earlier had been so certain their approach would define how people saw domain names now sensed things would move along with or without them. That very evening, Cohen began shifting millions of dollars into offshore bank accounts. And that same night, Carreon gave the go-ahead to dozens of subpoenas against companies that Cohen worked with. There was now no going back.

In the morning, Cohen entered his final day of deposition. He handed Kremen a t-shirt with "sex.com" printed on it. It was part of a new range of merchandise, Cohen told him. He also told Kremen's attorneys that he had decided to drop the defamation lawsuits against Kremen and Carreon.

In the room the tension between Carreon and Wagstaffe was growing. Carreon was irritated by Wagstaffe creeping into the main case. Kremen was scared of confronting his own friend, so he avoided it. Carreon also felt, with some justification, that Wagstaffe didn't know the case as well as he did. On the flip-side, Wagstaffe felt that Carreon was too involved, unfocused and unable to see the wood for the trees. As usual, Stephen Cohen sought to make the most of the situation.

"Let me explain something to you, sir," he told Carreon on one of his many conversational tangents during the deposition. "I've got one, two, three – four – attorneys in here. This is attorney number 15 or 16 I'm looking at representing Mr Kremen. You've got one attorney that flips off the bird at another attorney. You've got attorneys that can't get along. I've been in three days of depositions and I don't feel that it is right that I be badgered with questions that have been asked and answered not once, not twice but numerous times on the exact same subject."

Cohen was nothing if not perceptive. But the jibes, which he thought would set people against one another, only served to reinforce their desire to see him brought down to size. Cohen, for all his genius, had absolutely no understanding of people working together with a common purpose. For him, progression is a solitary occupation.

The last day's questioning covered Cohen's business affairs and his numerous run-ins with the law. Carreon took over the questioning at three p.m., and immediately the aggressive banter between the two began again. Almost nothing was learnt, but it was fun to listen to the two trading insults. Although Kremen was less impressed as he saw thousands more dollars go up in smoke. And then, exactly 18 hours into the deposition, Dorband ended it. Stephen Cohen left 1202

Kettner Boulevard on a warm summer's night, confident that he had managed to get through three days of questioning relatively unscathed, and a fortnight later, on 24 July, Dorband succeeded in having the main plank of Kremen's complaint – a claim for conversion – dismissed because of the NSI decision.

For the third time, Gary Kremen's case was hanging by a thread. And for a third time, the introduction of a new legal team resulted in its salvation. The collapse of Carreon's case was effectively the end of his involvement, as Kremen now gave Wagstaffe the lead prosecuting role. Wagstaffe then did exactly the same to Carreon's legal approach as Carreon had done to Diemer's – tore it up and started again.

"The previous lawyers were very creative," Wagstaffe explains. "They made these long, complex drafts, but they also gave a big target to shoot at. So Cohen attacked them – that's why there were so many amended complaints. When I took over, I just went for it. I told a simple story and went after the domain: remove the thing that was making the money that he was fighting us with." The result of Wagstaffe's rethink of the case, filed on 11 September 2000, was the fourth amended complaint in the case.

Wagstaffe stripped out the long list of defendants, focusing only on Stephen Cohen, his two main companies (Ynata and Sand Man), Network Solutions, and between one and twenty "John Does". He also replaced Carreon's long list of untested legal theories with five claims firmly held in existing law: declaratory relief, involuntary trust, fraudulent transfer, trespass to chattels, and unfair competition and false advertising. The complaint came with two damning back-up documents: a memorandum of points, and a declaration by Wagstaffe in which he distilled the extra information that had been pulled out during Cohen's three-day deposition. It pointed out how the information gleaned at the deposition tallied with all the previous assertions made about Cohen's past criminal behaviour. The document was enough for Judge Ware to believe there were grounds for the case to go to trial.

Wagstaffe's commanding authority in the courtroom also contributed to two vital victories against Dorband in front of Ware and Trumbull. First, he persuaded Ware not to grant Cohen's motion to dismiss the case, and then he managed to persuade Trumbull to compel more depositions of Cohen, and, crucially, of representatives of Sand Man Internacional and Ynata.

"When I saw the difference of having Wagstaffe in the courtroom, I was blown away," Kremen recalls. "Wagstaffe just cut to the chase. He said, the guy's a thief, he never had title." It wasn't just his conciseness though – Wagstaffe also commands immediate respect from members of the judiciary. Kremen saw it immediately: "You know, the judge would look him in the eye and go: 'Is this right, Jim? Is this guy a criminal?' That was the break. And it wasn't until that actually happened in court a couple of times – then I was 'Oh my God, I understand this – that's why he's treating us, me and Carreon, like scum'."

Cohen and Dorband had, as usual, gone out of their way to try to prevent the depositions of representatives of Cohen's companies from going ahead. But Dorband's stalling tactics were too well known by Kremen's lawyers by then, and they shut down every one of his exits as soon as he made for one of them. And so it was that on 28 September 2000 Charles Carreon, Richard Diestel and a San Diego court reporter flew to Mexico and set up in Hotel Coral, Ensenada, 50 miles south of the US border. They could have had no idea what was going to happen next.

37

MR SANDMAN

"May I ask a question?" were the first words that Roman Caso, the representative for Ynata – the company at the heart of sex.com's complex corporate web – spoke following his swearing in. It was three p.m. and Caso was facing Carreon and Diestel, with Dorband acting as his representative. Caso only speaks Spanish so a translator was acting as the go-between. "It's fine with me," Carreon responded.

"No one told me anything about testifying. I mean they told me to be here because it had something to do with something that has cost the company a lot. I thought maybe it was a negotiations meeting or something like that. They told me to be here because it had something to do with something where my name came up, and I'm with that company. Aside from that, I have nothing to do with it. I mean, I don't know what's going on here."

It was the first time that someone other than Stephen Cohen had been quizzed about sex.com, and in just a few seconds the entire edifice painstakingly built up by Cohen over five years crumpled. There was no international inter-connecting corporate structure with a series of boards overseeing hundreds of staff placed across the world. Stephen Cohen *was* sex.com, and the rest of it was pure invention – or, more accurately, bullshit.

Cohen had turned up an hour late and spent the morning testifying as the designee of Sand Man Internacional. The deposition played out the same tired old game, with Cohen providing none of the documents he had agreed to bring, talking in circles, giving nothing away and making a series of empty promises.

But the crucial fact was that the judge had also ordered that a designee from the other defendant, Ocean Fund International/Ynata, be made available. Since Cohen could not be the designee for Ynata as well as the other companies without completely undermining his own argument that all the companies were no more than alter-egos of Stephen Cohen, he had no choice but to put someone forward. That person was his business partner Roman Caso. The only problem was that Cohen didn't tell Caso anything about it – for the simple reason that Caso knew nothing about sex.com's business. We can only assume that Cohen hoped Caso would feel obliged to go along with the questioning, say he wasn't able to answer the questions, and Carreon and Diestel would leave with nothing. It was a huge gamble, and it very quickly became obvious that Cohen had misjudged his business partner.

"If there is a questionnaire, or something like that," Caso ventured. "If there's something planned, you should have told me. You just can't do this like this. I mean, I have a very impor-tant call. I'm having a problem with clients, so I have to go and take care of it. I mean, I can't be here."

This was all spoken in Spanish and translated, leaving the unusual pauses that these situations create, but even so it rapidly became clear that things were not going according to Cohen's plan. In his panic, Cohen exposed a five-year lie that he could speak "no more than two or three words" of Spanish by holding a long and increasingly angry exchange with Caso in his native tongue. Unfortunately for him, Carreon is also fluent in Spanish, and followed the conversation exactly, at one point breaking in to tell Cohen in English: "I would prefer not to be referred to in that way."

As Carreon would later explain, Cohen had referred to himself and Diestel as "fucking assholes", to which Caso had raised an eyebrow and told Cohen he wasn't sure who the fucking asshole was. Caso then told Cohen it was his problem and he would have to sort it out himself. He then stormed out of the room, swiftly followed by Cohen and Dorband, leaving Carreon and Diestel looking at each other in amazement. Even though both of them had spent months digging into his affairs, Cohen's extraordinary ability to build a false reality had caught them out. As the extent of Cohen's fabrications began to dawn on the two lawyers, Cohen and Dorband came back into the room and the deposition started up again.

Carreon spoke first: "I'm just going to go ahead and make a statement just to summarise what I observed in case it wasn't on the record. My understanding is that Mr Roman Caso appeared as secretary and vice president of Ynata Limited. He was sworn and then refused to proceed with his deposition for grounds that he appeared to state on the record adequately. And I don't know if it was on the record, but if you would confirm, Mr Dorband, that you do not represent him."

Dorband was flustered. The truth was that he was an extremely talented attorney who had taken on an exciting case; but he had got sucked further and further into Cohen's affairs. By the time it was over, the once ferocious Bob Dorband was left hiding from this author in the office of an insurance company in Portland, Oregon, pretending he hadn't heard the knocking at the door. He then pleaded that the name of the company he worked for be kept off the record in case it rebounded on him.

Dorband had in fact tried to get out of the case several times, filing official motions to be allowed to step aside as Cohen's attorney, but every one was fought and won by Kremen's team. Dorband was in this until the end, just like everyone else. And after it was all over, Wagstaffe was very kind, even sympathetic towards him: "Bob Dorband knew that his client was a crook – he must have known. But he was a good lawyer."

The tide was turning, and more than anything it was the experience in Mexico that finally broke the bond of trust between client and attorney for Dorband. Even so, he continued to fight for Cohen. With only Carreon and Cohen able to understand Spanish (and with Roman Caso having stormed off), it fell to Cohen to try to explain the link between the fantasy world he had built and the real one that had so rudely interrupted proceedings. "As a representative of Sand Man," Cohen began, "I will state for the record that Mr Caso came in his own individual capacity to testify. He knew he was going to testify. I don't know if he understood what he meant by testifying, because it's different in Mexico than it is in the United States. But he's extremely upset. I think the record show, it clearly shows, that I tried to calm him down. He is completely irate. He's livid."

What is he livid about, Diestel asked. Cohen casually stretched his arms: "What is Mr Caso upset with? Your client has cost our company a substantial amount of money based on a felonious complaint, and Mr Caso is aware of the damage it's caused. He's aware of the amount of aggravation it's caused. And if it was up to Mr Caso, he would go after individuals personally. He's that upset. I don't take that view. He does. And, unfortunately, I have to work with him. We don't always see eye to eye, but that's not something I can control. It's like a marriage: sometimes it's good, sometimes it's not so good."

In a single breath, Cohen had pinned the blame on Kremen, then on Caso, made implicit threats and held himself out as the peacemaker. Carreon and Diestel had seen and heard enough. They would never listen to Cohen or Dorband done through official letters. Diestel was so angry he looked straight into Cohen's eyes and told him: "As you have done your whole life, you speak with a poor tongue, sir," before both he and Carreon walked out and flew back to the United States.

They went straight to Judge Trumbull, who immediately ordered that a series of Ynata employees appear for deposition in San Diego in two months' time. Cohen claimed that none of them were able to attend because they couldn't get visas; Trumbull rejected his argument.

And so, two months later, Carreon, Diestel and a translator were waiting for Derrick Taylor (Ynata president), Fernando Rodriguez (senior vice president), and Rodolfo Gomez-Aguilar (the "sole shareholder" of Ynata) to turn up for their depositions when in walked, yes, Stephen Cohen and Robert Dorband. Stephen Cohen would, it turned out, be the only representative of Ynata appearing that day, but he was able to speak for the others. Incredibly, Carreon and Diestel went through the façade of interviewing Cohen, who said nothing of any value. It was a massive anti-climax, but at the same time it marked the end of normal legal interaction. Cohen had propped up his façade for as long as he could, but they all knew it was over: the Wizard of Oz had been exposed; Cohen's lies had run their course.

"I'm going to be out of town until probably the tenth of December, and then I will be able to continue this deposition," Cohen said just before leaving. But it wouldn't be until 5 December 2005, five years later, that any of Kremen's lawyers would sit down again in the same room as Stephen Michael Cohen. He knew the game was up and he was leaving town with his money in strong chests tied to the back of his wagon.

38

KINKO'S

"Gary has these wild delusions," Cohen explains. "He only won the case because of my own acts. I got nobody to blame but myself. And the only crazy thing I did was Kinko's. At times in life you make dumb decisions. In retrospect I wouldn't do it again."

Carreon had served literally hundreds of subpoenas to get hold of whatever information he could on Cohen's business dealings. Some of the recipients said they had no records regarding Stephen Michael Cohen; others refused point-blank to disclose them; some refused to disclose them until they were presented with a court order, and others simply handed them over.

The end result was hundreds of thousands of pages of material through which Carreon and his daughter and wife slowly sifted. Painstakingly they built up a picture of Cohen's complex and tangled corporate web. Everyone knew that all the different companies – Sporting Houses (× 3), Ynata (× 2), Ocean Fund, Sand Man – were Cohen under a different name, but what Kremen's team had to do was *prove* it.

It wasn't easy. Not only did Cohen have a number of businesses, he also had a wide range of bank accounts, in the US and abroad: the Union Bank of Florida, Washington Mutual in Washington, Federal Credit Union in California, and Charles Schwab in Nevada. But the most important account – the one through which Cohen passed most of his money – was with the local San Diego branch of Wells Fargo.

Cohen and Dorband fought for months to prevent Kremen

getting access to bank account details, but after Cohen had failed to provide anyone but himself as a representative of the various companies, Judge Trumbull approved the subpoenas. Despite the order, Cohen tried to prevent the release of documents by sending a letter to the banks threatening to sue them if they responded to the "illegal" subpoenas. He was ignored.

To deal with the huge volumes of documents arriving, Kremen's and Cohen's legal team had jointly developed a system for producing copies of them. They were sent by courier to a photocopying store – a branch of Kinko's – in Chula Vista, just a few miles south of San Diego. The staff there would copy the documents, charge Kremen's lawyers' credit card, and then forward the copies on to their various law offices. Each time they did this, Cohen's lawyer, Robert Dorband, was informed and provided with contact details for the Kinko's store in case he wanted to pay for his own set of copies.

This same system was used when documents from Cohen's main account at Wells Fargo were eventually produced. Dorband was informed by Diestel when the documents would be at the store and was also sent a reminder letter the day before with details of who to contact at the store, complete with phone numbers, if he wanted his own set of copies. He declined.

So on Wednesday 4 October 2000, the day before the documents were due to be released by Wells Fargo to Diestel, his office made the usual arrangements with Kinko's: the documents would be delivered to the store and a set of copies made for each of Kremen's lawyers, to be FedEx'd to the respective law firms.

Diestel's secretary was surprised, then, when Reggie from Kinko's called the following day to explain that, as the documents had been picked up, there would be no charge for them to be posted to the office. She was confused, as there was no record of anyone from the office going to pick them up, but Reggie assured her he had taken a call from someone at their offices yesterday telling him to cancel the FedEx order because someone would be coming in to pick them up, and a few hours later they came in, and he handed the documents over.

No one in the office knew anything about picking up the documents from the store, which made it all the more suspicious when, the next morning, a Friday, they received another phonecall, this time from Federal Express. They would not be able to deliver the package from Kinko's today, the caller explained, because they had been given the wrong zip code, but it would be there Monday. This would have been an understandable, if irritating, explanation were it not for the call the day before in which Reggie swore blind someone had identified themselves as coming from Bledsoe, Cathcart, Diestel & Pedersen before taking the documents away. And sure enough, on the Monday, two large sets of documents, totalling roughly 1,200 pages, arrived.

Diestel, Carreon, Wagstaffe and Idell had been dealing with Cohen for long enough to know that any unusual events, especially if they concerned information on Cohen, were rarely accidental. One of Carreon's team used FedEx's tracking system and found that rather than come from Chula Vista, the parcel had come from a FedEx depot 40 miles north of the Kinko's store, near Carlsbad airport, on the other side of San Diego. This immediately set off alarm bells – Cohen's home was only a few miles from the drop-off. In fact, it was the nearest FedEx drop-off to him.

Despite the pages not being numbered, the staff went through all the documents, box by box, and paper by paper, running the records together chronologically and noting any omissions. At the end of it, they found that nearly 200 pages were missing. As soon as Carreon found out, he drove straight to the Kinko's store and was delighted to find not just one but 18 security cameras in-store. He explained the situation, but the store refused to hand the tapes over.

Carreon's experience as a defence lawyer provided him with the solution to this problem: he immediately reported the theft of court-protected documents to the Chula Vista police department. And sure enough, Detective King turned up at the store soon after, requested security tapes of the crime, and booked them into evidence. When Carreon finally got a look at the tapes, he knew they had just won the case. There, bold as brass, was Stephen Cohen. The tapes caught him walking into Kinko's, strolling up to the desk, talking to the person behind the desk and leaving a few moments later with all his bank records.

Carreon quickly typed up a court filing, included a copy of the tape, and sent it to Judge Ware, who, predictably, hit the roof. And that was it. Game over.

"Judge Ware got very upset over Kinko's," Cohen recalls. "He went completely crazy, completely nuts. And then he issued some very crazy orders. You couldn't talk any common sense to him at that point."

Dorband agrees: "Things really accelerated when Mr Cohen did the Kinko's incident. That was pretty much when things started to slide downhill rapidly. I thought we always had a chance to win that case, up until then. Their argument all along had been that Mr Cohen was this con man, and an ex-convict, and all that, and we would try to downplay that, and say, 'That's not relevant', trying to keep his credibility. And when he stole the documents, it kind of undercut whatever credibility he may have had in the case. And the judge kind of said: 'You know what? Plaintiff, you're right. This guy is not to be trusted.'"

Dorband admits, with a wry smile, that shortly after Cohen was caught red-handed on tape he shared a "frank exchange" with his errant client. "I'll leave it at that."

Cohen isn't fully able to explain why he did it, except to argue, unconvincingly, that Kremen was "abusing the system" and "didn't have a right" to look at the bank documents. The truth was that Kremen and his lawyers had managed to get past his lies and see what was hidden behind, and Cohen's professional pride was hurt. There is no doubt that the Wells Fargo documents helped reveal a few final links, but Kremen's team had already outfoxed him. He was desperate to show to himself that he could still disrupt the case, and do so invisibly, using his cunning. But it backfired and now his only exit, Judge Ware, was giving Kremen's lawyers what orders they needed to nail the case down.

Shortly after, Carreon, Diestel and Wagstaffe produced an extraordinary document, based on hundreds of hours of determined legwork. This document finally put down on paper the exact outline of the vast corporate web surrounding sex.com. It was a moment of rare comradeship. "It is very rare that you will establish, by proof, to the satisfaction of a judge, that some individual is using corporations in a manner that is fraudulent," Carreon says with pride. But they did it. Money from advertisers was being sent by wire transfer to Union Bank in Florida. The money would accumulate and then be transferred off, in pulses of about a hundred thousand, to Wells Fargo in San Diego, where it would then be pushed offshore.

"So we were able to say, 'Judge, this is a pipeline.' That was the key. To be able to say, 'This bank account fills up, it empties, it fills up this bank account; this bank account fills up, it empties … At the end of the month there's never more than twenty, thirty grand in there. At the peak time there's four or five hundred. It's moving, Judge! It's getting out of here! You've got to stop that!'" Carreon had worked for over a year nailing it down and he finally had it.

Kremen's team filed a motion for preliminary injunction requesting that sex.com be handed back to Kremen immediately. On 27 November 2000 – five years, one month and nine days since it had been stolen, it happened – Gary Kremen was finally given back sex.com.

Cohen was ordered not to move or dispose of any asset or property without the permission of the court. He was to inform anyone holding his money or doing business with him of the court's order and, most dramatically, he ordered that $25 million be deposited with the court by Cohen pending the trial and full judgment.

Cohen was given three weeks to provide a full accounting of the entire sex.com operation from the moment he gained control in October 1995 to the present day, including copies of all agreements and contracts. He was ordered not to do anything with his mansion in the hills north of San Diego. And he was ordered to sign document waivers within seven days. Ware gave Kremen another 60 days of discovery, and banned Cohen from contacting any company that had been subpoenaed.

From that point on, it was just a mopping-up operation. Grab a few pieces of final evidence, appear for trial in front of a judge who had already made it clear what he believed, and then savour the look on Cohen's face when he knew once and for all that he had been beat.

39

MONEY, MONEY, MONEY

If only.

"I never put the time into the case because I never believed we would lose," Cohen claims. "The judgment came as a great shock." The first part is rubbish, but there is no doubt about the second. In one fell swoop, Cohen had lost his baby – sex.com.

Not only that but he had an enormous list of conditions he had to meet in less than a month. It was too much to take in. Having carefully strung out the court case for more than two years, things had suddenly accelerated to the point where he had just days to provide everything he had fought so hard to protect. He was out of his mind with rage at Ware's order.

He made no fewer than 20 calls to Dorband in the 48 hours following Ware's judgment. But of far greater significance, it turned out, were the 33 phone calls over three days Cohen made to an old friend, John Brownfield. Brownfield is a convicted cocaine trafficker Cohen had met back in the 1970s when he was still a kid and into cheque fraud. Cohen called John – or Jack as everyone knows him – to ask his advice. He knew Kremen and his lawyers would be crawling all over his bank accounts within days. He had to decide fast what to do and then do it. Judge Ware had delivered his judgment at 10.15 a.m., and at 12.12 p.m. ordered Dorband to call Cohen immediately and inform him of the order. Literally 30 minutes later, Cohen began wiring money out of US bank accounts.

At 12.42 p.m., $109,000 was moved from the main Wells

Fargo account to one of Cohen's other accounts in Luxembourg. Less than an hour later, at 1.22 p.m., another $233,000 was wired to one of his Mexican accounts. And then, two hours after that, at 3.15 p.m., the entire balance of a different Wells Fargo account – an enormous $840,687 – was wired to the same Mexican account. Consciously and deliberately breaking Ware's court ruling, Cohen was cleaning up and clearing out.

What made this all the more infuriating from Kremen's perspective was that he and his team had predicted this was exactly what Cohen would do and had prepared for it. The job of sending an advance copy of the injunction to Cohen's banks had been left to Carreon. The idea was that as soon as the judge approved it, Kremen's team would simply call the banks and explain the injunction had been approved, if necessary faxing a copy to the office. But Carreon had completely forgotten to set this up thanks to extended victory celebrations, so when the order was finally given, rather than simply call the banks and give the green light, Kremen found that he was having to dig out the banks' telephone numbers, fax them the details (after finding their fax numbers), and then talk them through the implications of the injunction. By the time he'd done all this, all of Cohen's money had gone. Every last cent.

Kremen has never forgiven Carreon. "What he should have done – what he was supposed to do – what Wagstaffe *told* him to do – what he was supposed to be in charge of was calling all the banks and telling them 'We have the injunction.'"

Cohen did more than just shift money around. He knew that with such a strong court order against him he had little choice: either pay up, or skip the country. Cohen spent a lot of his time just across the Mexican border in Tijuana anyway, so he made the decision to make the move permanent. He would be outside the US courts' jurisdiction and Kremen could go fuck himself.

The biggest problem was persuading his fifth wife, Rosa Montano, and her two daughters, Sarai and Jhuliana, to leave their mansion in the exclusive Rancho Santa Fe area and move back across the Mexican border. Rosa was very, very far from happy. She had been living in a stunning $3 million home that she herself had chosen, and her children were benefiting from the very best that the United States of America could offer, including schooling at the exclusive Torrey Pines High School. Rosa wasn't very bright, but she was a fiercely protective mother. She had been willing to put up with a lot from her husband – as any of his ex-wives will testify – but when it became clear that the high life was being pulled away from her, suddenly Stephen Cohen wasn't quite as appealing. It was the beginning of the end of their marriage.

Cohen was still hoping he might be able to work his way out of the case. He was torn. He could give the court some of what it wanted in order to retain some credibility, but he was only too well aware that the court was likely to order that he hand over any money he admitted to. As ever, the money won.

Cohen claimed he couldn't produce company accounts because he had been fired. He then filed a laughable set of personal accounts that showed him making no money whatsoever from sex.com between 1995 and 1997; $150,000 in 1998; $300,000 in 1999 and $1 million in 2000. Even admitting to these figures made Cohen feel ill, so he included expenses to help reduce the figure: $8 million of expenses in fact.

Kremen's team hired a financial expert, Martin Moroski, who proved the accounts were a sham by documenting monthly transfers averaging $150,000 from Cohen's US accounts to his other banks in Mexico, Liechtenstein, Luxembourg and the Netherlands. Dorband kept filing arguments against Kremen's lawyers' motions, but Ware simply dismissed them one after another. The whole case had disintegrated. The defamation case against Kremen and Carreon was killed. Cohen's remaining trademark cases against "sex" domain owners were kicked out of court.

And then Ware appointed a court receiver, George Fisher,

and gave him sweeping powers to locate and take control of Cohen's assets. Fisher started by seizing two Cohen cheques worth $1 million, and then a trust account set up by Cohen. He then moved onto Cohen's enormous stock of domain names. Cohen was being swiftly and systematically shut down. For his part, Cohen was working just as hard, if not harder, on the other side trying to shift and hide his multitude of accounts, businesses, buildings and so on.

"It's like shadow boxing or nailing a jellyfish to the wall," Wagstaffe complained to Ware at the next hearing. "We're at best Wile E. Coyote and they're the Road Runner." Cohen failed to turn up to a contempt hearing; an arrest warrant was issued.

Just six days later, on Thursday 8 March 2001, the trial of sex.com started, 973 days after Kremen had first filed his complaint, and five years, four months and 18 days since sex.com had been stolen. The thief, Stephen Michael Cohen, was nowhere to be seen.

40

TRIAL

The actual sex.com trial was something of an anticlimax. It had been scheduled to last three or four days, but it barely took two. Cohen had no intention of fighting, and didn't even turn up, so ending his right to a jury trial. Kremen had lined up 18 witnesses and 95 exhibits; Cohen 0 and 0.

Even Bob Dorband was jittery. Wagstaffe threatened him with a Rule 11 motion, which effectively accused Dorband of knowingly misrepresenting the reality of the case. Kremen and Wagstaffe were sick of Dorband's constant motions that served no purpose but to confuse and delay the case. They were in the ascendant, and it was time to make Cohen's attorney feel a little bit of the pressure.

Dorband complained to Ware immediately that he was being intimidated into not doing his job properly. After a brief discussion, Wagstaffe promised that whatever Dorband did during the trial would not be used as part of a complaint against him. Not that it made the slightest difference: the evidence against Cohen was overwhelming.

Wagstaffe opened by explaining that the domain had been transferred by means of the Dimmick letter and an email that Cohen had sent to NSI changing Kremen's contact details. He then showed that the Dimmick letter was a forgery, and that Cohen's testimony about it was false.

The real Ms Dimmick was "Sharyn" not "Sharon". A handwriting expert said the signature was not Ms Dimmick's, but bore a striking resemblance to Cohen's. And the landlord of the flat where "Vito Franco" had got her – or someone who may have claimed to be her – to sign the letter had checked his records and found at the time the flat was rented by two men. Ellen Rony explained how the domain transfer had happened, and why it was fraudulent. Computer forensics expert Jon Berryhill explained exactly how he knew that Cohen's French Connection BBS printouts that purportedly showed Cohen had used the term "sex.com" since 1979 were fake. And specialist accountant Richard Ainslie testified that Cohen had made $43 million from his use of sex.com between October 1995 and November 2000.

Dorband knew the case was already lost. His opening statement lasted less than a minute; he gave no arguments or counter-arguments; and he had no witnesses. In the end, all Dorband had to fall back on was the proof of his extraordinary papering skills. "The mere fact that we have three binders full of documents, and counsel has been prosecuting this case for years shows that things are not quite what they appear to be," he ventured. "Speculation is one thing; proof is another."

But the proof came in buckets. The nomenclature "sex.com" didn't exist in 1979, and Cohen's "proof" that it had was printed out on a printer that didn't exist at the time. A seemingly innocuous reference to "COH0198" also referred to a piece of legislation passed years after the date Cohen claimed the evidence was produced. A deposition with Cohen's ex-wife Karon Poer helped to outline Cohen's shady past and history of lying and forging.

The second day of the trial was unusual in that the courtroom was already discussing how to get hold of Cohen's assets. Wagstaffe's associate lawyer Pamela Urueta ran through Cohen's previous convictions, and then outlined the evidence that Cohen had personally authorised the transfer abroad of vast amounts of money from his US accounts.

Then the entire hearing became devoted to the issue of Cohen's mansion in Rancho Santa Fe. Everyone knew the judgment was in the bag, but Kremen and Wagstaffe also knew that virtually no money remained in the US. Cohen's expertise and determination in hiding money would make tracking down the funds a huge challenge, so they were keen to get their hands on any and all assets still within Judge Ware's jurisdiction.

Dorband fought desperately to have any discussion of the house ruled inadmissible, particularly since the owner was not Cohen or Sand Man or Ynata, but a Montano Properties. Montano Properties was of course, yet again, no more than an elaborate Cohen shell. Records showed that Cohen had bought the house for $3 million with sex.com money, and also that he had "sold" it for nothing. Some careful detective work also uncovered deeds from Cohen handing over control of the property to his wife and step-daughters – but with a clause giving Cohen the right to buy back their entire holding for one dollar. Wagstaffe's case was slow and methodical, and at the end of it Ware agreed to put the property under constructive trust – effectively preventing Cohen from doing anything with it. Kremen had already filed an entirely new lawsuit against Montano Properties, and Ware had just provided that case with extra weight.

And then before you knew it, it was over. Ware wouldn't release his final judgment for nearly a month, but in his summing up he made it quite clear what it would be. "I should say as I have listened to the evidence here, that I have become further convinced that Mr Cohen has misrepresented himself, has committed fraudulent acts, has attempted in various acts to deceive the various lawyers and others who have been trying to get to the truth of what occurred initially and how the funds have been moved and managed.

"And so one of the functions of the court is to judge the credibility, and his credibility has been seriously, seriously damaged as a result of the evidence which has been presented to the court." Ware did have some words of support for Dorband, however, saying that even though he had been sanctioned by the court for previous conduct, he wanted to compliment him for the job he had done in a "very, very difficult circumstance to be in before the court".

On Friday 30 March, the Court of Appeals dismissed Cohen's claim against Ware's previous decision to hand sex.com over to Kremen. And on Tuesday 3 April 2001 Ware released his damning final judgment.

But just as one painful legal case closed for Kremen, another opened up between him and Charles Carreon, his attorney, confidant, fellow warrior and one-time best friend. Carreon had been growing increasingly bitter at being sidelined by Kremen in favour of Wagstaffe. He had fought incredibly hard for over a year, and at a reduced rate, to help Kremen fight his case, but the glory of beating Cohen and winning back sex.com was given to Wagstaffe, not him.

The resentment had been building up for a while, and was only made worse by the fact that Kremen and Carreon were now in business together running sex.com – in which Carreon now had a 15 per cent stake. The problem was, as Kremen explains, Carreon felt this meant he could make 50 per cent of the decisions. "He didn't understand the concept of 85–15. He was like 'We're both equal, it's just that you have 85 per cent.' And it just won't work like that. You have to have some process to decide. You need a decision process."

It didn't help that, in business, Kremen likes to make the decisions – *all* the decisions. Even though Carreon was getting 15 per cent of the proceeds, amounting to tens of thousands of dollars every month, he had become dazzled by the huge sums everyone else was making. Cohen had made $40 million; Kremen was taking most of the money from sex.com; Idell and Wagstaffe were being paid huge hourly rates; how come he got stiffed? It was clear as well that Carreon's domineering wife had been expecting a big payday and didn't get it. She blamed Kremen for easing Carreon out of the case, and worked on her husband until he believed the same.

"Charles wanted money up front all the time," Kremen complains. "And he kept calling himself my partner, but he wasn't treating me like a partner. Partners don't demand payment up front. Partners take the same risk. That just drove me nuts. And when I would ask him, 'So what do you need it for?' he wouldn't tell me, or he'd tell me, like, 'Oh, my wife wants plastic surgery.'"

This tension was compounded by the fact that Carreon was a fine lawyer but a dreadful businessman. Carreon felt he had the right to make business decisions without consulting Kremen – something that also drove Kremen crazy. Kremen was particularly incensed when Carreon threatened to kill the contract with a major advertiser if they didn't sign up to new terms he had devised.

But the matter came to a head when a bill from Wagstaffe and his firm arrived for services rendered over much of the case. It was no ordinary bill. "We started getting money in from sex.com and then this literally million-dollar bill from Wagstaffe came. In fact, it was $1.2 million – the cumulative pay. I think this is what happened because, you know, I was doing drugs so I don't remember everything.

"I go to Charles, 'Okay, well we have to pay the Wagstaffe bill off first,' and he goes 'No, that's your responsibility,' and I said 'What do you mean that's my responsibility?' He goes 'You've got to pay that out of your side' and I'm like 'No – we have to pay it 85–15.' And then I realised the right thing was for him to pay it all – because it was legal expenses."

Needless to say, if Carreon was querying 15 per cent of a $1.2 million bill, he wasn't going to take too well to the idea of paying the whole thing. Kremen went to his other lawyer, Idell, for advice. Kremen soon realised he didn't even have a copy of the contract he and Carreon had signed. And then the whole story about how the contract had been drawn up came out.

Idell knew straight away that the contract wasn't worth the paper it was written on, "because I didn't get a chance to show it to anyone", Kremen explains. "I took it, I signed it, never had a copy." It was a contract drawn up between a lawyer and his client in which the lawyer stood to benefit far beyond providing his services. What's more the contract was not standard in that it gave Carreon 15 per cent of everything, rather than 15 per cent of the money recovered from the case. Unsurprisingly, such an arrangement is deeply frowned upon by the legal establishment, and Carreon should have insisted that Kremen seek a second lawyer's advice. "To get interest in a client's property, the other guy has to have a lawyer, and I didn't have a lawyer," Kremen sums up.

So Kremen took the opportunity to fire Carreon and refused to send him any more monthly cheques covering 15 per cent of sex.com's profits. Carreon's decision to refuse to pay up his side of Wagstaffe's legal bill was to cost him dearly.

It was in this poisonous atmosphere that Carreon, in a fit of pique, decided to sue Kremen for wrongful termination. And he chose the first day of the trial to file the complaint. But what really annoyed Kremen was that Carreon personally provided Dorband with a copy of the lawsuit during the lunch break of the first day of the trial, and Dorband couldn't resist raising the issue repeatedly during the trial. Kremen made sure Carreon paid for that.

The antipathy between the two men then became as intense as their friendship had been. Using Idell, Kremen countersued Carreon, claiming professional negligence. So Carreon sued Idell, which got Idell's insurance company involved. It went to the Bar Association of San Francisco, who decided that Carreon was not entitled to 15 per cent of sex.com, but since Carreon had worked at half his normal fee, ordered Kremen to pay him retrospectively at his usual $200-an-hour rate. Carreon won $269,000, but lost a stake worth millions.

But Kremen was still angry, and continued with his lawsuit even after the Bar Association's decision. It wasn't pretty –

Carreon's wife physically attacked Idell in the courtroom at one point – and much of what was said remains under seal, but the two former comrades finally reached a settlement. It was years until Kremen and Carreon felt able to talk to one another again.

41

JUDGMENT DAY

"The Court hereby enters judgement in favour of Plaintiff Gary Kremen against Defendants, Stephen Michael Cohen, Ocean Fund International Ltd., Ynata Ltd. and Sand Man Internacional Ltd., jointly in the amount of $40 million, plus punitive damages in the sum of $25 million.

"A constructive trust is imposed upon all monies and properties of the Defendants. The Receiver is ordered to collect and hold such properties pending further order of this Court. The warrant of arrest issued on March 2, 2001 shall remain outstanding until defendant Stephen M. Cohen surrenders the property of each defendant to this Court."

That was the judgment that finally decided sex.com. Kremen got ownership and $65 million. In a more extensive "findings of fact and conclusions of law", Ware was unequivocal. Cohen had "devised and executed a fraudulent plan to steal the domain name sex.com from Gary Kremen". He had forged the Dimmick letter with the intent to steal sex.com. Cohen had no right to the domain, and had submitted bogus documents in an effort to prove his prior rights.

Cohen had "substantially interfered" with Kremen's use of the domain and deprived Kremen of its use and of "earning substantial rents, income and profits". Cohen had failed to provide any meaningful documents for the business through sex.com so the precise profits could not be ascertained. But from what was found, Cohen made "in excess of $40,000,000".

Contrary to his sworn testimony, Cohen had transferred his profits to "undisclosed offshore locations" and continued to conceal funds. He wilfully, and against the strict orders of the court, transferred assets to offshore accounts. The evidence was "clear and convincing" that Sand Man and Ynata, as well as Omnitec, were "the alter egos of Stephen M. Cohen", and that Cohen had acted "with malice, fraud and oppression, as well as engaging in despicable conduct".

Cohen had bought the Rancho Santa Fe mansion with sex.com proceeds and then, against his own testimony, transferred it to Montano Properties for no consideration. As a result, the property, the funds transferred abroad, as well as Cohen's domain names and his IP addresses (the vital addresses used by computers to connect to the Internet) were all to be held in constructive trust for Gary Kremen.

The court ruled that Cohen did not have a valid trademark in the term "sex.com", and that Kremen was entitled to recover punitive damages – calculated at $25 million. Finally, Ware declared that "none of the affirmative defences asserted by defendants in their answers have any merit".

If being awarded $65 million can ever be regarded as an anticlimax, Kremen felt it. "The number is big, but it is unlikely that I will ever see more than a small fraction," he told the *Los Angeles Times*. The lawyers felt the same, Wagstaffe's assistant Pamela Urueta describing the chances of getting any money out of Cohen as "slim to none". From the lawyers' perspective, however, this was still a big victory for the Internet as a whole. Wagstaffe told *Wired* magazine: "The substantial size of this damage award sends a message that the Internet is not a lawless wasteland." Urueta told the BBC: "This ruling sends out the clear message that the domain name is a valuable property right ... that can and should be protected."

You can imagine what Cohen said. But at the same time, the sex.com thief did raise a pretty fair point: "In the O.J. Simpson case – a guy accused of homicide in civil court – the decision was $25 million. The Exxon Valdez oil leakage was only $30 million. $65 million?! Ware was pissed. Livid. He was disgusted by Kinko's and this was an emotional act." And while Cohen had indeed made many millions from sex.com, was it right that Kremen should be awarded everything that Cohen had earned from the domain rather than just the value of the domain? Cohen may have been a lazy businessman, but it was undeniable that he did build a business; it didn't create itself. Not that it mattered: the judgment could have been $10 million and Cohen would still have refused to pay it.

If there was one consolation to Kremen's Pyrrhic victory, it was the enormous press attention. Not only did it give Kremen a temporary sense that the fight had been worth it – even though it had cost him years of his life and millions of dollars – but it gave him an opportunity to outline his new plans for sex.com. Cohen's maximum sleaze for maximum profit approach was out. A new, softer approach was coming in. "We have done what we said we were going to do – reduce the amount of pornography on the site as we transition the site to more mainstream content," Kremen told the *LA Times*. He told MSNBC: "We're working on a deal [for content on] sex education, disease prevention, women's oriented stuff, stuff that you normally don't see. And we're doing it because we think we can make money at it." He told *Wired*: "It may be kind of dumb of me, but I think I can actually do it. I think I can make more money by transitioning it into a more mainstream kind of thing."

It wasn't long before Kremen realised just how wrong he was.

42

THE PORN INDUSTRY

Kremen was the least likely porn baron that ever lived, a fact he was constantly ribbed about. At his surprise 40th birthday party, the guests sported lapel badges featuring a young, wild-haired Kremen with the legend "accidental pornographer" printed underneath. It was a joke shared between family and friends.

As owner of the Internet's largest porn website, Kremen did his best to get along with the adult industry, but no matter how hard he tried, his disdain for pornographers showed through. Kremen was a well brought-up, highly educated and ultimately shy man who now found himself working in an industry full of Stephen Cohens: streetwise, ruthless, amoral extroverts. It was not a good fit.

Kremen was ashamed of the hardcore pornography ads on his site, so one of the first things he did was to pull them down. But just as he moved toward what he called "a *Maxim* magazine model – softer, with more context around the content", the adult industry was heading in the opposite direction, towards more explicit material that pushed the boundaries of legality.

Websites were so easy and cheap to set up, and the profits so huge, that the Internet was soon awash with hundreds of thousands of porn sites. Then exhibitionists discovered the Internet, and suddenly there were tens of thousands of free pictures plastered all over the Web. The adult industry is nothing if not pragmatic, so it moved to where the money was – unusual types of pornography that people would pay for out of desire or curiosity. By going against the market, Kremen marked himself out as a businessman making decisions with his heart rather than his head. To everyone already in the adult industry, it also indicated that Kremen felt himself to be above them. When he then appeared all over the press promising to clean up sex.com, implying that the adult industry itself was something to be ashamed of, it turned the fiercely competitive but tightly knit industry against him. They began an unofficial boycott of sex.com.

Since sex.com had never hosted much original content – and Kremen didn't want to get into providing his own pornographic content either – the bulk of the money came from the large and colourful ads on the site that clicked through to other adult websites. Thus sex.com largely depended on the rest of the adult industry for its income. When other sites started refusing to do business with sex.com, it took just a few months for the website that had been making $1 million a month at its peak to see its monthly revenue collapse to a paltry $50,000.

There were two other factors: Kremen's personality, and Cohen's interfering fury. Kremen was still strung out from his battle with Cohen when he was forced into the fight with Carreon. He had also moved on from cocaine and developed a serious addiction to crystal meth, which even Kremen admits is "much worse". San Diego was recognised as the "methamphetamine capital of North America", so with plenty of money and an easy supply, not to mention a number of hangers-on thanks to his new-found fame, Kremen was on a rapid downward spiral.

Why had Kremen got so caught up in drugs when all his drive came from work? "Oh, I know why," he answers immediately. "Because I didn't have any fun at university. I didn't have any fun, and then I started companies and things like that and I didn't have any fun. I didn't even try drugs until I was 28, 30. And the thing is, if you have free drugs, women come to you. And you feel good. Of course it's the drugs and not you – but you don't feel like that at the time. And I didn't really care."

Cohen would mock Kremen all the time about his drug problem, constantly calling him a hopeless junkie. "He would come into depositions and curl up in a ball on the floor and sleep," Cohen sneers. "He would come to court in wrinkled up shirts, and he hadn't showered, he smelled. The first time I saw him at my deposition, he was a joke. I never believed we would lose after that. He's in la-la land." Kremen admits that it got bad: "It was horrible. I had two [really bad] moments, you know. After one, I got rid of cocaine. And that was good. But I was living on Third Street. It looked okay during the day ... I'm kinda attracted to those kind of things, I don't know why."

Kremen then became involved with a group of old friends who were all addicted to heroin. "There was this poet. Paul O'Leary. Called himself England's Greatest Living Poet. But to make money he was an executive recruiter and he would call all the time. And he called me one day. Must have been a liquidity event, I had a lot of money, and I was either going to put it up my nose or buy something. He called me and said let's go hang out. He drinks up a storm and takes a lot of drugs and he would take me to the bars and say 'You should take this!' and it felt really good. And he got me in bed with his whole low-life set – that's how I got involved."

Kremen's drug habit was not his only problem. He was rapidly becoming a pariah in the adult industry, and the sex.com cash cow was starting to look distinctly underfed. Cohen was also adding his own special blend of pressure by calling up contacts in the adult industry and telling them tales of what Kremen was like and how he couldn't be trusted in business. He also made more and more phone calls to Kremen himself, boasting about how much money he had and the luxurious life he led. He mocked Kremen for screwing up sex.com, and taunted him with the fact that he was never going to get his $65 million.

The sudden drop in revenue from sex.com meant that money was tight, and Kremen started struggling to pay his lawyers.

Wagstaffe was still fighting to bring NSI back into the case and to get hold of Cohen's Rancho Santa Fe mansion. Richard Idell was dealing with the lawsuit between Kremen and Carreon and other general legal issues that appeared.

It became so bad that in December 2001 – eight months after Ware had awarded Kremen $65 million – Kremen's lawyers had to inform Judge Ware that there was a problem paying for the court receiver. Ware was stunned: "I'm somewhat surprised when you say there are financial difficulties in this case. When I last heard about the income being generated from this website, I was told a very impressive number. Those numbers have apparently changed?" They had, Kremen's lawyers replied. Ware was not impressed and pointedly remarked that his $65 million judgment had been based on the income he had been told sex.com was bringing in.

Fortunately for Kremen, he had made a decision that saved his business, his legal fight and quite possibly his life: he hired a smart young business manager to act as chief operating officer and chief financial officer of his new company, Grant Media. Steve Klopf, a young man who was looking for a challenge and who thrived amid chaos, arrived just as sex.com hit rock bottom. "Gary had got some hotshot in to run the business, and he started bringing in $100,000 consultants who were spending more than the company had," Klopf explains. "I asked the hotshot what he was going to do when next month he had no money and he said 'Go to Gary and ask for more.' I told Gary this and he went crazy."

The general belief was that the owner of sex.com – the man who had won such a public legal battle – had money to burn. In fact, the opposite was true. "The big problem was always money," Klopf says. "I would have to money manage. Pay people off in small chunks over months. It was really tough for a while. For a year and a half, everyone was beating on us, slagging us off." It wasn't just the business cut: Kremen's drug addiction made working for sex.com a rollercoaster. "The pressure got to him. He was hanging around with these guys and he got into drugs because they were all drug addicts." Kremen's flat was directly above the sex.com offices in downtown San Francisco and the visitors to Kremen's flat would invariably find their way downstairs into the offices. "It was crazy, I would arrive at work to find needles on the desks," Klopf recalls. "Every day someone would turn up saying Gary had invited him to work there. I would ask: what are you going to do? 'I don't know.' So I would kick them out."

Other mornings, Klopf would arrive to find a stack of printouts on his desk with instructions scribbled all over them. Kremen had pulled an all-nighter and decided he knew exactly what had to be done. "Gary was crazy, crazy. He would have a whole set of changes and forget about them the next day and have a whole different way of doing it." Worried about his finances, Kremen was also constantly looking for opportunities to fire staff. "You didn't want to take up any room in his mind. People would get stuck in his mind and every day he would tell me they had to go," Klopf reveals. "Someone would have produced a graph and because it didn't have a box around it, or it was in the wrong font, he would say: 'They have to go.' And then two days later, he'd forget about it. I thought about hiring a temp agency so Gary could say 'Fire them!' and I'd say okay and get rid of them and just get a new person in."

It is hardly surprising then that sex.com went through three management teams in the first year that Kremen had control of the business. Many of sex.com's original advertisers refused to work with Kremen; Kremen refused to take money from people offering more distasteful types of pornography such as bestiality; and he didn't want to get into producing pornographic content himself. His publicly stated plan to offer sex-education information on the site also never came to fruition because the advertising money simply didn't exist – and the one thing he needed more than any other at the time was cash. But it was then that the business brain that had created

Match.com and Net Angels, sold security software off the fledgling Internet and registered sex.com kicked in: sex.com would become a sex search engine, an X-rated Google. Klopf may have had to deal with piles of late-night scribblings, but he had never lost belief in the man who would spend days on end upstairs and ring down to find out what was going on. "The overall focus was always there," he maintains. "Gary's a genius. He would insist on something, and then three months down the line you would suddenly realise where he was going with this."

Klopf managed to get sex.com back on its feet using Kremen's plans, and within a year revenue had climbed back to $200,000 a month. But even then, the huge legal bills Kremen was running up were killing the business. An extraordinary $175,000 a month was being spent on paying Wagstaffe, Idell and a number of private investigators and financial specialists that Kremen had hired to track Cohen and his funds down. Klopf started selling future advertising at a cheaper price just to cover that month's shortfall, and he and Kremen took to passing a book about the Apollo 13 mission, *Failure is Not an Option,* back and forth between them as inspiration. It wasn't just business that was disrupted by Kremen's drug habit; it was taking a heavy toll on him personally. "At one point I was worried about his physical health," Klopf says. "He got fat, was losing hair, he really damaged himself."

Perhaps just in time, there was finally a breakthrough in the exhausting six-year battle with Cohen, a vitally important victory that turned Kremen's entire life around and helped him put some of his demons to rest.

43

RANCHO SANTA FE

"Welcome to the house of Stephen Cohen!" exclaims Gary Kremen as he strolls out onto the veranda into the warm Californian sunshine more than two years after the $65 million judgment.

Stretching into the distance are the hills of one of the most exclusive neighbourhoods in the world, Rancho Santa Fe in San Diego. Past the hills, out of sight, is San Diego itself, the first American city north of the Mexican border. Off to the west is Highway 5, stretching all the way up the American west coast – from Mexico to Canada past Los Angeles, San Francisco, Portland and Seattle. Just beyond that lies the Pacific Ocean.

"This is where he used to sit in the early hours of the morning, figuring out new scams, working out how to screw people," Kremen explains from his patio chair with a mixture of awe and disgust. Behind him, the hot tub lazily bubbles away, and from it steps lead down to a large, curved swimming pool. Beyond the pool lies an immaculate landscaped garden and a sand volleyball court, while off to the left there is a combined tennis and basketball court. The place is at the same time impressive and welcoming, qualities that are carried over into the huge Mexican-style villa behind. This was the house, the extremely exclusive residence, of Stephen Cohen, but now it belongs to Gary Kremen.

Rancho Santa Fe has a strict no-street-light policy. If you drive in the neighbourhood after dark and turn the car lights off, the wall of trees lining the road and marking estate boundaries produce an unnerving darkness. Pitch black. This lack of artificial light, the quietness, the gentle cricket buzz and the soothing warmth creates an atmosphere of serenity that lets the mind wander untroubled. It is the perfect spot for recuperation and for clear, focused thinking.

It is all too easy to picture Stephen Cohen sitting here planning his next scheme to separate people from their hard-earned cash. And sitting here, you suddenly understand why he fought so hard and then exploded with such rage when Kremen managed to pull ownership away from him.

Cohen bought the six-bedroom, eight-bathroom bungalow at 17427 Los Morros for $3 million in November 1998. Four months earlier, Kremen had finally come good on his threat to sue over the theft of sex.com, so Cohen was looking for somewhere to invest and hide the money he had made from it. He settled, naturally enough, on property. Perhaps the name appealed to him: *morro* means "mouth" in Spanish – the tool of the con man's trade.

No sooner had he bought the house than he signed over ownership to a company called Montano Properties, a company that made no goods, offered no services, had no shareholders, employed not a single member of staff, produced no reports, and made not one single dollar in the course of its existence. It was just another Stephen Cohen shell company, which existed solely as a place to hide his ill-gotten gains.

But Kremen had found it. Figuratively at least. "I found out about it and pulled the title records, and realised he was associated with it and owned it, and I realised it was bought for like $3 million. So I realised it had to be worth something." Kremen decided to go and check out where the man who had stolen his domain lived. "But I didn't know Rancho Santa Fe. I was trying to find the house and I got lost, stuck on Black Mountain Road. I kept circling and circling and I couldn't find it, and it was like two in the morning so I went to sleep on the edge of the highway. I know the space where

I slept. There was one bit of cover. I slept on the ground." Kremen's failure to find the house wasn't that ridiculous – the whole place is pitch black at night, and the road it is in – Los Morros – changes name several times along its length for no obvious reason.

It wasn't long before the house became the focus of all of Kremen's – and hence his legal team's – efforts. It was the one thing of Cohen's they were sure they could get, and, what's more, it was so personal to Cohen – it was his home after all – that Kremen wanted it all the more. Kremen wanted to inflict some pain.

The result was an extraordinary series of complex legal manoeuvres and counter-attacks. Cohen tried several times to shift ownership of the house, but was caught each time. He then persuaded an old criminal friend, James Scott, a convicted counterfeiter, to pose as the president of Montano Properties, and persuaded another criminal associate, Jack Brownfield, to say he had been renting the mansion's guesthouse with a long-term non-cancellable lease. That was also picked apart and exposed as untrue. And finally, when all else failed, Cohen forced Montano Properties through the bankruptcy courts, calling Kremen the evening before to tell him what he was doing and assuring him he would never get the house.

But Kremen fought every inch of the way. Unlike his money, Cohen could not wire a six-bedroom mansion across the border. All he could do was put obstacles in Kremen's path, which Kremen would then pull out of the way and plough on. In the end, it took nine months of relentless legal pounding for Kremen to get his hands on the property. And it was then that Stephen Michael Cohen showed just how far he was willing to go to deny Kremen the pleasure of beating him. He may have lost his home, but he was damned if he was going to let Kremen enjoy it. Three truckloads of Mexicans turned up at the house, supervised by three of Cohen's henchmen, and proceeded to tear the place apart. Literally.

Photographs taken shortly afterwards of the subsequent devastation show that all the ornaments, furnishings and furniture have been taken, and all the handles, doors, units, lights and wiring torn out. The plumbing had been destroyed, the wooden panels in the study prised off the walls, the toilets removed, and the gutters pulled down. Water gushed through the house, destroying the carpets and floors, and all the doors were purposely left open, attracting wild animals. Even the trees in the garden had been uprooted and taken away. There was no kitchen sink. There was no kitchen.

Incredibly, it could have been worse. Kremen had hired a private detective to watch the house to see if anything was going on – particularly if Cohen decided to pop back for a quick visit. When the trucks arrived, the detective called Kremen, Kremen called his lawyer, and his lawyer called the court receiver's representative in San Diego. The representative turned up, with the police, and both were greeted by the president of Montano Properties claiming that he was within his rights to remove personal property from the mansion.

Even though the whole process only took a few hours, when the police chief asked for a look around the property, the receiver was stunned to see the damage that been caused. With the situation threatening to descend into violence, the chief shut the situation down, allowing the workers to drive off in their trucks, and taped the house off. It was a few days before Kremen flew down to find Cohen's multi-million-dollar message: you won't beat me. In defiance, Kremen moved in.

Or, more accurately, he moved into the guest house, which still had a functioning toilet and a floor that wasn't rotting and infested. Kremen was also paranoid that Cohen might send someone round to mete out some punishment. Once such a thought enters your head, it can be difficult to beat it, especially when you are sleeping in their house. He refused to succumb though and slept with a baseball bat by his side.

To make matters worse, the refitting of the house was a complete fiasco. Kremen had recovered one of the three trucks that had driven off loaded with the house's possessions, handing over a wad of cash to a Mexican in a car park, no questions asked. But his big mistake was to put an old junkie friend in charge of fixing the place up. The result was kitchen-cabinet doors used as shelving, blinds jammed into place, and holes and cracks in the walls as things didn't fit were smashed into place.

Even though it was a disaster, the move saved Kremen. The drug crowd he had been hanging out with wouldn't make the journey from San Francisco, and the tranquillity of the place helped Kremen to settle down. "It was good for me," Kremen reflects. "I was doing a lot of drugs and to get down here was good. And I needed a chilling-out period because it was such an intense experience, the whole thing. I mean, it took up years of my life."

He threw occasional big parties for the adult industry, which at least one guest has confirmed were pretty wild, but Kremen didn't really enjoy them. "I felt that people felt I should be doing it. It was weak on my part – it was dumb. I never enjoy parties – I'm not a party enjoyer. Unless it's go out and have a party and drink. That I enjoy – some crazy bars."

It was the fact that it was Cohen's house that really pleased Kremen. "For a couple of months to a year, this was the biggest thing ever." But after more than five years in Stephen Cohen's house, the sense of victory has long since gone. The house is enormous, beautiful and calming. Kremen hates it. "If it had no maintenance I would keep it, but it costs two hundred and fifty thousand dollars a year just to run this place. How much do you think the pool guy costs? Six hundred dollars a month. You think this pool works all the time? It's four to five thousand dollars a year to repair. Take all the water out, repair the tiles."

He gestures at the stone patio: "To clean this thing – this is four thousand dollars a year right here. This is fifteen hundred bucks a month – this landscaping. These trees – I gotta remove these trees because they're breaking the foundation. Trees are like forty to fifty thousand dollars – palm trees. I gotta remove a bunch of them, I gotta get the permission, I gotta hire a certified arborist. And then propane: fifteen hundred dollars a month. Electricity: seventeen hundred dollars a month – and I don't even use the air-conditioner.

"Just add it all up. Property taxes: four thousand dollars a month. Just add it all up. And it stresses me out. For all that money, I could be investing in another company every month – which gives me more enjoyment than the house does. That's my logic. Yeah it's beautiful, but I don't see it like that any more. I just see a tennis court and I see, bugs – exterminator – seventeen hundred dollars. I see – oooh beautiful palm trellis – twenty-one hundred dollars. I'm over it."

When Kremen tells an old friend about his plans to rent the house and eventually sell up, the friend is relieved. "Thank God for that. Bad juju. Get rid of the last of that man."

The house wasn't the only property that Kremen prised from Cohen. But the Rancho Santa Fe mansion is far more impressive than the ramshackle and derelict house that overlooks the Mexican border and Tijuana. It was also owned by Montano Properties, having been expertly conned from its bondsman owner for just one dollar by Stephen Cohen, who had persuaded him the title deed was worthless. It was infested with vermin and lies in a confined zone – you had to drive past the US border police to gain access to it.

It still hurt Cohen to lose it. Perched above the border, the land presented a unique business opportunity – sending cheap bandwidth from the United States several hundred yards across the border into Mexico using satellite dishes where higher prices meant he could sell it at great profit. It was highly profitable before Gary Kremen won the house and the land and turned up with a pair of bolt cutters to cut the data link.

Cohen again forged an elaborate but entirely false paper trail to keep the property out of Kremen's hands – and again he failed. There was no point in Cohen trashing the border house, however – it was already no more than a dilapidated shack. It was only the data-link Cohen wanted, so the situation called for something a little more inventive. When Kremen arrived to cut the locks off the property, and with every intention of using the bolt cutters on Cohen's data-link too, he was sternly informed that the land on which the link stood did not belong to him. An eight-foot square steel cube, painted white and with Cohen's Pacnet company details stencilled on the side, was only ten feet from the house – but in between stood an old wire fence, which, Kremen was informed, represented the border of the property he had won from Cohen. He would be breaking the law if he cut the link.

Kremen smelt a rat and hired an experienced surveyor to review the land. A week later, the surveyor discovered the fence was in the wrong place. A careful study of the ground revealed old posts and the original border, which, surprise, surprise, *did* encompass the data-link. Traces of fresh sand were found in the links of the existing wire fence, confirming the surveyor's suspicions: Cohen had installed a new fence and then weathered it with a sand blaster. It looked as if it had been there for ten years.

As Kremen got off the drugs and settled down, the adult industry soon grew to appreciate the search technology that sex.com was now offering – technology that Kremen himself had masterminded. In many ways it was the same as his classi-fied-ads business back in the early days of the Net. Back then people wanted to tell others what services they had to offer. Five years later, there were so many services that it had fallen to individuals to type what they wanted into so-called "search engines". Kremen was offering the sex version of Google. He still wasn't one of the boys, but people were happy to do busi-ness with him. Revenue hit $300,000 a month and kept rising, enabling Kremen to fund his ongoing legal battles without hurting his business.

Soon after, Judge Ware declared Cohen a fugitive from justice, and Kremen decide to put his new-found wealth to good use by offering $50,000 to anyone who could grab Stephen Cohen and pull him back across the border.

44

SHOOT-OUT

"What your client may have thought to be a prank has back-fired. Seven people have been arrested in Mexico attempting to abduct Mr Cohen. Two have been shot. There is now blood on your client's hands, and I sincerely trust that you have previously advised him, based on my letter to you several weeks ago, that the reward offer should be immediately withdrawn.

"Your client has now exposed himself (and those acting in concert with him) to serious civil, and possibly criminal, liability. I trust you will take the appropriate action to prevent further bloodshed and even greater exposure to liability on the part of your client and his agents."

The letter was from Dorband to Idell. Kremen has it framed and on his study wall.

Kremen and Cohen had been trading insults almost daily, and Kremen decided he had had enough. Having completely ignored the US court's authority, Cohen then had the audacity to appeal the decision against him. Kremen knew Cohen was in Tijuana, so he hired private investigators to find him. It didn't take them long. They knew his work address and simply tailed him to his house, which was literally just around the corner at 2532 Avenida Diego Rivera. They also compiled a huge dossier on Cohen, his wife, associates and step-children (Kremen actually went to court to find out where they were being schooled). There was nothing that Kremen didn't know about the man who owed him $65 million.

Judge Ware was nearly as frustrated. Cohen was claiming, without any form of proof, that he was being held under house arrest by the Mexican government so couldn't attend court. The court receiver checked out the claims and concluded they were rubbish. As a result, Ware had taken the extraordinary step of making Cohen a fugitive from justice, opening the way for the extradition of Cohen back to the US.

Kremen took the opportunity to mock up a "Wanted" poster for Cohen, and stuck it on sex.com. It was a joke, but then Kremen started thinking seriously about it. Having been talked through the tortuously slow extradition laws by his lawyers, he decided that the modern equivalent of a wanted poster might not be such a bad idea after all.

And so, on the morning of 30 May 2001, Kremen posted a $50,000 reward on sex.com for Stephen Michael Cohen in both English and Spanish, and tipped off the press. Within days, it had been reported in newspapers across the world. The reward offer gave extensive details about Cohen: "white male, 53 years old, with brown thinning hair, brown eyes, a grey/brown mustache, high forehead, approximately 5' 6" to 5' 8", weighs approximately 220–230 pounds". It also gave his likely whereabouts, as well as the slightly bizarre information that he "has a florid face and nose, and is partial to wearing imprinted t-shirts". A still from his video deposition was also put up, as well as maps and a long list of Cohen's associates, along with their telephone numbers and email addresses. When a number of those associates complained, they were withdrawn from the list for one day, but only on the condition they call to discuss their links with Stephen Cohen. If they didn't call, they went back up.

The posting stated that anyone who provided information leading to the arrest of Stephen Michael Cohen by officials of the United States was in line for a $50,000 cash reward. A telephone number was provided as well as an email address – reward@sex.com.

The United States has a proud culture of bounty hunters (although they prefer the term "bail bond investigator"), where freelancers do the work of stretched state authorities by locating and arresting individuals who have skipped bail or are otherwise recognised by the courts as fugitives. The problem with Kremen's reward was that a US bounty hunter is only allowed to work within the United States. Seizing Cohen in Tijuana and dragging him back across the US border was illegal. Not that there weren't those willing to take the risk. With even successful bounty hunters rarely making more than $100,000 a year, a $50,000 cash lump sum was very tempting. Kremen got a number of phonecalls, but they all fell through when Kremen insisted on a contract that would remove – or at least, reduce – Kremen's liability. The problem with such a contract, the bounty hunters knew only too well, was that they would be signing to say they were planning to break the law. From Kremen's side, however, having made the reward so public, he couldn't risk doing an under-the-table deal.

If Kremen's intention was to worry Cohen, it worked. A number of his associates called up pretending to be bounty hunters in order to find out whether Kremen had hired anyone yet. The reward turned out to be a psychological masterstroke. A few months earlier Kremen had been sleeping in Cohen's house with a baseball bat; now Cohen was sleeping in his house in Tijuana terrified that any second some meathead from Kentucky was going to kick his door in.

The result was the letter from Dorband claiming that seven people had been arrested and two shot attempting to abduct Mr Cohen. Kremen didn't believe a word of it, and promptly posted the letter on sex.com alongside the reward notice. Despite Cohen's claims getting wide attention, popping up not only in court but newspapers across the world, it turns out that Kremen was right. The event never happened, and we know that because the only person who has any recollection of the event is Stephen Cohen himself. Considering that the shoot-out happened in broad daylight in the centre of Tijuana, and involved Mexican police and US bounty hunters, it is more than a little unusual that the violence-obsessed Tijuana press failed to pick it up. Cohen even went to the trouble of forging a confession from one of the Mexican policemen he claimed was guarding him, but if anything it was worse than the other countless forgeries that had already appeared in the case. It was clearly the end of the line for Dorband as well. The letter, in which Dorband appeared to believe that people had actually been shot, was the last he ever wrote for his soon-to-be ex-client.

Having a client like Cohen must be difficult, Dorband was asked long after his final letter. "It *is* difficult. It is difficult. But you keep your eye on the legal aspects of the case, and you are protecting the legal system as much as you are any particular individual." Phoney shoot-outs in order to help bypass that legal system were, however, a step too far.

In Dorband's place, Cohen hired his old friend Michael Mayock to act as his attorney, and just three days later this resulted in a furious court filing asking Judge Ware to lift the arrest warrant against Cohen because Kremen's reward was causing "emotional distress and life threatening fear" to Cohen and his family. Mayock appeared to have no trouble believing Cohen's wild tales and upped the ante, claiming that three groups of men had now attempted to kidnap Cohen on three separate occasions. This time it turned out that only six men had been arrested, but an extra one had been shot, taking the total number of casualties up to three. "Unless something is done," Mayock cried, "more people will undoubtedly be injured and perhaps killed."

Ware threw the complaint out, calling it "implausible", and refused even to review the "proof" Cohen promised to provide. That evidence, which purported to be a Mexican court order, ended up being another poorly typed-up sheet of A4 with a cheap stamp claiming to be a government seal. Ware was just as angry with Kremen, however, and Kremen wisely decided to take the reward down straight after the hearing.

Despite claiming later that the documents proved his total innocence, Cohen confided that he didn't have copies to hand of the evidence provided to court. Nor did Dorband. Nor did Mayock. Extraordinary, considering they detailed a moment when Cohen says he feared for his life as three men were shot on his lawn.

But Cohen had achieved his aim of getting the reward pulled. And Kremen had achieved his aim of scaring the hell out of Cohen. Cohen moved house – no doubt in the dead of night, sneaking past the Mexican policemen who he said were keeping him under house arrest. He went out of his way to keep his new address secret. Having ditched, or been ditched by his lawyers, paranoid that at any moment he was going to be grabbed and bundled across the US border, sitting in a new and unfamiliar home, and with his old friends and colleagues furious with him for having dragged them into the crosshairs over the Montano Properties case (Kremen threatened Jack Brownfield, Rosa Montano and a number of others with criminal prosecution over the destruction of the Rancho Santa Fe house), Cohen appeared to have a breakdown.

Six months after the "shoot-out", he filed a sudden series of rambling, ranting and frequently incoherent motions to the court.

On 2 January 2002, he applied to become the attorney of record in his case, and in the same filing demanded that Kremen's lawyer Richard Idell be "criminally prosecuted for wilful violations".

On 4 January, he requested that his affidavit be put under seal because it covered confidential matters concerning himself and his attorney, Dorband. Except the court didn't appear to have received any such affidavit.

On 10 January, he complained bitterly that Kremen had reposted the reward on sex.com. In fact, the printouts he attached made it quite clear he was simply looking at a saved copy of the reward notice on his computer, rather than an actual live page on the Internet.

On 27 January, Cohen demanded that the injunction against him be lifted, raving that it amounted to a death warrant against him and that he wasn't able to afford even toilet paper. The court's decision had reduced his status to that of a slave, Cohen ranted, and so broke the 13th Amendment of the United States Constitution.

On 30 January, he complained again that the reward was still on the sex.com site, and that the issue had appeared all over again in the press. But all the printouts he provided showed the reports were dated from May and June 2001. Cohen had circled the date in the bottom right-hand side of the pages, which showed only the date they were printed out.

On 31 January, Cohen filed another motion. This one claimed that someone at the courthouse was destroying Cohen's faxes and letters to Judge Ware. He demanded an investigation into the obstruction of justice, and then filed an affidavit from himself stating exactly the same thing.

Each filing gave a postal box address in Tijuana as the contact address, betraying Cohen's paranoia. Cohen also appears to have slipped again into his fantasy world where he was a lawyer who had once been advised by General Manuel Noriega to stand for the Panamanian Bar. Unfortunately, a non-existent licence to practise in Panama did not provide Cohen with the right to file motions into a California court – something only a qualified attorney registered to practise law in California can do. Ware reviewed the first three of Cohen's filings and found them "unclear and rambling in nature". He then refused to accept any more filings from Cohen unless they went through a lawyer. We don't know how many filings Cohen sent after that, but within days Dorband wrote to the court giving notice of his formal withdrawal as Cohen's attorney, noting that no substitute counsel had been named.

And that was the last that anyone heard from Stephen

Cohen for over a year. Plagued by paranoia and in the depths of a mental breakdown, he had put his millions to good use and flown to Europe, where he bought a flat in Monte Carlo and tried to settle down to a life of carefree luxury.

Kremen's investigators were still trying to find Cohen's millions, but by the summer of 2002 Kremen's attention was most definitely elsewhere. NSI had just been pulled back into the case, and he was straining at the leash to get the people who had caused the problem in the first place.

45

NSI REDUX

In many ways, Kremen's fight with Network Solutions was the most important part of his ten-year legal campaign. His personal conflict with Cohen had certainly consumed his life, but the battle with NSI was to consume his money.

Kremen was aware that he might be forging a legacy. Having not had a day in seven years in which he didn't wake up thinking about domain names, he was actually in a position where he could change the law surrounding these building blocks of the Internet. Plus of course have revenge on the company that caused his problems in the first place and then treated him with such disdain.

NSI had been excused from the case on 8 May 2000 – more than anything because Judge Ware wisely realised he would live to regret making a judgment at that time. Besides, if his decision was wrong, there was always the right of appeal.

Kremen was determined to mount a challenge. As soon as Ware's final judgment on Kremen versus Cohen was entered, Wagstaffe appealed Ware's earlier decision to let NSI out of the case. It was the job that Kremen had originally hired him to do, and it was the prize that Wagstaffe wanted. On 9 May 2001 the Court of Appeals agreed to look at the case, and the wheels of justice were once more set in motion. Of course, Cohen had also appealed the decision against *him*, which added to the delay, but eventually, nine months later, the Appeals Court requested more information. On 11 February 2002 Wagstaffe filed his case on behalf of Kremen.

The 58-page appeal brief can be divided into two parts: one dealing with Cohen and his various legal contortions; and the second dealing with NSI and why it should still be held liable for passing Kremen's rights in sex.com to Cohen.

The situation was complicated by the fact that NSI had been allowed out of the case on the basis of Carreon's third amended complaint – a complaint that was subsequently redrawn and rehashed by Wagstaffe, ensuring final victory over Cohen. Thus Wagstaffe found himself in the odd position of arguing a legal position that he had himself considered inadequate first time round. He chose the elements of Carreon's argument that were strongest: conversion; conversion by bailee; and breach of contract.

The main thrust of the case was simply expressed: "Although Cohen is primarily responsible for stealing the domain name, he would never have been able to do so without NSI's ready assistance. Even the most rudimentary attempt to verify the Dimmick letter would have detected Cohen's crude forgery. But NSI made no such attempt. It handed over Kremen's domain name – worth millions of dollars – without even notifying Kremen and in violation of its own published process. The district court mistakenly held that, as a matter of law, NSI is not responsible for its ineptitude."

Despite filing their arguments in February, it took until August 2002 for the busy Appeals Court to hear oral arguments. In the room were Mayock for Cohen; a new entry, Thomas Hogan, acting for Montano Properties (which was still pretending to be a separate entity); Wagstaffe for Kremen; and Dolkas back in the ring for NSI. Judges Kozinski, McKeown and Fitzgerald gave Mayock and Hogan 20 minutes; Wagstaffe 20; and Dolkas 20.

Hogan simply stated that he wanted more time for the whole Montano case, almost immediately ceding to Mayock – who proceeded to blow what little chance Cohen had in his first sentence. "I feel sorry in a way for Judge Ware," he began, "he's sort of like the person in a B movie who gets hit with the sucker punch ..."

"Who's this?" Kozinski asked.

"Judge Ware," Mayock said.

"Judge Ware?" Kozinski asked with a mixture of surprise and amusement. "People don't often feel sorry for us being judges ... they are powerful people."

Mayock laughed, and foolishly ploughed on: "Well, essentially what happened he was told 'Hey, look over there!', and he did, and he got blind sighted. He got blind sighted by Kremen, whose entire focus in the case has been to point to Cohen, call him a thief, call him a liar, call him an ex-convict ..."

Kozinski cut him off. "You know I think you did in fact call him a sucker, I didn't quite get it ... I mean you're here standing there telling us he got fooled."

Mayock kept going: "I think he did."

It was a big mistake, as Kozinski immediately made clear: "It's perfectly fine to say that the district court erred, but I don't think it is appropriate to start off by telling us the district court is a sucker. Why don't you start over again?"

Just over a fortnight later, on 30 August 2002, the Appeals Court threw out Cohen's appeal in a single, damning paragraph: "In light of Cohen's status as a fugitive from justice and his egregious abuse of the litigation process, we exercise our discretion to dismiss his appeal pursuant to the fugitive disentitlement doctrine."

In comparison to Mayock's street-hustler approach, Wagstaffe radiated authority and class. Confident, comfortable and witty, he ripped apart Cohen's arguments and then launched into the real issue: NSI. The judges had already agreed between themselves that the Dimmick letter was transparently a fraud, but Judge McKeown warned straight away that "It would have to still fit under a legal theory." "I understand," replied Wagstaffe. The argument therefore soon centred around the issue of whether a domain name was property that could be converted ("conversion" again being a legal term that defines the injury that occurs when someone takes or uses your property without permission). Wagstaffe accepted that a domain is not tangible in the sense that you cannot touch it, but it was tangible in that its removal denied someone else the right to use it.

Dolkas didn't agree, of course. There was no formal certification provided for a domain name, he argued. But the judges were already swaying toward Wagstaffe's explanation, and Wagstaffe supplied them with a number of analogous examples to show why Dolkas' model didn't hold up. What about company stocks, where ownership lives only on a computer? What about cash machines, where you type in a number and the cash in the machine is deducted from your account instead of someone else's? That is all done electronically. Dolkas argued that all NSI did was link domain names to computer IP addresses, but real-world examples of what domain names had already become made his argument sound bizarrely antiquated.

Nevertheless, the same problem that Ware had faced in 2000 still existed when the Appeals Court was discussing the case in 2002: what were domain names? And was it time to start defining them in law? The concern was such that McKeown and Fitzgerald out-voted Kozinski and decided to refer the question of whether a domain name could be viewed as convertible property to the Supreme Court. Just getting to that decision itself took another five months. In the meantime, the case was put on hold.

This was Kremen's worst fear. He was sick of bankrolling a high-level legal discussion about what domain names were to the tune of hundreds of thousands of dollars. What he wanted was for NSI to admit it had done wrong handing over control of sex.com to a crystal-clear con man. He also wanted them to compensate him for the millions he had lost as a consequence of losing sex.com, and the millions more he had spent as a result of having to fight them through the courts. But as Judge Kozinski had predicted, the Supreme Court was too busy, and told the Appeals Court it would have to decide the issue itself. That little circle took two months. It was now March 2003, and the appeal judges started all over again discussing what the nature of a domain name was. It was at this point that the importance of beating NSI became apparent not only to Kremen but to the wider Internet community.

There had always been tension between NSI and the engineers who had designed and built the Internet. Having been handed an effective monopoly over the Internet, NSI had started to believe that it *was* the Internet. Even when the US government realised its mistake and created ICANN to prevent NSI from ruling what was supposed to be an open and inclusive system, the company was so entrenched it managed to beat off the assault. But in a January 2003 filing to the Supreme Court, in which NSI argued its philosophy of what domain names were and therefore what the Internet was, the immensity of the company's delusions of grandeur was openly revealed.

If the case were decided against it, NSI claimed, it would "cripple the Internet and jeopardise the national economic benefit for e-commerce". NSI was arguing, with some seriousness, that if it was found legally responsible for what it did with the products that it made billions of dollars from, then the entire domain-name system – and therefore the Internet itself – would fall apart. Not only that, but the cost of registering domain names "would become unacceptably high" as it was forced to fight countless legal battles. The argument had Internet experts across the world spluttering out their morning coffee. Even if the Doomsday scenario as outlined by NSI actually happened – and there was no reason to believe it would – all it would mean was that NSI as a corporate entity would collapse. The data tables, computer servers, private contracts and fabric of the Internet would remain unaffected, and the Internet would continue with barely a blip. But to NSI's mind, an Internet without NSI was incapable of existing.

As ridiculous as all this was, it was a serious motion by a

serious and important company, and when the issue of what domains were was returned to the Appeals Court, it became clear that the judges were taking NSI's perspective seriously. Fortunately for the wider Internet community, Judge Kozinski was an Internet enthusiast, and he carried out a huge amount of research to make sure the Appeals Court knew what it was talking about when it made one of the biggest legal decisions ever to have affected the Internet.

By the time the court finally came to a conclusion on 25 July 2003, it had been an unbelievable seven years, nine months and seven days since Stephen Cohen had stolen sex.com. The decision, however, was ground-breaking.

"'Sex on the Internet?', they all said. 'That'll never make any money.' But computer-geek-turned-entrepreneur Gary Kremen knew an opportunity when he saw it. The year was 1994 ..." So begins a surprisingly lively decision written by Kozinski, a decision that made domain names convertible property for the first time, and pulled the law regarding the Internet into line with reality. The decision read like a magazine article about the theft of sex.com, complete with details of Cohen's past, his trashing of the Rancho Santa Fe mansion, the claimed Tijuana shoot-out and so on, before finally getting down to the nuts and bolts: "Given his limited success with the bounty hunter approach, it should come as no surprise that Kremen seeks to hold someone else responsible for his losses. That someone is Network Solutions."

The decision found that Kremen did not have a contract with NSI because he hadn't paid any money for sex.com, but that he *did* have an intangible property right in the domain name, and that Network Solutions had wrongfully disposed of that right by handing it to Cohen. Judge Ware's tight reading of the conversion law – that the domain had to be linked to something tangible – was dismissed as a "rigid limitation" that "many courts ignore or expressly reject". Instead, the Appeals Court agreed with Wagstaffe and Kremen that the domain name system itself was a document. "That it is stored in electronic form rather than on ink and paper is immaterial," the decision read, explaining that if the opposite were the case, "torching a company's file room would then be conversion while hacking into its mainframe and deleting its data would not".

But the review of NSI's behaviour was the most damning element of the decision. "The district court was worried that 'the threat of litigation threatens to stifle the registration system by requiring further regulations and potential increases in fees.' Given that Network Solutions' 'regulations' evidently allowed it to hand over a registrant's domain name on the basis of a facially suspect letter without even contacting him, 'further regulations' don't seem like such a bad idea. And the prospect of higher fees presents no issue here that it doesn't in any other context. A bank could lower its ATM fees if it didn't have to pay security guards, but we doubt most depositors would think that was a good idea."

The decision concluded: "Kremen had a viable claim for conversion. The judgment of the district court is reversed on this count, and the case is remanded for further proceedings. AFFIRMED in part, REVERSED in part and REMANDED. No costs." Finally, NSI had no choice but to sit down at the table with Kremen and start talking compensation.

But that wasn't the only matter that had finally been decided. A month earlier, and almost unnoticed, an appeal by Cohen to the Supreme Court had been decided. Michael Mayock had put together a ten-page argument explaining why it should review the Appeals Court's dismissal. It was sent on 2 April 2003, but in the Supreme Court's equivalent of the blink of an eye, the decision came back on 9 June. It consisted of one line: "The petition for a writ of certiorari is denied." Cohen's legal fight was over.

If Kremen thought that NSI had changed in the three years since he had last dealt with them, he was in for a rude awakening. The company was pulled back into the district court four days later to decide the compensation, and the case was off again on an apparently endless series of motions and counter-motions.

NSI's loftiness was gone, however – it had been found guilty of wrongfully disposing of sex.com and it would have to pay for that. Ware also allowed Kremen's team to add a civil theft charge to the complaint which automatically tripled any damages. It had no choice but to talk options, and the big issue was where the figure came from and how much it was going to be. Kremen wanted to make it a simple exchange: NSI would pay the $40 million Judge Ware had ordered Cohen to pay, but would not be liable for the $25 million punitive damages. NSI said it would pay no more than $500; so Wagstaffe upped Kremen's claim to $43 million.

This went on for another 40 case filings, and another six months, before the case even reappeared in front of Ware. And then the whole thing started all over again. NSI was playing the long game in the hope that Kremen would tire of the financial burden. At the same time, Kremen started making some wild allegations (any evidence for which is currently under seal): he had uncovered evidence of collusion between Cohen and NSI's head of investigations, which was covered up by senior management; that same person had a drink problem; Cohen had also stolen another domain using the same method; there was a 37-minute phone call between Cohen and a senior NSI staff member during which he moved 37 ill-gotten domains; there was an internal NSI scam where people could jump the backlog of domain-name registrations for a fee.

But with the case entering a strange pace of its own making, it became clear that it was also potentially in Kremen's lawyers' own interests to keep the case rolling on, thanks to the arrangement they had reached with their client. "If we solve it on Tuesday [30 September 2003], they get 30 per cent, which they split among themselves," Kremen explained two months after the Appeal Court decision. "If we solve it within ten days before trial they get 33 per cent. If we solve it any other time, 40 per cent." It may sound counter-intuitive, but the reasoning was that the longer the proceedings dragged on, the higher the payout would eventually be.

Another 80 court filings later and suddenly it was February 2004. Then came the good news: Ware had set a date for trial – 10 June 2004. At the same time, VeriSign bought Network Solutions. Despite a short argument over liability, it became clear that now was the time for settling. Kremen wanted to get on with his life – to continue the fight meant at least another year of legal tennis, and two to five years before it was finally over. Wagstaffe and Idell warned him that this was probably the last chance he had to avoid going to trial. "Wagstaffe pressured me, said it was time to settle," Kremen explains. "And I had a headache. I'd been doing it for a long time and I had had enough." Kremen took the settlement that VeriSign were offering.

The two sides reached agreement and turned up for the last time at a special hearing in front of Judge Ware on 22 March 2004 to get a protective order to keep secret the settlement and several of the documents in which both sides had made very strong allegations against one another. But the case was finally over, and Ware allowed himself a few moments reflection: "The Court wants to express its appreciation to the parties for their conduct during the litigation. This was a matter that raised very novel legal issues and one of the things that we owe to those generations that have preceded us and those generations that follow us is to bring the very best thinking and analysis to novel legal issues, because that's how law develops … This was a case where I was pleased to have excellent lawyers appear before me, and I'm pleased to sign the dismissal as well as to involve the Court in the future enforcement of the settlement by the protective order." How much did NSI/VeriSign pay Kremen? Somewhere between $10 and $20 million – probably a little over $15 million.

"I'm ecstatic that we have reached a settlement so we can put the case behind us," Kremen told the dozens of reporters who were covering the end of the epic legal battle. Wagstaffe was more reserved. "Law works very slowly. Sometimes there's a drop down and sometimes a step up. And sometimes something comes along – I call it old wine in a new bottle. The Internet is messing about with the law at this moment. What Kozinski said was that the Internet could be dealt with by existing law. And the implications of that will continue for the next fifty years." Wagstaffe also summarised his time on the case more informally: "It's been a lot of fun." It was over, and Kremen had a handsome pay-off. And in an ideal world that would have been the end of it.

Except there remained one person never far from Kremen's mind. Having fled Mexico for Monaco, Stephen Michael Cohen attempted to retire. Like so many ageing crooks before him, Cohen appeared destined to live out the rest of his life leading the luxuriously lazy existence of the wealthy exile, whose true identity is only discovered by neighbours and friends after his death. But Cohen couldn't do it. Life without scams was too boring. He had started investing in casinos and hotels – Monte Carlo's stock in trade – and began looking for new opportunities on the still-blossoming Internet. Before he knew it, schemes were opening up again before him.

Cohen also started keeping an eye on sex.com and Kremen's court case with Network Solutions. He would get hold of filings as they were lodged with the court, and if they looked bad for Kremen, he would call him up to tell him he was going to lose. He started trying to gauge how keen Kremen was to continue chasing him. Kremen was ambivalent. He openly admitted that he knew he would probably never get a cent of Cohen's money. Towards the end of 2003, he even suggested that he would be willing to let the whole thing drop for a token gesture from Cohen. Cohen decided it was safe to return to Tijuana. Back in Mexico, his marriage to Rosa Montano soon fell apart, leading to his fifth divorce in May 2004. However, he was back among friends.

Then, in October 2004, just to tie up the final loose ends, Kremen applied to the court to make both his ownership of the Rancho Santa Fe mansion and the sex.com trademark application permanent. It was no more than a formality. But settled in Tijuana, back among his friends, and within walking distance of the US border, Cohen decided to break the uneasy truce built up between two doughty and exhausted fighters. On 8 November – more than seven months after the case had been closed – Cohen filed an appeal against its final judgment. Stephen Cohen was back on his feet and spoiling for another fight.

What he possibly hoped to achieve, it is difficult to know, but it was a major miscalculation. The Gary Kremen he had fought between 1995 and 2001 was a very different man from the one he would face in 2004. Kremen was now battle-hardened, legally ruthless and had no money concerns to force restraint. Kremen was stunned to see Cohen intervene at the eleventh hour. He knew then that there would be no end to it, that Cohen would never be able to leave the matter alone, so he made up his mind that this time he was going to get him and settle it once and for all.

46

SHUT-DOWN

Cohen didn't know what had hit him. Kremen had fired a legal broadside, and he kept on firing while not only Stephen Cohen, but also his wife Rosa, his stepdaughter Jhuliana, and his associates Jack Brownfield and Miguel Betancourt all dived for cover. The irony of the situation must have struck Cohen. Here was pupil turning on master. Gary Kremen's case against Cohen seven years earlier had been all but destroyed by Cohen's legal onslaught. Kremen had learnt the lesson: go in hard and go in fast.

Despite having all his money carefully secreted in offshore accounts and being based in Mexico, Cohen was still hugely reliant on the motherland he wasn't able to visit. Due to the unreliable Mexican postal system, Cohen used a box in the US as his main collection point. He also used American credit cards and American mobile-phone companies, and he had vital business assets on the US side of the border. The same was true of his family and his business associates. To Kremen's mind, all of them were now legitimate targets.

Cohen had been careful to make sure nothing was in his name – "I have no bank accounts, no savings accounts, no trust accounts. I haven't written a cheque in two years," Cohen confessed. But it wasn't long before Kremen's team of lawyers, on both sides of the border, and his new private investigator, Stanford MBA-holder Margo Evashevski, had drawn enough connections to convince Judge Ware to issue a series of new orders. The team issued dozens of subpoenas and then, when they had accumulated enough evidence, made filings into court under seal so that Cohen wasn't aware of what they were up to.

Ware issued secret orders that gave Kremen access to Cohen's credit-card accounts, his mobile-phone accounts and his mail. Each step accumulated more evidence of Cohen's involvement in a series of companies. Once this was proven beyond doubt, the investigators then went after the businesses, which included several Internet service providers (Pacnet, WL Com), a lending company (Mexico Lending), an Internet voice company (Ezcallme), a shrimp farm (International Sea Farms) and a strip club called The Bolero. One court order gave Kremen's investigators access to Cohen's computer servers, on which they discovered months' worth of his emails.

"But he was quicker than we were," explained Kremen's lawyer Tim Dillon, who was coordinating the charge. "We got into a couple of his accounts, but by the time we really started getting in there, he changed everything."

Before Cohen knew it, his stepdaughter Jhuliana was being sued for fronting Cohen's $800,000 investment in The Bolero, his associates found their vital business facilities had been seized, his Internet domains had been taken over, and a journalist from *Playboy* magazine had walked up to him outside his Mexican attorney's office to ask for an interview. If Cohen had known that just across the street, sitting in a 4 × 4, was Gary Kremen, he would have really freaked out.

Kremen had had enough of Cohen, and was playing hard-ball. The lawsuits and the seizures were just the opening salvo, designed to bewilder and confuse. Kremen's big plan was to build enough of a case to whisk through the complex and confusing extradition process and grab Cohen before he got wind of it and fled for Europe a second time. Kremen had prepared a dossier comprising tens of thousands of documents covering every aspect of Cohen's personal and private life: records of his cars and their number plates, his addresses, his businesses, known associates, favourite hang-outs …

Cohen was certainly feeling the heat. He was effectively helpless in the US since no serious lawyer would take him on as a client, and his Mexican attorney – a notorious figure in Tijuana, Gustavo Cortez – had more enemies than friends. The net was closing in, but stubbornly Cohen refused to budge an inch – because it was Kremen applying the pressure. He kept trying to find ways to outmanoeuvre him. And then, unexpectedly, the whole situation blew up.

"Is this your car?"

"Yes."

"Do you have anything to declare?"

"No."

Jhuliana Aramis Cohen – Stephen Cohen's 21-year-old step-daughter – had crossed the Mexican border hundreds of times before, and the questions were completely routine. She was alone in her maroon 2005 Kia Optima, with Californian plates, in a dedicated lane for trusted travellers. Unfortunately, the transmitter that recognised the car as being granted special privileges wasn't working that day, so Customs Officer Nguyen asked her to move to a secondary inspection area for a cursory check.

A second customs officer inspected her papers and asked her to open the trunk. He went around to look and immediately saw, uncovered and in plain view, ten large packages wrapped in brown packaging tape and coated in some kind of liquid detergent. Officer Castro asked Ms Cohen to get out of the car, and she was escorted to the security office. A sniffer dog was called over, and it instantly alerted its handler to the presence of drugs. One of the packages was opened, and at midday on 22 June 2005, Jhuliana Cohen was arrested for attempting to smuggle 202 pounds – 92 kilograms – of marijuana into the United States.

Cohen was close to his stepdaughter, and they both lived in the same penthouse flat in Tijuana's expensive Chapultepec district. Cohen immediately set about getting her the best legal representation he could, apparently unaware that her arrest had already set the clock running on his own freedom. When Kremen's lawyer Tim Dillon learned that Jhuliana had been arrested, he contacted the authorities, explained that there was an outstanding lawsuit against her, and applied for a deposition date to quiz her about her multi-million-dollar holdings. On the other side of the border, helpless, Stephen Cohen went nuts. His anger and impotence were revealed in a series of changes he made that night to a number of Wikipedia articles that covered him, Gary Kremen and sex.com. In a series of eight changes in the early hours of 28 September 2005, Cohen first corrected his own entry to say "Stephen M. Cohen is the true owner of sex.com" before sabotaging Gary Kremen's. "Gary Kremen is a pathological liar who was able to convence [sic] a federal judge that he was the true owner of sex.com," read the Cohen-edited version. He then changed the estimated settlement value between Kremen and NSI to $150,000, amid other alterations.

If this childishness wasn't enough, Cohen returned a second time, making a further eight changes between seven and eight a.m. on 13 October after he had heard what Kremen's lawyer had asked Jhuliana. The $150,000 was further reduced to $50,000. Then he deleted Kremen's entry altogether. And then, a few minutes later, changed his mind to make it read, simply: "Gary Kremen is bi sexual freek [sic] who is also hooked on speed."

The pressure had got to Cohen a second time. As Kremen had accurately surmised two years earlier: "He'd never met anyone like me who wouldn't stop – I was just not gonna give up." The arrest of Jhuliana had also raised interest in her stepfather, under whose name the car was insured. Immigration officers became aware that there was an outstanding arrest warrant for this Stephen Michael Cohen.

"Cohen's arrest was a lucky confluence of events on our side," says Dillon. "On this side we are calling the authorities, telling them where Cohen is, and getting them to pay attention to it. Here's this guy, he owes a lot of money, he's in contempt of court ... Cohen had to go renew his visa in Mexico, and what's funny is that he could have paid somebody $100 to do it.

"But he chose to do it in person, it is somehow flagged when he goes into the visa office, and they tell him he needs to come back tomorrow. And he didn't think anything of it, he left, came back down and by that time they had the authorities there to deport him back to the US."

On 27 October Cohen was arrested and, despite desperate attempts to talk his way out of it, was driven the short distance to the border, where US marshals were waiting to pick up their man. He was housed in the same detention centre as Jhuliana, and the next morning appeared in a white prison-issue jumpsuit, looking a little worse for wear. Denied bail, Cohen pleaded with the judge to let him stay in San Diego for a few days as he was negotiating a settlement. That settlement, made to Kremen's lawyer a day later, was $100,000 in cash and three properties. Tim Dillon laughed it off. The next day, Cohen offered him $75,000 and two pieces of property.

Cohen was shipped up to San Jose, where his arrest warrant had been issued, and on 14 November he was brought before Judge James Ware, the man who three and a half years earlier had made him a fugitive from justice. "Mr Cohen, I presume," the judge inquired, never having actually had him in his court before. Cohen's old boss, and a friend for over thirty years, Roger Agajanian, was representing him. He offered to act as Cohen's guardian and to put him up in his own home. Ware commended the gesture, but made it clear that Cohen was going nowhere until he had begun purging himself of the various contempt charges that he – Ware – had personally issued. Incredibly, at the end of the hearing, Cohen stood up and began to explain why he had been unable to come to court in 2001: house arrest, bail, a heart attack (an old Cohen faithful) and surgery, which of course had to be done overseas. Needless to say, Ware was completely uninterested. He set the date for the next hearing: 21 November, at 1.30 p.m.

And so began the most bizarre episode of the entire eleven-year fight between Stephen Michael Cohen and Gary Kremen. A fascinated media leapt on the fact that the man who had walked away with millions and defied the US legal system for so many years had been caught and jailed. No one had thought it possible, particularly Stephen Cohen. Kremen had beaten him fair and square. Kremen cleared his entire calendar of work and gave himself a new full-time job: chasing Cohen's assets. Judge Ware granted Kremen's lawyers two depositions, on 5 December and 27 December, and made it clear to Cohen that he would keep him in custody until Cohen had provided sufficient information for Kremen to recover the $65 million that he owed – a sum now increased, with interest, to $82 million. As it turned out, there was a third deposition on 30 December, but each proved to be as pointless as the others.

Despite being behind bars and being warned that until he provided real, usable details of his bank accounts he would be detained indefinitely, Stephen Michael Cohen refused to be beaten. The hours of questioning verged on the surreal. Cohen promised in the most wide-open terms to sign anything, provide anything, do anything he could to help with investigations, but despite a team of lawyers that had picked apart two of Cohen's previous intricate corporate webs, none of the information provided led to a single discovery.

Kremen's lawyers eventually confessed that they had been unable to trace any funds beyond November 2000 – when sex.com was handed back to Kremen and Cohen began in earnest his movement of funds. While playing the forgetful and confused old man, Cohen had managed to retain the names of bank accounts (and even sometimes their numbers) that he had cleared out and shut down six years earlier. He happily looked into the camera of the video deposition, stated his name, and agreed that any bank holding his funds should make available whatever bank records they had to Mr Kremen and his lawyers. It was an elaborate bluff: only Stephen Cohen knows where he has moved his funds, under what name, in what country.

Monthly hearings with Judge Ware were scheduled to review what progress had been made. Very quickly, a pattern was established: month after month, Cohen pushed to see if he would be allowed out on remand, and month after month, his request was refused. Every time Ware told him he would be going back to jail, Cohen had a different explanation as to why Ware's judgment in the case, four years earlier, had been wrong.

Cohen first faced Ware on 14 November 2005. On 21 November, he was informed that until he provided account details he would remain in custody.

On 12 December, after the first deposition, and against the judge's express wishes, Cohen insisted on speaking, and told Ware that his entire judgement was flawed. Ware sent Cohen away, telling him that until he provided Kremen's team with sufficient financial details to recover the millions he owed, he would be kept in custody.

A month later, on 9 January 2006 – after a further two depositions during which Cohen had given Kremen a list of banks he held accounts in but claimed not to remember what the account numbers were – Kremen's team explained they had still been unable to trace a single dollar. And Cohen had another criticism of Ware's judgment. He was sent down again, this time for two months.

When Cohen appeared before Ware a fourth time, on 13 March, his orange jumpsuit was red and he was chained to the floor. "I had my life threatened," explains Dillon. "I can show you the threatening emails we got. We ended up getting them traced back to Cohen's lawyer – Gustavo Cortez ..." Somehow Cohen had also managed to get through on the phone to his now ex-wife Rosa Montano just when she was about to sign over some property to Kremen. By the end of the call, she was too scared to do it.

And so Kremen's team started tracking back how Cohen had found out about Rosa's deal, and then subpoenaed the jail to provide phone records, claiming that Cohen was interfering with the case.

While Cohen was making calls from prison, Kremen's team was following behind him watching closely. And then they heard a rumour that Cohen was planning to pay some people to do a hit on Kremen. They added that claim to a long court filing covering other information they had gleaned, and details of the threatening emails. Ware decided it was enough to throw Cohen in solitary confinement and to kill his phone privileges. The phone was Cohen's lifeline, and without it for five months he slowly started stewing.

When the phone calls stopped, even Cohen's old crook friends realised that the master con man might finally be heading for his biggest fall. Dillon's office received an anonymous tip-off that someone was willing to give them what they wanted – live bank-account numbers. In return, they wanted a ten per cent cut of what was recovered. A deal was cut, and Kremen's team got hold of the details for three bank accounts, one of which, in Luxembourg and under Rosa's name, was still warm.

Dillon explains the clandestine manner in which the bank details were delivered. It was like something from a spy movie. "I was on my way to northern California and I pulled over in one of the LA freeways into one of the restaurant parking lots and did the exchange. This guy was in a car, and he had backed it into the bushes, so you couldn't see his licence plate. No licence plate on the front; sunglasses on. I basically pulled up next to him, rolled down the window and he handed over a manila envelope with one page of A4 with the three bank-account details in return for my exchange of the agreement. I'd never seen him before."

Cohen was unable to find out what was going on, or get in the way, giving Kremen's team valuable time to chase the money down. Cohen's isolation was taking a heavy toll on his mental state. When he returned to face Ware for the fifth time, on 4 April, he had dismissed his lawyers and was now representing himself. In a worrying repetition of 2002, when he had made himself the attorney of record despite having no qualifications or legitimacy to do so, Cohen then proceeded to file a long series of increasingly incoherent motions to court, scrawled in a peculiar mix of upper-case and lower-case letters, and running through wild and paranoid assertions. Ware sent him down again.

On 9 May, Cohen was up in front of Ware again, and still refusing to give in. When he was brought before Ware again on 19 June, still maintaining his performance of confused innocence, even Gary Kremen thought Ware was going to let him go free. Cohen had been in jail eight months, and had given away nothing.

On 27 June, Cohen got his answer to a last-ditch request of the Court of Appeals. He had asked the higher court for an emergency writ of mandamus, filed in his position of "in forma pauperis". In non-legal language, Cohen had petitioned the Court of Appeals to use an extraordinary and rare power to overturn all of the motions, contempts and convictions held against him on the grounds that he was penniless and unable to fight the legal guns ranged against him.

Cohen had again slipped into his fantasy land where he existed both as an attorney – the supreme defender of rights – and as the put-upon victim of society. It was a thin membrane that separated Cohen from this fantasy land, and throughout his life, usually when his real misdemeanours had caught up with him, Cohen crossed the divide. Cohen's fantasies formed a protective barrier between him and the rest of the world, a barrier that gave him an unnatural confidence to do more, live more and achieve more than anyone else he knew. He was there again.

The petition was denied and Ware ordered that Cohen be returned to jail for six months. A month later, on 19 January 2006, Gary Kremen sold sex.com for $12 million. It was the greatest sum of money ever paid for a domain name.

47

JAILBIRD

The main jail for Santa Clara Country is a tall imposing building overlooking the main road near San Jose airport. Outside, parked on the road, you will find, even at eight a.m., a hotdog seller who will provide gentle chitchat and a fully loaded sausage in a bun for two dollars. Round the corner is the main pitching spot for "Bad Boys Bail Bonds". A luridly painted truck advertises the loan service, complete with a cartoon of a man trying to tear his way through some jail bars. An employee hands out branded neck ribbons, ideal for clipping on a jail-visitor pass.

Inside the jail it is all uniforms and clean-but-sparse furniture. The rules here are everything. You follow the rules, and you learn the rules by following others or by finding yourself shouted at for breaking them. And this is only the visitors' lounge. Inmates are allowed one half-hour visit per week. It's first come, first served, so if someone visited four days ago and you turn up, unaware, you're not getting in. Fortunately, Prisoner 05063735, in bunk 2-4W – one Cohen, Stephen Michael – hasn't had any visitors in a year, apart from Gary Kremen's lawyers.

The system is as precise as it is pointlessly bureaucratic.

The first step is to fill in a visitation request slip with your own personal details and those of the prisoner you wish to see. The requisite details for all the prisoners in the jail are listed on a sheet of paper on a clipboard that is supposed to stay at the front desk.

Take a slip, and then try to locate the clipboard. Every five minutes, it goes missing, earning the whole room a rebuke. Once it has been located, you look up your jailbird, and try to figure out which details need to go in which box. And then you add all your details and sign various declarations that you are a law-abiding citizen and so on. You then try to find the end of the queue, from where you edge forward to hand this slip to a booking officer who appears apparently at random and stands at a special desk where they take an inordinately long time going through each slip for no discernible reason. At some specified time the officer then exclaims that the time slot for the next visit in 30 minutes has closed, meaning that everyone who has already been standing at the same spot for an hour will have to wait at least another hour and a half until they get to see their loved ones. Assuming, that is, the booking officer gets through enough slips before the next cut-off point is called.

Stephen Michael Cohen, it turns out, is in the "old jail" behind the main jail, at 180 West Hedding Street. As you turn the corner you can hear the reverberations of a basketball game on the other side of a 20-foot high brick wall. A big sign on the wall warns you not to try to talk to the prisoners, but fortunately the laws of physics got there first.

In the old jail, which looks like a rundown doctor's surgery except for the huge square-jawed desk sergeant in permanent standby mode, the slip is given further intense scrutiny before the rules are outlined: no cameras, no tape recorders, no phones, no magazines or newspapers, no paper, no keys, no pens, no pencils. A jacket? A slight whirring can be heard as the answer is slowly retrieved. "Nothing in the jacket." What makes the rules all the more remarkable is that prisoner and visitor are separated by a three-inch thick piece of Perspex, with communication only possible through a telephone.

This then is the reality of the United States penitentiary system, a system where the one overarching and unwritten rule is that you do not complain, discuss, suggest or even hint that there is anything at all wrong with all this. It is sheer purgatory for a man like Stephen Cohen.

"This case is subject to a federal investigation. I am unable to discuss any aspect of the case with you." Cohen has absolutely no idea who the person facing him is, and would only have learned 20 minutes earlier that he had an unknown visitor. "I can't talk about any aspect of the case." Or, it would seem, about himself. Or even about jail. Nothing. Except of course he does: given the opportunity, he cannot help but talk.

"I was expecting investigators from the Department of Justice. I have a new lawyer and he is going to the DoJ, there has been some serious fraud in this case." But Cohen wouldn't give the name of his new lawyer, and he certainly hadn't informed the court of this development. He was in fact still submitting handwritten filings to the court, written on prison paper and largely incoherent, claiming to be representing himself. It was a worrying echo from five years earlier, when Cohen lost his mind in Mexico. "There will be new filings in a week, and I am going to be out of here in three weeks."

And so began a bizarre rundown through the entire sex.com case in which Cohen threw out all the old angles, apparently unaware that every one of them had been reviewed, researched, dissected and discarded by Kremen's lawyers and Judge Ware years earlier.

"There has been a massive fraud perpetrated here. The documents that prove I was being held by the Mexican government are missing from the court records. They were filed by Dorband and Mayock but the judge says he never saw them." In fact, Ware had refused to review them years earlier, and Mayock and Dorband feign ignorance of them for the simple reason that they are so weak it is best to pretend they don't exist.

In fact, Wagstaffe had dealt with the documents specifically in front of the Appeals Court judges when he beat NSI. "Cohen submitted what he purported to be a Mexican court order your honour, but ... he actually submitted something from a district attorney's office, and our expert looked at those documents and said that is not a house arrest." One of the other documents was clearly a Cohen forgery, and another purporting to be another government document Wagstaffe dismissed as purchasable on any Mexican street for $50.

Cohen then returned to his trademark application. "I have had a trademark in sex.com since 1979." The rigid determination with which Cohen has stuck by this lie for over a decade is extraordinary. After all, it had enabled him not only to get control of sex.com, but also to grab countless "sex" domains from his competitors. But the fact was that the documents submitted to the trademark office were demonstrably fake, and Ware had again ruled as much. Cohen's infringement lawsuits were ended. Cohen has an explanation: "I only handed over a small amount of the documents I sent to the trademark office to Kremen during discovery."

Kremen himself was faced with this absolute refusal to budge. "Still to this day I would accept a reasonable amount to settle," Kremen explains. What about $1 million? "Who's being greedy, I'll take $500,000!" And had he told Cohen that? "Uh-huh." And he said? "He goes: 'You don't deserve it – I invented sex.com in 1979.'"

Meanwhile, in jail, Cohen starts on the Kremen standing issue. "He had no right to bring the case in the first place – he didn't have any standing." In fact, Ware had ruled at least twice that Kremen had standing; Wagstaffe had also argued the standing issue in the Court of Appeal, where his argument was accepted. The law says that Kremen registered sex.com and had it stolen from him. It had been decided in 2001. It was now October 2006.

Cohen embarks on an analogy, one that he repeats no fewer than three times during the half-hour interview, each time as if thinking of it for the first time. "Imagine it's 1969. You're in Russia, and a KGB officer comes up to you, taps you on the shoulders and says, 'You're guilty of espionage.' Forty minutes later, you're told you've been found guilty on the evidence. Evidence that you've never seen. That's what's happened here."

But it's not 1969, it's not Russia, Kremen isn't the KGB, and the case was tried in public court under the spotlight of the world's press for three years. "Kremen has never got a cent from me. He only got my ex-wife's house. Ware was going to let me out in June and told Kremen's attorneys they had to prove the evidence, so they produced this email which is false. That's the only reason I'm here."

The "false" email had been discovered in the 'sent mail' folder of Cohen's Gmail account. It was signed "Steve", and moved 3.5 million euros to a branch of Nordia Bank in Europe. Cohen claims that it was a plant by Kremen. "But how would I have got his password?" Kremen asks. "Well, he hasn't figured that part of his lie out yet," Tim Dillon adds.

Cohen moves on to the next charge. "You have an attorney filing 300 subpoenas without informing the court. The theft of documents. I have got DoJ investigators coming in today." Cohen's claims of illegal subpoenas by Kremen's lawyers were dealt with in court and dismissed. But what had infuriated Cohen was how Kremen found out so much about his private businesses so quickly. The answer is that Ware signed several Draconian orders giving Kremen access to Cohen's credit-card accounts, post and phone records and then placed them under seal.

Where did the money go? "Who says I made loads of money?" Cohen argues, adding in a not-so-subtle threat: "There are a lot of false stories and I'm going to go after reporters. These stories have been put out there by Kremen. We have freedom of press but this whole false impression was created and I'm going to go after them with a racketeering action."

Why doesn't he just pay Kremen $500,000 and walk away? "This case isn't going to settle. I've been incarcerated for a year because of this."

And then, just when it starts getting uncomfortable, there is a noise in the corridor. "Sorry, the investigators are here, I have to go." And he puts the phone down and walks off.

It is a moment of the old Cohen brilliance, but he fluffs it. He is too hesitant, too aware of his observer's reaction, and, after twelve months in jail, he is too desperate to talk to someone from the outside world other than Kremen's lawyers. Moments later he reappears. "Sorry, the investigators are talking to my attorneys first." But there is no record of anyone else visiting Cohen that day.

He starts talking again about abstract legal issues:

"Look at it from my perspective. The reality is that ..."

I can't help but jump in: "The reality is that you're in jail ..." An uncomfortable pause, and I change tack. "It can't be pleasant in jail."

"Oh, it's okay. I play cards every night. But I'm going to be out of here soon. As soon as they look at this, I'm going to get straight out of here."

And the extraordinary thing is, less than two months after that conversation, he was. Judge Ware had given Kremen's legal team six months and an extraordinary amount of legal backing to track down Cohen's money, and they were unable to turn up a single thing. Cohen was just too good.

Under the civil contempt law, Ware was obliged to keep Cohen in jail *only if* he felt that more time in jail would encourage him to provide sufficient details to lift the contempt. It was clear that Cohen was never going to divulge any information, and Ware was forced, after 14 months of keeping him in jail, to consider Cohen's claim that he would only be able to find out where his money was if he was out of jail and able to talk to people. Ware released him, with an order to return on 26 February 2007 to explain how his search had got on. He was given his passport.

Just eight hours later, Cohen's Mexican lawyer, Gustavo Cortés Carvajal, known locally as El Sapo or "The Toad", was the target of an assassination attempt in Tijuana.

Cortés was in a Mercedes van being driven by fellow lawyer Jose Luis Alamillo, when it was blocked in by two trucks in central Tijuana. Alamillo broke free, and at this point the would-be assassins opened fire. Alamillo was shot several times, as was a four-year-old boy in a car at the scene. Cortés escaped unhurt.

Suspicion immediately fell on Cohen, although there remains no evidence at all that he was involved. Cortés had access to Cohen's accounts and knew more than anyone about his hidden empire. It was also widely rumoured that when Cortés paid off a $1 million kidnapping ransom the year before he was $350,000 short and so took it from one of Cohen's accounts. It is impossible to know what the truth is in the murky criminal world of Tijuana. Some question whether it was possible to order and carry out a hit on Cortés in just a few hours. Others point out that El Sapo had no shortage of enemies, any number of whom were known to be handy with a gun. Cohen himself has never resorted to violence to further his interests, preferring instead to out-think his opponents.

But at the same time, it is very, very foolish to underestimate Stephen Michael Cohen. The man who seemed a little unsure in jail, perhaps even showing the first signs of dementia at age 58, is a dangerous man if he feels wronged.

"Winning was everything to Steve," recalls Frank Butler. "Just because you prevailed in a case against him that did not mean that you would ever collect anything. The winning wasn't malicious, although he would do a lot to get ahead of someone he believed had done him wrong, and I mean a *lot*. By wrong, I mean someone who did not play by the rules that Steve played by. Something deep inside of Steve simply makes him that way."

All of Kremen's team know that they are unlikely to walk away from the case and Cohen without some problems. Tim Dillon – who has led the charge against Cohen, his associates, his wife and his stepdaughter in an effort to get at his assets – said he was "uncertain" what would happen when Cohen was out. Kremen's private investigator Margo Evashevski admits to being worried and slightly scared over what could happen. And Gary Kremen asked pensively one day when driving through San Francisco: "So what do you think he'll do?"

"He'll make a few phone calls, try to make your life difficult and then give up," I replied.

"Hmmm," Kremen replied, entirely unpersuaded.

"So what's the plan when you get out of here?" I asked Cohen.

"I'm going to get a house here in San Jose and fight this case."

"San Jose is not the best place in the world to live."

"It doesn't have to be the best place. I will move here and fight this case all the way."

The old con man's eyes flickered into life. "And I'll tell you what. You'll get a call from me one day and I'll say meet me at this place. I won't tell you why. I'll turn up in a big car and then I'll let you drive me to the Grand Jury investigation."

48

PERPETUAL MOTIONS

Judge Ware's court is far less grand and much smaller than you would expect. Courtroom 8 on the fourth floor of the United States District Court in San Jose. Take a right out of the lifts, a right again and it's at the end of the corridor.

There are four other cases being heard this morning, nine a.m. on Monday 26 February 2007. The big question is: will Cohen turn up? "He'll be here, he's in town," Kremen's lawyer Tim Dillon says.

And sure enough, a few minutes later, Steven Michael Cohen pops up round the corner wearing light blue jeans, a dark blue jacket, and a half-blue, half-yellow sweatshirt with "Amsterdam, Holland" written on it.

Dillon stands up and wanders over. "Hi Steve." "Hey." Cohen hangs around waiting for his lawyer, Steven Teich. He arrives shortly after and they take a seat at the back of the courtroom. Kremen's other lawyer, Richard Idell, spots them, walks over and extends his hand. "How are you doing, Mr Cohen?" Cohen shakes his hand quickly. "Fine." "Richard Idell," he introduces himself to Steven Teich.

As soon as Idell is out of earshot, Teich turns to his client. "I don't like this, predators about everywhere." He pauses. "It doesn't look like they have anything though."

And he's right. Despite all the thousands of hours spent prosecuting Stephen Michael Cohen, the tens of thousands of pages of court documents, the long and bitter battle, the countless judgments, Kremen's team "don't have anything". Cohen is still playing the long game.

A reporter wanders over. "Are you saying anything?" she asks. "No," Cohen responds abruptly. She asks Steven Teich the same. "Nope." Teich turns to Cohen again. "What can we say, 'the case is finished?' You need to declare bankruptcy." "I can't do that," Cohen tells him, although it not entirely clear why.

And then a woman calls out: "All rise for Judge James Ware", and the court is in session.

Case 20718-cv-98, Kremen versus Cohen, is third up. It is clear immediately that nothing is going to be agreed today. Dillon predicted as much. "I guess Steve will make us drag him in front the judge a few times. There'll be a lot more of these." The entire discussion this time revolves around a single point that should never have come up in the first place. Kremen's lawyer wanted an address for Cohen so they could serve him with papers. Cohen stretched the argument out: he is staying with friends, he doesn't have a set address. He has given Kremen's lawyers an address in Salt Lake City, Utah. They can use that.

Judge Ware walks through the points and eventually decides that Steven Teich's offices in San Francisco can be used as a legal address for Cohen. Cohen also wants to substitute himself in for another of his lawyers. Ware looks him squarely in the eyes. "One of my desires – as a judge," he tells Cohen carefully. "And I have had your case since I *was* a judge – is not to have this case until I retire. I'm looking forward to have to substitute no-one in because the case is over."

And then he tells the two sides to go to the library on the floor above and have a further discussion about settling the case. Three hours later, the lawyers emerge having got precisely nowhere. Cohen denied he had any money. Faced with another piece of paper showing him moving millions of dollars around European banks, he denied that the signature was his. And so the roundabout made another turn.

All this is costing Kremen $25,000 a month and yet despite promising he would be there, he hasn't turned up. I call him. "Yeah, I had everything booked. I had the last flight out and then I thought 'why should I go to all these hearings?' I think I'm only encouraging him [Cohen]. I'm over this."

Dillon isn't sure how much longer Kremen will keep chasing Cohen. "Will Gary keep paying $25,000 a month to chase Cohen? Gary's a businessman and he is looking for a return. Does he think he'll get that return? Well, that's the question isn't it?"

As for Stephen Cohen. He refuses to discuss the case, turns his back, pretends not to hear his name and walks off. Teich explains: "Steve doesn't want to talk to you. You have written some horrible things about him. I haven't read the stories but Steve told me. Horrible things. Terrible things. Things like 'con man'."

And if you looked across the road at that moment, you could see the man who is not a con man, the man who did not steal sex.com and the man who does not have millions of dollars secreted away in dozens of offshore accounts. The man who was not beaten by Gary Kremen.

INDEX